The Dixie Cragger's Atlas

A Climber's Guide to Tennessee
Volume 2 - The Hinterlands

Warning

Rock climbing is a dangerous activity. The publisher and author assume no responsibility for injury or death resulting from the use of this book. The information contained herein is unverified and the author and the publisher cannot guarantee its accuracy. Assessments of the difficulty, danger and risks associated with rock climbing and rock climbing routes is completely subjective. No climb is safe and you could be injured or killed while climbing any of the routes described in this book. It is up the user to evaluate ability, assess risk and take all precautions necessary to engage in climbing any of the routes in this book. This book is NOT an instructional manual. The authors and publisher make no representations or warranties, express or implied, of any kind regarding the contents of this book, including accuracy or reliability of the information presented herein. The user assumes all risk associated with the use of this book.

Proudly printed in the USA, using domestic materials and providing American jobs.

Cover Photo: Jamie Dial and Jeff Noffsinger on the Terrorarium Roof pitch of Vertigo, O&W Wall, Big South Fork. Photo: Matt Thomsen

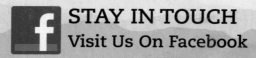 STAY IN TOUCH
Visit Us On Facebook

PROTECTING CLIMBING **ACCESS** SINCE 1991

Jonathan Siegrist climbs the Third Millenium (14a) at the Monastery, Colorado. Photo by: Keith Ladzinski

About The Guide

I'm an author, but I'm foremost a climber, and I love to travel to new places. I am also a guidebook aficionado and have bought and used many guidebooks over the years. Some were great and others have been terrible. Some were dangerously inaccurate, while others may have had good info, but fell apart the first time they got thrown in a pack. I'm sort of old school as well, and feel that guidebooks should include information about the first ascent party and dates if possible. In this regard, guidebooks are a historical document, conveying the efforts of climbers, the history of climbing areas and tracing the evolution of the sport. In this way, new climbers come to appreciate the past and hopefully develop a sense of history and the ethical considerations that are so important to climbing.

This new edition of the Dixie Cragger's Atlas continues in the above vein, and boasts many improvements over previous editions. If you already own the Dixie Cragger's Atlas, why should you buy the new one? Here's why:

A two volume set – one book for Tennessee and one for Alabama and Georgia. Keeps your pack lighter and guarantee that your skinny legs won't get bigger on the approach hikes.

These are the first Dixie Cragger's editions to be presented in color!

Info on new climbing areas that have never been published before.

Hundreds of new routes at existing areas.

Clear and concise route descriptions.

Grade revisions and changes (by consensus) at all areas.

New cliffline and individual route photos.

Super accurate bird's eye topo maps, where applicable.

A new format in which numbered routes correspond with numbers on all maps and photos.

A quick navigation section for each chapter, with scanable QR codes for your smartphone.

Quick visual reference for the grade breakdown at each area.

WHY JOIN THE  SCC

THE SOUTHEASTERN CLIMBERS COALITION

is a 501(c)(3) non-profit corporation dedicated to preserving climbing access in the Southeast. We started in 1993 when a group of climbers banded together to help with ongoing access issues at Sunset Rock, atop Lookout Mountain in Chattanooga, Tennessee. The group had positive results from the start and has gone on to sponsor cleanups and trail days at climbing areas. We've expanded our scope to include fundraising and land preservation, purchasing many historic and threatened climbing areas around the southeast. The SCC's volunteers are climbers from Tennessee, Alabama, Georgia, North and South Carolina and the Ozarks who have joined forces to resolve local climbing access issues. The goal of the Southeastern Climbers Coalition is to provide ongoing means for climbers throughout the area to respond effectively to access threats at our crags and mitigate the impacts of their increased use

SO THIS NEVER HAPPENS AGAIN

Boat Rock, Atlanta, GA - 2004

Photos by Wes Powell

www.seclimbers.org

2002

Photo: Wes Powell

Raised $100,000 for the purchase and preservation of the severely threatened **BOAT ROCK** bouldering area, just 20 minutes from downtown Atlanta, GA. Over 260 boulder problems to date, and counting!

2003

Photo: Sean Stewart

Received a donation of the **KING'S BLUFF** cliffline, a limestone sport climbing area near Clarksville, TN. More than 160 routes from 5.3 to 5.13 on 9.78 acres along the Cumberland River.

2005

Photo: John Liles

Purchased 1550 linear feet of classic sandstone cliffline on a 3.14 acre tract at **JAMESTOWN**, Alabama. Climbers had been visiting Jamestown since the 70's, but it had been closed since 1993.

2005

Photo: Brad McLeod

Negotiated a lease agreement for **CASTLE ROCK**, a sandstone cliff near Jasper, TN. Castle Rock is home to more than 50 established lines, including one of Tennessee's hardest, "Apes on Acid" - a 5.13d.

2009

Photo: Andrew Kornylak

Raised funds to purchase a portion of **YELLOW BLUFF**, near Huntsville, AL. Yellow Bluff is an historic sandstone cliff with both sport and traditional lines. The property had been closed for over 25 years.

2009

Photo: Will Eccleston

Purchased a 25 acre tract that includes a portion of cliffline at **STEELE**, AL. The property includes over 40 established climbing routes, both traditional and sport. Steele had been closed since 1987.

ACKNOWLEDGEMENTS

All rock climbing guidebooks invariably draw from many sources. Most often, a guidebook author is merely a collector or curator - an editor in charge of assembling bits and pieces of information. This guidebook borrows from and references previous guidebooks, articles from Climbing Magazine, Rock and Ice Magazine, websites, the author's personal knowledge and reams of information submitted by active climbers within the community. I am also appreciative of all of the excellent photography made available for use in the book. As anyone who shoots can tell you, it's a tough thing to set up, get in position and hang around for hours getting good pics. A heartfelt "Thanks" goes out to everyone who helped along the way.

Scott Perkins, Mike Cork, Joshua Livasy, Nathalie DuPre', James Putnam, Jeff Mekolites, Steve Jones, Darryl Bornhop, Micah Gentry, Mike Cork , Harrison Shull , Jonathan Hollada , Brad McLeod , Jerry Roberts, Kelly Dalton , Stewart Robinson, Rene Pirolt, Andrew Kornylak , Stan Wallace , Jeff Gruenberg , Travis Griggs , Travis Eiseman, Lance Brock, Andrew Miller, Nathan Brown, Jeff Noffsinger, Tyler Stracker, David Draper, Luis Rodriguez, John Dorough, Lori Walden, Anthony Meeks, Todd Wells, Arno Ilgner, Greg Kottkamp, Tony Robinson, Glenn Ritter, Wayne Roy, Matt Thomsen, James Pullum, Paul Mashburn, Daniel Worley and others too many to mention.

Last but not least a special thanks goes out to Mary Ann, Ava and Liza, who endured my long hours driving, hiking, climbing and (mostly) sitting at the computer.

A CAVEAT

I am not a graphic designer/layout artist nor an expert in those fields, as will probably be clearly in evidence to some who are using this book. I executed the layout and design myself, but I am self-taught - no doubt resulting in much to gripe about or critique from those who work in the design/print industry. This process has made me keenly aware of how much work and talent goes into producing a publication, and I applaud those who make it seem effortless.

In some cases, I have strayed from commonly accepted practices or conventions in an effort to keep the book size to a minimum, given the amount of information contained within. I welcome constructive criticism and advice, and am truly sorry if the lack of a drop shadow or a font size irregularity is offensive to you. I strive to make the information as complete, accurate and up to date as possible.

GRADE COMPARISON CHART

Yosemite Decimal	French System	United Kingdom		East German	(UIAA) West German	Australian System
5.5		4a	VS			
5.6		4b	VS			
5.7	5a	4b	HVS	VIIa	5+	
5.8	5b	4c	HVS	VIIb	6-	16
5.9	5c	5a	E1	VIIc	6	17
5.10a		5a	E1	VIIc	6+	18
5.10b	6a	5b	E1	VIIIc	7-	19
5.10c	6b	5c	E2	VIIIb	7	20
5.10d	6b	5c	E2	VIIIC	7+	21
5.11a	6c	6a	E3	IXa	7+	22
5.11b	6c	6a	E3	IXb	8-	23
5.11c	7a	6a	E4	IXb	8-	24
5.11d	7a	6a	E4	IXc	8	25
5.12a	7b	6b	E5	Xa	8+	26
5.12b	7b	6b	E5	Xb	9-	26
5.12c	7c	6b	E6	Xc	9	27
5.12d	7c	6c	E6	Xc	9	28
5.13a	8a	6c	E7		9+	28
5.13b	8a	7a	E7		9+	29
5.13c	8b	7a	E7		10-	30
5.13d	8b	7a	E8		10	31
5.14a	8c	7b	E8		10+	31
5.14b	8c	7b	E9		10+	32
5.14c	9a	7c	E9		11-	33
5.14d	9a	7c	E9		11	33

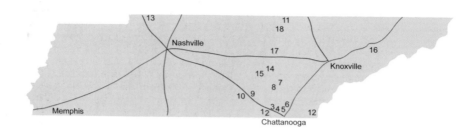

Table Of Contents

VOLUME ONE

VOLUME TWO

INTRODUCTION

Every climber, if they stick with it long enough, will eventually look back and realize that they have been climbing for a longer period of time in their life than not. For twenty-seven years, climbing has been a constant and consistent love and has taken me all over the country and abroad. Indeed, climbers may be among the most well-traveled participants of any sport. Nothing gives a climber itchy feet and a wandering urge like a photo in a magazine or a story around a campfire of a place they haven't visited yet. Sometimes I think we are more enamored with the routes we haven't climbed than the routes that we have. Who can resist the heartstopping exposure of Yosemite, the grandeur of the Rockies, the sweeping vistas and red towers of the Desert Southwest? The perfect white stone of the Gunks? Heck, those are just a few places in this country. How about Australia? Spain? Africa? Mexico? Pick a point on the map and you're nearly guaranteed that there will be climbing opportunities there- all fantastic in different ways and all sure to provide life-changing experiences that will be carried to the grave.

Most of us however, spend the majority of time at our home crags, in familiar surroundings, frequenting the same areas weekend after weekend. Here in the south, the sheer volume of rock and the number of climbing areas can make choosing a place to go the biggest hurdle. The major cities of the Deep South - Atlanta, Birmingham, Nashville, Chattanooga and Knoxville, all lie within two hours of of nearly forty climbing areas, some highly publicized and others held in secrecy. The point is this - we don't have to travel far to find adventure and new experiences. There's plenty in our own backyard!

Though Alabama and Georgia have their fair share of excellent rock, the best areas lie in central and eastern Tennessee. It's been said that there is more unclimbed, undeveloped rock in Tennessee than climbed rock. It's been said that Chattanooga, often referred to as the "Buckle Of The Sandstone Belt" has more rock in close proximity to a major metropolitan area than any other city in the country. It's been said that the Big South Fork National River and Recreation Area contains more climbing potential than the rest of Tennessee combined! All true? Perhaps.

On a map of the southeast, locate the town of Gadsden, Alabama...put another finger on the Red River Gorge near Lexington, Kentucky...got it? Everything between your fingers is known as the Cumberland Plateau (Sand Mountain as it enters Alabama). Essentially a long ridge coves, canyons, creekbeds and river valleys, the Plateau runs diagonally for nearly 300 miles, filled with an abundant supply of high quality sandstone. Characterized by a dense, fine-grained texture, this escarpment sandstone is one of the finest climbing mediums around. The variety is endless; a smooth polished face is likely to give way to a perfect hand or finger crack; steep walls may have huge jugs as well as solution pockets. Though most sandstone routes are steep, strenuous and relatively short (usually around 100' or less, with a few exceptions) this guide includes some long multi-pitch routes as well, mostly in Suck Creek canyon and the Big South Fork.

If there is any downside to climbing in the deep South, it is the sometimes grueling summer heat. Climbing is possible however, even on hot days, since many of the crags are north facing or have shaded caves and corners. The up side is that the winters are very mild, with only a few days that are too cold. It is not uncommon to spend Thanksgiving and even Christmas Day in short sleeves! The best times to visit are late March through June and late August through December.

The topography and geology of the Cumberland Plateau provides for a myriad of other recreational activities, so bring your kayak or open boat, mountain bike as well as backpacking and caving gear. (The Karst topography of the region makes the Cumberland Plateau home to the highest concentration of caves in the United States) Read each chapter intro carefully as every attempt has been made to note this information where applicable.

Those of you who purchased the first Dixie Cragger's Atlas will find that these new editions contain several new areas and lots of new routes! This guidebook represents thousands of hours of effort and I couldn't do it without help. Though I have personally visited, climbed at, hiked, mapped and gathered information for every area, this guidebook could not happen without the hundreds of active climbers and first ascensionists who graciously provided information. Please see the acknowledgements section. I am grateful to everyone. It is my hope that with this comprehensive and informative guidebook in hand, you will be prepared to explore some of the best rock climbing in the United States. The focus of this book is on the most popular, publicly accessible climbing areas in Tennessee. Nearly thirty crags are represented, with over 2000 routes documented in a concise, user-friendly format. No matter how hard you climb, or whether you prefer sport or traditional climbing, there's plenty to whet your appetite: the steep, tiered roofs of Foster Falls, the perfect cracks and corners of the Tennessee Wall or the outback adventure climbing in Suck Creek Canyon and the Big South Fork....just name it and you can find it here in the Deep South! And you can get there using this guide-The Dixie Cragger's Atlas for Tennessee!

A Few Notes About This Book

- It is my belief that any good guidebook should make an attempt to document first ascent information. In this sense, a guidebook also becomes a sort of historical document or record; painting a picture of each area and its development through the years. The routes that climbers enjoy today, whether sport or traditional, are the result of someone else's drive, commitment, determination. Sorry if it's boring.

- Every attempt has been made to verify the accuracy of the information contained herein. Where possible, approximate route lengths have been given, as well as bolt counts for sport routes. Do not rely solely on bolt counts in the text or on the topos! Always carry extra draws.

- Traditional routes will have a concise, but thorough route description. Sport routes are fairly self explanatory, and may be detailed using a simple topo/diagram.

- The cliffline and route photos should adequately direct you where you want to go, but some areas are difficult or impossible to get photos of, leaving little choice but to use maps, diagrams and topos/drawings. Sport routes are numbered in blue, trad routes in red. On the topos, roofs are denoted with darker colors, while ledges have a lighter color. • FA - refers to the first ascent of a route, either on aid or free. FFA - refers to the first free ascent of a route, if the first ascent was on aid.

- Assume that the FA was free, if there is no FFA mentioned. Toprope ascents of routes are not noted, unless the route remains a toprope route. Such information is erroneous, since many routes, especially sport routes, were toproped for years before they were bolted.

- P1, P2, P3 etc- refers to the given pitch of a route, and the grade for each pitch is included.

- Both in the text and on photos and topos, sport routes will be notated in blue and traditional routes in red. Mixed routes are counted as trad routes.

- Please send any corrections, additions and suggestions to: Chris Watford at info@dixiecragger.com or callwild@earthlink.net. Look for updates and revisions available on the web at www.dixiecragger.com

RECOMMENDED GEAR

While several of the climbing areas in this book offer predominantly sport climbing, the vast majority are traditional in nature or at the very least, offer a mixture of both types. While it is possible to climb a number of routes with only a few quickdraws, to experience and truly appreciate all that the region has to offer, it is best to bring along a complete and thorough rack, as well as the skill and knowledge of how to use it. A standard (and recommended) rack might include the following:

A set of brass or steel nuts
Two full sets of wired stoppers
Cams from 1/4" to 5" (doubles in the small/mid sizes)
Twelve full length runners
Ten to twelve quickdraws
Plenty of extra carabiners
A nut tool

The above list is merely a recommendation. Some routes may require extra gear or an odd piece of gear. Every attempt has been made to note this in the route descriptions if such is the case, but in the end, it is up to you to make the final assessment as to the gear required. For toproping, it is necessary to bring an ample supply of long 1" webbing slings. Indeed, several 20' and 40' slings are extremely useful. A few things to consider when toproping:

- Always pad trees, underneath your slings, with a rope bag, towel or your shirt. Some areas, such as Sunset Park, make this a requirement, but it is a good idea anyway, since it saves the tree and your rope from abrasion and wear.
- In recent years, many routes at the popular areas have had ring anchors placed at the top of the routes, a welcome addition, especially as pine beetles have devastated most of the trees that were previously used. Some routes do still end at trees or sometimes cold-shut anchors. Should you encounter them, never toprope directly through "cold shut" type anchors, which are dubious at best and terribly unsafe at their worst. Use a few 'biners or quickdraws for the rope to pass through, thus limiting the amount of wear on the cold shuts themselves. There are many instances of cold shuts and chains that are nearly worn through, but cannot be replaced because someone has foolishly pounded the bolt threads to prevent removal.
- Please make sure to never toprope directly through the stainless rings. The amount of time and effort required to install and maintain them is enormous, so use your own slings and biners.
- Make sure your slings are not running over any sharp edges.
- Never, ever toprope through a pulley, no matter what your summer camp ropes course instructor told you! This is a great way to get killed or seriously injured. Always use a few 'biners with the gates opposed and reversed.

DIFFICULTY RATINGS

This guidebook utilizes the popular Yosemite Decimal System for grading free route difficulty, and is, of course, highly subjective. The YDS doesn't address the level of danger or risk, so serious runouts or poor protectionare noted in the route descriptions and may occasionally be noted using an R or X rating. Aid climbs are graded using the A0 through A5 scale. Please refer to the chart comparing the YDS grades with those of other grading systems from around the world. Note: The "5." has been removed from the grades.

ROUTE QUALITY

This guide uses the common "3 star" system for grading the relative quality of a particular route. The quality rating is based in relation to other routes at the same area. A two star route at one area might scarcely deserve a star at another area, and a route with no stars might still be worth doing. If your favorite route didn't get all the stars you think it deserves, pencil some more in.

ROCK CLIMBING SAFETY

This guidebook is NOT an instructional manual! It is not meant to teach the vast body of knowledge required for safe climbing. This book was written with the intended purpose of getting the competent and experienced climber to the crags and describing the routes he or she may find. Along with the excitement, rewards and joy that climbing can bring, it is nonetheless a sport that carries with it a certain amount of inherent risk. Serious injury and death are a very real possibility, so tread lightly as you explore the vertical realm. If you are new to the sport, seek competent instruction. Proceed cautiously. Make every attempt to learn and understand the complex and intricate systems that climbing requires. The vast majority of rock climbing accidents can be traced back to human error - a split second lapse of judgment or an attempt to use a skill or technique without proper knowledge. The list is endless. Keep in mind that experience is the best insurance and gravity never sleeps!

RAPPELLING

Rappelling is the most dangerous aspect of climbing. Indeed, the vast majority of accidents occur while rappelling because the climber is completely reliant on gear and the quality of the anchor. Triple check all systems. Make sure that buckles are securely fastened; that knots are securely tied; that you aren't relying on a single anchor. Confirm that both ends of the rope reach the ground and tie BIG knots in the ends if you're in doubt. Lastly, it's best if the second climber (or last, whichever the case may be) clip in, thread the rope through the permanent ring anchors and rap off, thus greatly limiting wear and tear on the rings, which are expensive and time consuming to install.

BELAY ANCHORS

Just as in rappelling, it is important to triple check all belay anchors. Never trust a single anchor. Make sure all locking carabiners are locked or that non-locking biners have their gates opposed. Resist the temptation to be lazy. Equalize all anchors with a cordelette system whenever possible. Again, do not toprope directly through the fixed ring anchors! Rappel down whenever possible to avoid wearing out the ring anchors.

OBJECTIVE DANGERS

- These include falling objects, weather, and other uncontrollable variables. Loose rock is always a possibility at any climbing area. It can fall on it's own, or more likely, is dislodged by another climber. Climbers often drop pieces of gear as well. Wearing a helmet is always a good idea, but is no substitute for keen attentiveness and cat-like reflexes.
- For the most part, weather in this part of the country is fairly predictable. You can generally see it coming. Be aware of thunderstorms. Get off the rock at the first hint of lightning.
- Be aware of the summer heat and the toll it can take on your body. Drink lots of water to curb heat exhaustion and heat stroke.
- There are many varieties of poisonous and non-poisonous snakes in the region. Keep an eye out for them in and around the rock and scree at the cliff base, as well as under fallen logs and the like. Watch for stinging insects such as wasps and hornets. Carry a

good repellent, as well as a can of wasp/hornet spray.
- By far the worst "critter" you will encounter anywhere in the Deep South just might be the indigenous species known as the Lowlife Meth Head, who seem to be most prevalent in the rural, mountainous nooks and crannies where climbers like to play. Advice? Be careful where you camp. Think twice about leaving your tents, sleeping bags and cook gear set up while climbing. Always take wallets and cell phones with you to the cliff and lock all valuables that you can't take with you out of sight (admittedly a difficult thing to do in an SUV or similar). In essence - be smart and hope for the best.

OTHER POINTS TO PONDER

Several of the areas covered in this guide have a fairly longstanding climbing history - some dating back to the 1960's and 70's. It stands to reason that, depending on the area, many of the routes presented are traditional in nature, using generally, though not always, clean protection. This style of climbing may seem foreign to those initiated in rock gyms or on sport routes, yet it is what makes the TAG region such a treasure.

The joy and sense of accomplishment of placing gear, setting up belay systems and looking back down a pitch and seeing nothing but chalked holds is a great feeling. Tennessee is home to some of the finest (and boldest) traditionally protected routes (as well as some of the best sport climbing) in the United States, which contributes to the widely-held notion of Southern climbers being "All 'Rounders". Take the time to learn about all forms of climbing. Learn to set up natural anchors and toprope setups. Gain an appreciation for the legacy left by previous climbers. As Chattanooga climber Craig Stannard aptly put it, "Today's climbers should realize that they are simply riding the wave, and are not the wave itself."

This is not a diatribe for, or against either climbing style, just a few thoughts from the perspective of someone who has seen the sport evolve into what it is today. Long gone are the days of heated and fractious arguments between "tradsters" and "sporties", and fortunately, traditional climbing and sport climbing peacefully co-exist. Having said that, it's still best not to go sinking bolts without thoughtful consideration of the nature of the crag in question, lest you bring much ire and wrath upon yourself. As we are all aware, crags that contain predominantly sport climbs tend to be more crowded, almost to the point of overuse, a fact that does not go unnoticed by land managers, Park Service personnel and the like. It is very important, at a time when climbing resources are under the very real threat of closure or severe restrictions that all climbers act responsibly, do as much as we can to help with access issues, and treat other users with respect. We are all responsible for how the public perceives us.

THE CUMBERLAND TRAIL

Several climbing areas covered in this guidebook now find themselves in, next to or managed by, the State Of Tennessee as part of the Cumberland Trail, and as such, the State now has jurisdiction over the management of all recreational activities on these lands. The trail begins by passing through Prentice Cooper State Forest, which includes Suck Creek Canyon, the Tennessee Wall and the Promised Land. Continuing northward, it passes through the North Chickamauga Gorge (Leda) and the Soddy Gorge (location of Deep Creek, one of the newer climbing areas in the region) Continuing north, the trail passes by Devil's Racetrack, Black Mountain, and the Obed/Clear Creek just to name a few. Luckily, Bobby Fulcher and the gang at the state have a very good working relationship with climbers and the Southeastern Climber's Coalition. Both organizations work together to come up with management strategies and plans to ensure that recreational opportunities are enjoyed, while protecting the resource.

The Cumberland Trail is an ambitious hiking trail project under development in East Tennessee. When completed, the Cumberland Trail (CT) will extend 300 miles from its northern terminus in the Cumberland Gap National Park (KY) to its southern terminus at the Chickamauga Chattanooga National Military Park located on Signal Mountain just outside Chattanooga, Tennessee. This scenic footpath follows a line of high ridges and deep gorges lying along or near the rugged, eastern edge of Tennessee's Cumberland Plateau, offering a unique wilderness experience and many scenic views, waterfalls, landscapes, gorges, wildlife, and widely varying flora. As a remote, backcountry trail it will meander through eleven Tennessee counties primarily on public lands. These lands are managed by Tennessee's Departments of Environment and Conservation (TDEC), Wildlife Resource Agency (TWRA), and Forestry. The trail also passes through two national parks and a national scenic river area. In 1998, the trail was designated the Justin P. Wilson Cumberland Trail State Park, Tennessee's first linear state park. The CT is an official component of the Tennessee Recreational Trails System and a legislatively designated State Scenic Trail. Furthermore, the Cumberland Trail is a part of the Great Eastern Trail, which is under development and will extend from Alabama to New York when completed.

The continued development and maintenance of the Cumberland Trail has been accomplished through a working relationship between the CTC and TDEC. The CTC, other nonprofits, private corporations, foundations, individuals, and others assist TDEC in raising funds for land acquisition, providing maintenance, and further developing the Cumberland Trail.

This extensive trail is being constructed and maintained largely by volunteers from Tennessee and across the nation, organized and managed by the Cumberland Trail Conference, an affiliate of the Tennessee Trails Association (TTA), a non-profit 501c3 membership organization. The CTC's mission is to design, construct, maintain, and raise funds in support of the Cumberland Trail. Building the Cumberland Trail is a grassroots effort, driven by the communities along the trail and a broad network of individuals from across the US. This very successful private/public partnership is a model often cited to demonstrate the power of volunteerism, and public/private partnerships.

Still a work-in-progress, the Cumberland Trail is a remote footpath that will pass north to south through 11 Tennessee counties on the eastern escarpment of the Cumberland Plateau. Once completed, the trail corridor will be contained on public lands. Presently, 190 miles are maintained and open for hiking and other outdoor activities. These miles are divided into 15 different segments. Between these segments, land acquisition for the proposed trail corridor is an on-going process, so gaps in the proposed trail route do exist. The Cumberland Trail Conference working with Tennessee's Department of Environment and Conservation, other government agencies, and private organizations are all diligently working to acquire the needed land and close the gaps. The open sections are all uniquely different and allow hikers access to remote areas preserved for their natural or scenic beauty that cannot be otherwise accessed. For more information, please visit **www.cumberlandtrail.org**.

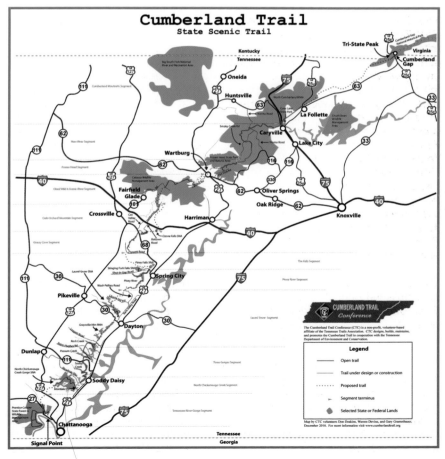

Cumberland Trail State Scenic Trail

Cumberland Trail State Scenic Trail
- - Open Trail
- - Proposed Trail
■ State Natural Areas
■ TWRA WMAs
■ Cumberland Trail SST *
■ State Parks
■ National Park Service

Map produced by James Brannon, GISP - Cumberland Trail SST - 02/11/2013

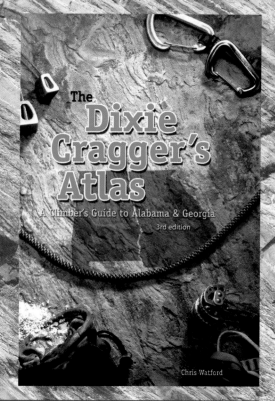

Chris Chesnutt on Soul Sounds
Photo: Bill Hatcher

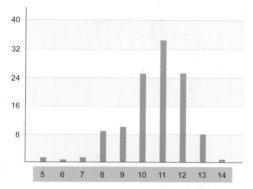

PARKING

WEATHER

CHAPTER 7

Buzzard Point, along with nearby Laurel Falls, lies in the Laurel/Snow Pocket Wilderness, near Dayton, Tennessee. Perched high on the rim of a spectacular gorge, it's one of the most beautiful areas in the Cumberland Plateau. For climbers, Buzzard offers an outstanding array of steep, difficult sport routes, typically on excellent stone, as well as a few crack lines. There are easier routes, but they are often short, slabby or just plain uninspiring. Possible drawbacks? Buzzard Point is mostly south-facing, so summers can be brutal. A fairly stout hike is required, but since it is primarily a sport crag, just divide the gear and hoof it - you won't be disappointed!

History

Most likely, the first climbers to visit Buzzard Point were Rob Robinson, Bruce Rogers and a few others in 1977. Route development was intermittent through the early 80's, until a highly motivated group of Atlanta and Chattanooga climbers, among them, Jeff Gruenberg, Charlie Kable, Ron Davis, James Dobbs, Shannon Stegg and Chris Chesnutt, began in earnest. Many noteworthy lines were put up during this time period, culminating with Gruenberg's testpiece, Pieta (one of the hardest routes in the East and still unrepeated). In 1990, Knoxville climbers Glenn Ritter and Tony Robinson put up many of the remaining lines in a flurry of activity. Today, Buzzard is just about "climbed out". (Famous last words, huh?)

Location and Directions

Dayton, Tennessee lies northeast of Chattanooga, along the eastern rim of the Cumberland Plateau. To get there, follow Highway 27 North to Dayton, bearing right on the Dayton Bypass, to the Medical Center. Turn left on Walnut Grove Road, at the 8th traffic light and follow it 1.5 miles. Turn left on Back Valley Road, and proceed one mile and turn right on Richland Creek Road. Follow this to a parking/picnic area. The trail follows Richland Creek, then cuts uphill and right, across a metal foot bridge,to a fork. The right trail goes to Laurel Falls, while the left soon crosses a series of metal footbridges and continues up to Snow Falls. The trail will climb up through the forest for roughly a mile, to intersect the cliff base. Walk left along the base to Buzzard Point, or go right and up through a cleft in the rock to Snow Falls.

For the hale and hearty, there is also the Shinbone Ridge approach. This is basically a bushwhack that involves hiking from the parking lot about 8/10 mile, then crossing the creek to the left. This steep "trail" follows the obvious ridge that shoots down the mountain and is rumored to be somewhat easier since the hillside burned a lot of the undergrowth a few years ago. This trail hits the cliff near Crack Of Dawn.

Camping

The closest camping is at the Laurel/Snow Pocket Wilderness trailhead or along the trail in designated spots. There is no camping in the vicinity of the aforementioned top drive in.

Luxuries

The small town of Dayton is pleasant enough, and offers gas, groceries, etc. but for most everything else, it is necessary to drive south the Chattanooga.

Emergency Services

Dayton Police Department	(423) 775 - 3876
Rhea County Sheriff's Department	(423) 775 - 2442
Rhea County Medical Center	(423) 775 - 1121

Regulations

The Laurel/Snow Pocket Wilderness is owned and managed by Bowater Paper Company. It is open to the public and the only regulations involve horseback riding and camping. Bowater asks that only designated campsites and fire rings be used.

FYI

Dayton, Tennessee, aside from being located in a beautiful part of the planet, also has a bit of historical significance. It was in the Rhea County Courthouse that noted attorneys William Jennings Bryan and Clarence Darrow fought a court battle to determine whether the theory of evolution could be taught in public schools. This legal battle later became known as the Scopes Monkey Trial. You may remember it from your ninth grade history class, if you weren't asleep.

The Laurel/Snow drainage, like many parts of the Plateau, was once a thriving coal mining area, as evidenced by the remains of an old rail line running along Richland Creek. Abandoned mine shafts are visible on the hillside above the trail, as are stone arches and remnants of the old pipeline which was once the water supply for the city of Dayton.

The Laurel/Snow Pocket Wilderness, home to both Buzzard Point and Laurel Falls, was once part of Bowater Paper Company's Pocket Wilderness Program - a goodwill venture designed to utilize non-productive land for recreation, Bowater has proven that its forests can be used for purposes other than pulp wood production. It is an excellent program, with ten wilderness areas currently in the system. Although they do not all offer climbing opportunities, they usually feature trails, waterfalls and scenic overlooks. For more information and a current map/brochure, contact:

Bowater
Calhoun, Tennessee 37309-0188
(423) 336-2211

Cliff Layout

The routes are listed right to left, from where the trail from the bottom intersects the Point. Please refer to the diagrams and topos.

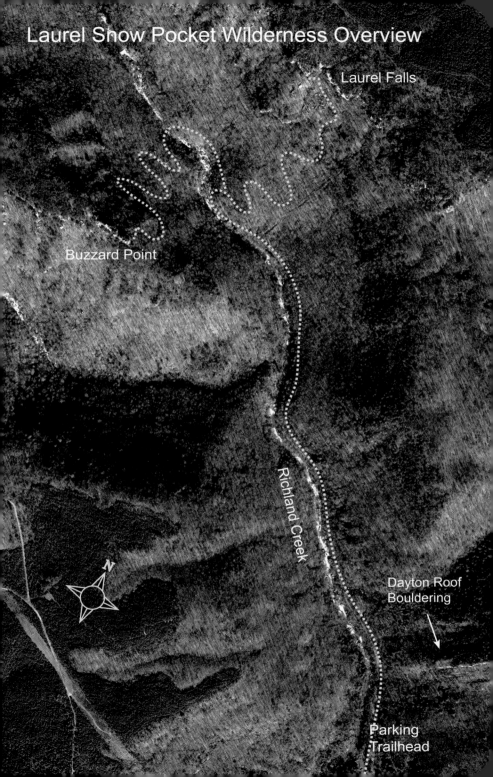

Laurel Snow Pocket Wilderness Overview

Laurel Falls

Buzzard Point

Richland Creek

Dayton Roof Bouldering

Parking Trailhead

Buzzard Point

The Point

The Boulder

1. *Crack Of Dawn 11b
Start: Climb up to a thin crack splitting a roof and face above. At the end of the crack, step right and follow an arete to the top. 60' *FA: Jerry Roberts and Chris Chesnutt, Tony Robinson (direct finish)*
Direct Finish 11b - At the end of the crack, follow two bolts up the face to the top. 60'

2. **Pump It To The Sky 12a/b
Start: 15' left of COD. Climb past six bolts to anchors. 60' *FA: Glenn Ritter, 1990*

3. ***Off To The Wild Blue Yonder 12a
Start: 5' left of Wild Blue Yonder. Clip past four bolts to the top. 60' *FA: Glenn Ritter, 1990*

4. **The Tall Cool One 11d
Airy and pumpy, this route was featured on the cover of Climbing magazine several years ago. Start: 15' left of Wild Blue Yonder. Climb a white arete, past a bolt just off the ground. *FA: Chris Chesnutt, 1990*

5. **Pocket Wilderness 12c
Start: 5' left of Tall Cool One. Climb a clean, white bolted face. 70' *FA: Glenn Ritter, 1992*

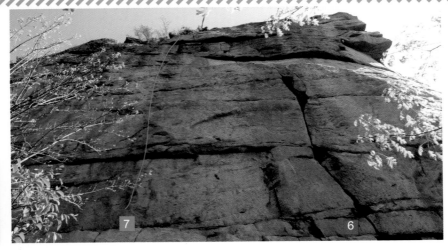

6. **Cracksmith's Delight 10d
Start: 5' left of Pocket Wilderness. Climb a finger/hand crack and face to the top. 70'

7. **Leapin' Lizards 12b
Start: 10' left of Cracksmith's Delight. Climb past five bolts to anchors. 70' *FA: Glenn Ritter, 1991*

8. *The Beefeater 11c
Start: 15' left of Leapin' Lizards, on a steep, orange face. Follow a thin, vertical seam to anchors. 50' *FA: Glenn Ritter, 1992*

9. Ambition Ammunition 11a
Start: Just left of The Beefeater. Climb past three bolts to a ledge. 35' *FA: Glenn Ritter and Tony Robinson, 1990*

10. *AIDS Crack 7
Start: 5' left of Ambition Ammunition. Climb a hand crack splitting the face. 60' *FA: Arno Ilgner*
*Alt. Finish (Ruby Falls) 10a
Climb the crack, then step left and follow the arete, past a bolt, to the top. 60' *FA: Glenn Ritter and Tony Robinson, 1990*

11. **Cuyahoga Falls 12b/c
Start: 5' left of AIDS Crack. Follow a line of bolts up a white face to the top. 60' *FA: Glenn Ritter, 1991*

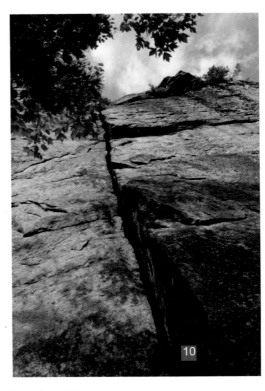

💲 12. **Cinderella 12a
Start: 5' left of Cuyahoga Falls. Climb a short, bolted seam and small, right-facing corner. Finish via the top of Cuyahoga Falls. 60' *FA: Glenn Ritter, 1991*

💲 13. ***Snow White 12a
Start: Just left of Cinderella. Climb a long, thin seam in a steep, white wall, past a few bolts. 50' *FA: Chris Chesnutt, 1990*

The next seven routes are located just left of Snow White, in a shallow recess/alcove. From the back of this recess/alcove, it is possible to see through a hole, to the other side of the cliff.

💲 14. *Who Shot Bambi? 10d
Start: 20' left of Snow White. Take aim on a blocky arete past two bolts to the top. 60' *FA: James Barry, 1990*

💲 15. *Dakota Blues 8
Start: 10' left of Bambi. Climb past two bolts, and finish just right of a small tree. 60' *FA: Erik Herbert, 1990*

💲 16. *The Theater 11b
Start: On the face opposite of Dakota Blues. Climb the face and arete, past three bolts, to anchors 50' *FA: Glenn Ritter, 1991*

🕕 17. Throb 10a
Start: 5' left of The Theater. Climb the right side of a big hollow flake to a stance, then up the face to anchors. 50' *FA: Tony Robinson, 1990*

T **18. Steal The Air 10a/b**
Start: 5' left of Throb. Climb a big, hollow flake, past a bolt, then finish up a nice crack to anchors. 60' *FA: Tony Robinson, 1990*

T **19. *Fit Makes The Fashion 11d**
Start: 10' left of Steal The Air, atop a boulder. Climb the face past two bolts and nice TCU placements (#0 critical). Trend up and left to anchors. 50' *FA: Glenn Ritter, 1990*

T **20. The Ugly Route 10b**
Start: Same as Fit Makes The Fashion. *FA: Arno Ilgner and Glenn Ritter, 1990*
P1: Move left past a horizontal slot, then follow a corner to a ledge. 40'
P2: Move left and follow an arete to the top. 30'
Alternate Finish (The Swan) 10a/b
Climb pitch one of the Ugly Route, then proceed past a bolt to the top. 70' *FA: Tony Robinson, 1990*

T **21. High Plains Drifter A3**
Start: 15' left of The Ugly Route. Pull a low roof and follow a short, thin seam, over a fixed rurp (?) and machine heads, to the top. 80' *FA: Erik Herbert, 1990*

T **22. Love It Or Leave It 11c/d**
Start: In the right side of a shallow recess, 25' left of High Plains Drifter. Follow a corner for a little ways. Step right and follow loose dirty holds to a roof. Continue to the top. 60' *FA: Tony Robinson and Glenn Ritter, toprope 1990*

23. Black Heart
Project just right of Incredalocks that goes out an obvious black bulge. Bouldery roof down low.

S **24. **Lost Horizons 11a**
Start: 50' left of Love It Or Leave It. (Rappel to the belay.) Follow several bolts up a steep face to anchors. 70' *FA: Tony Robinson, 1990*

T **25**Incredalocks 12a/b**
Start: 10' left of Lost Horizons. Climb a long finger/hand crack to the top. 80' *FA: Rob Robinson and partner, 1985*

The following four routes start from a ledge above the trail, left of Incredalocks.

26. *Joker's Wild 11b/c
Start: 15' right of Hard To Fathom. Wander up and right past two bolts to a small, left-facing corner. Continue over a third bolt to the top. 60' *FA: Glenn Ritter, 1990*

27. **Hard To Fathom 11d
Start: 15' left of Joker's Wild. Climb Hyperfathom (see below) but instead, angle right to anchors. 60' *FA: Glenn Ritter, 1991*

28. *Hyperfathom 11a/b
Start: Same as for Hard To Fathom. Climb the crack to a "T", then step left and climb past two bolts, along a right-arching crack to the top. 60' *FA: Tony Robinson, 1991*

29. Balisk 5
Start: Just left of Hyperfathom. Climb an easy flake/corner system to the top. 60'

30' left of Balisk, an enormous roof hangs over the trail. The next eight routes start from bolted, hanging belays above the lip. To access them, it is necessary to climb Balisk to the top, then walk left along the edge of the cliff to a rappel tree.

30. **Nine Hundred Foot Jesus 10a
Start: The furthest right route above the lip. Follow six bolts to top. 60' *FA: Tony Robinson, 1990*

31. **Jesus And The Prom Queen 11c
Start: Just left of 900 Foot Jesus. Move up and right past five bolts to the top. 60' *FA: Tony Robinson, 1991*

32. *King Jesus 11a
Start: Same as for Jesus And The Prom Queen. Follow five bolts to the top. 60' *FA: Glenn Ritter, 1990*

33. **Eleven Long Haired Friends Of Jesus 11c
Start: Just left of King Jesus. Follow a line of bolts up a steep face. 60' *FA: Glenn Ritter, 1992*

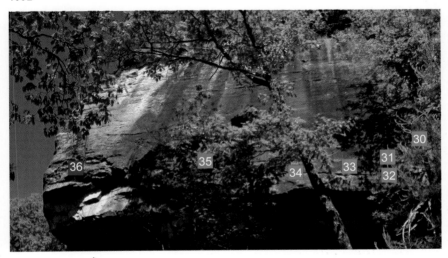

ⓢ 34. *Jesus Does The Rambo Hang 8+
Start: At a double bolt hanging belay, same as for Eleven. Follow bolts up a face and arete to the top. 60' *FA: Tony Robinson, 1991*

ⓢ 35. **Jesus! Get Away From The Edge! 9
Start: From a hanging belay, climb up and then step left to the left side of a prominent arete, past two bolts to the top. 60' *FA: Tony Robinson, 1991*

ⓣ 36. ***Life's Rich Pageant 11c/d
Airy, but with good holds and ample protection.
Start: From a single bolt belay, 30' left of Jesus, Get Away From That Edge! Climb the steep, orange wall above the lip of the roof, passing a fixed pin just off the belay. 60' *FA: Charlie Kable and Jeff Gruenberg, 1988*

The next five routes start from a ledge system above the trail. The first three share the same start.

ⓢ 37. *Antigone 10d
Start: Left of Life's Rich Pageant, trailside. Clip the first two bolts. Traverse right to a crack, then proceed past a third bolt to the top. 50' *FA: Tony Robinson, 1991*

ⓢ 38. Pride Goeth Before The Fall 10b
Start: Same as for Antigone. Clip the first bolt, then move up and right past three more bolts to anchors. 50' *FA: Tony Robinson, 1990*

ⓣ 39. *Dead Parents Society 11a
Start: Same as Antigone/Pride. Clip the first bolt, then move left over two more bolts to a hand crack. 50' *FA: Tony Robinson, 1990*

ⓣ 40. *Meridians Of Light 12c
Start: 20' left of Dead Parent's Society. Climb a rounded prow, over a bolt, then meander up a lichen-covered face to the top. 60' *FA: Chris Chesnutt, 1990*

ⓣ 41. **After The Fire 10d
Start: 50' left of Meridians Of Light, just right of an obvious prow. Pull a small roof. Follow a thin, left-facing flake over a roof and finish up the face to the top. 75' *FA: Jack Mileski, Mark Cole, Jennifer Cole, and Jeff Gruenberg, 1987*

The main access gully from the top is just to the left. There is a small ledge system halfway down the gully on the right wall, when looking up the gully. There are two routes on this ledge:

ⓢ 42. **Bottle Rocket 12c/d
Starts just right of Viper and takes the slightly overhanging face past 7 bolts to anchors. Note: The anchors are too high, sitting squarely in the middle of a

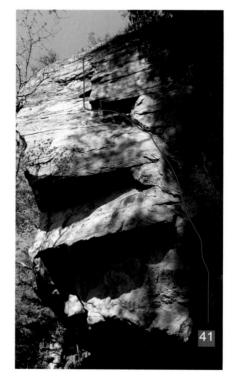

41

perennially-wet slab at the top. Hopefully they will be moved lower, but for now they have been lengthened with a long sling (?) *FA: Jerry Roberts, Anthony Meeks*

⛊ **43. Viper 13b**
Wanders a little, but essentially follows an overhanging arete feature. 5 bolts, anchors. 50'
FA: Jerry Roberts

The next few routes can be found by scrambling uphill to a small recess/amphitheater

⛊ **44. *Infant Of Fusion 9+**
Start: Left of the aforementioned gully. Follow three bolts past a ledge, to anchors. 50' *FA: Tony Robinson, 1991*

⛊ **45. Tiers Of My Years 10a**
Start: 15' left of Infant Of Fusion. Follow three bolts over a large flake to anchors. 50' *FA: Tony Robinson, 1991*

⛊ **46. *Humpty Pumpty 12c**
Start: 20' left of Tiers Of My Years. Stick clip a bolt and maneuver over roofs and up the face. 50' *FA: Glenn Ritter, 1991*

⛊ **47. ***Gargantua 12a**
Start: On the left side of the recessed alcove, 15' left of Humpty Pumpty. Yard out a roof past three bolts, then proceed up the face to the top. 50' *FA: Glenn Ritter, 1991*

⛊ **48. King Of Dreams 11a**
Start: 80' left of Gargantua. Follow bolts over a low roof and face to anchors. 35' *FA: Tony Robinson, 1991*

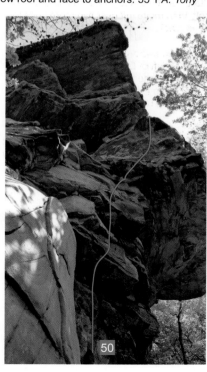

🆃 **49. Quark 10b/c**
Start: 15' left of King Of Dreams. Climb a white crack/corner system passing a roof midway. 40' *FA: Jay Arp, 1991*
Variation 10d
Start: 10' left of the regular start. Climb a shallow, right-facing dihedral/thin crack and finish on the regular route. 40' *FA: Tim Roberts, 1991*

⛊ **50. Sharon The Ho 11c**
Start: 25' left of Quark. Climb over two bolts to a ledge, step right and follow a bolted arete to anchors beneath a huge roof. 40' *FA: Tony Robinson, 1992*

⛊ **51. *Wild Virus 11b**
Start: 10' left of Sharon The Ho. Follow bolts to, and up, a corner, then through a roof to anchors. 50' *FA: Glenn Ritter, 1992*

⛊ **52. *Paul & Todd's Bogus Adventures 11a/b**
Start: 10' left of Wild Virus. Follow bolts through a notch/weakness in a roof to anchors. 55' *FA: Tony Robinson, 1992*

50

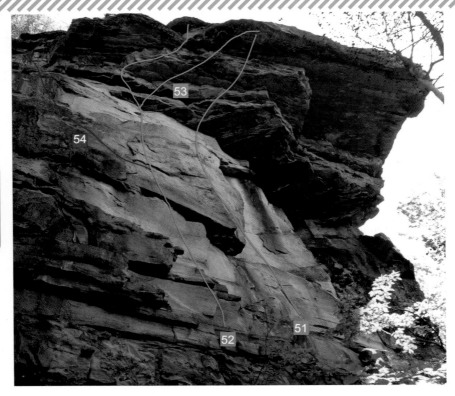

⑤ 53. *Legends In Their Own Minds 11a
Start on Paul and Todd's. Move right along a line
of bolts in the roof, then pull the lip (bolt). Finish on
Wild Virus. 55' *FA: Tony Robinson, 1992*

⊤ 54. I Should Have Stolen A Cadillac 8+
Start: Same as for Paul And Todd's. Climb over
two bolts, then angle left bypassing a large roof, to
the top. 55' *FA: John Martin, 1991*

⑤ 55. *R&R Productions 12b
Start: 20' left of Cadillac. Follow four bolts over a
roof and up face to anchors. 40' *FA: Glenn Ritter,
1992*

⑤ 56. *Knoxrageous 12a
Start: 30' left of R&R. Climb ledges and a face over
seven bolts to anchors. 40' *FA: Glenn Ritter, 1992*

⊤ 57. Way Out Back 11a
Start: Same as for Knoxrageous. Follow a
discontinuous system of cracks over bulges and
over a small overhang to the top. Reportedly tricky
and sandbagged. 40' *FA: Ron Davis, 1988*

CHAPTER 7

58. ***Slim Pickins 11a

Start: 50' left of Way Out Back. Climb a steep face past a few bolts to a thin crack in a steep slab. 90' *FA: Rob Robinson and Tim Cumbo, 1985*

59. ***Soul Sounds 13a

Start: 20' left of Slim Pickins. Follow a few bolts to a right-facing dihedral. Move left, turn the large, flat roof and continue up the headwall to the top. 70' Note: Used to require gear, but may have been fully bolted some years ago. *FA: Jeff Gruenberg, 1988*

60. ***Oh Man 13a

Start: 10' left of Soul Sounds. Follow a few scattered bolts through roofs and bulges to the top. 70' Note: Used to require gear but may not now. *FA: Jeff Gruenberg, 1990*

61. ***Wild Thing 12a (mixed)

Start: 5' left of Oh Man. Cruise up the wall over a roof. Labor into a small, left-facing dihedral. Continue over a small roof and up the steep headwall to the top. 70' Note: Requires gear. *FA: Jerry Roberts, 1988*

62. Meeks Route 12c/d

Left of Wild Thing. Another mostly bolted route that requires a light rack of cams. *FA: Anthony Meeks*

63. Big Timers 13a

Left of Meeks Route. Mostly bolted, but carry a light rack of mid-sized cams. *FA: Jerry Roberts, Anthony Meeks*

T **64. ***Talking Flakes 13a** (mixed)
Start: Angle right through a roof past a bolt. Step left to a small point/arete, then follow the steep headwall to the top. 70'
Note: Used to requires gear but may not now. *FA: Jeff Gruenberg, 1989*

T **65. ***Shake, Rattle And Hum 12c/d** (mixed)
Start: Same as Talking Flakes. Easy moves lead to a bolt. Step left past a bolt and layback a few hard moves. Rattle up the headwall to the top. 70' Note: Requires some gear. *FA: Ron Davis and Jeff Gruenberg, 1989*

S **66. ***Prime Time 12a**
Start: 40' left of Shake Rattle and Hum, from atop a ledge. Pull a flat roof and angle left past several bolts to the top. 60'
FA: Ron Davis, 1989

S **67. **Va Voom 12a**
Start: 10' left of Prime Time. Follow bolts through stacked roofs to the top. 40' *FA: Ron Davis, 1990*

S **68. Guns For Higher** (Project)
Start: 15' left of VaVoom. Climb up and left through stacked roofs to anchors. 40'

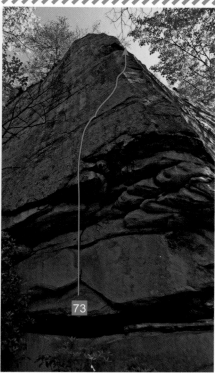

S **69. Imagine** (Project)
Start: 20' left of Guns For Higher. Follow bolts through stacked roofs to anchors. 40'

T **70. ***Bird In Hand 11a**
Start: 15' left of Imagine. Pull through a roof to an impressive corner above. Follow this to the top. 60' *FA: Rob Robinson and Tim Cumbo, 1985*

S **71. **Rhea County Gun Club 12b**
Start: Same as for Bird In Hand. Pull through the low roofs to a corner. Step left and climb over bolts to the top. 70' *FA: Glenn Ritter, 1992*

Continue walking left past an unnamed project for 50' or so to the next route…

T **72. *Grand Arch 9**
Start: Ascend a right-arching crack/flake system. 60' *FA: Chris Chesnutt, 1989*

S **73. Sly Man 12c**
Start: 15' left of Grand Arch, on a blunt, rounded face. Climb the smooth slab/face. (6 bolts, anchor) *FA: Travis Eiseman*

74. Nubian Tribes 11b
Start: On the right edge of a shallow recess, just left of Sly Man. Climb a thin crack that angles left. 60' *FA: Chris Chesnutt and Fritz Lovingood, 1992*

75. French Curl 6
Start: 50' left of Nubian Tribes. Climb a wide crack in an arching dihedral to the top. 60' *FA: Chris Chesnutt, 1988*

76. ***Tweekasaurus 12d
As the name implies…
Start: 30' left of French Curl, on a crimpy face. Crimp up a steep face over seven bolts. 70' *FA: Jeff Gruenberg, 1990*

77. ***Crankasaurus 11a
Start: 10' left of Tweekasaurus. Climb the bolted face above a large hole/hueco. 70' *FA: James Dobbs, 1988*

78. *Seepasaurus 10d
Start: 20' left of Crankasaurus. Climb over five bolts to an anchor. 60' *FA: Tony Robinson, 1991*

79. **Dynosaurus 10c
Start: 5' left of Seepasaurus. Climb over three bolts to anchor. 60' *FA: Tony Robinson, 1991*

T **80. Nomadosaurus 10a**
Start: 10' left of Dynosaurus. Climb past a bolt, then over small roofs to an anchor. 60' *FA: Tony Robinson, 1991*

T **81. Solosaurus 5**
Start: 50' left of Nomadosaurus. Climb past low-angle flakes. Wander to the top. 80' *FA: Ron Davis, 1989*

S **82. *Loonasaurus 11b**
Start: 35' left of Solosaurus. Climb past bolts and a fixed pin. Continue up the headwall above. Often done in two pitches. 90' *FA: Kent Ballew and Bear Thurman, 1988*

T **83. Megasaurus 8**
Start: 10' left of Loonasaurus, near the center of an obvious buttress capped by huge overhangs. Follow a crack system and a flared chimney. Move left, avoiding the roofs above. 80'

T **84. Pussified 9**
Start: 100' left of Megasaurus. Climb a thin crack in a short corner. 40' *FA: Kent Ballew and Bear Thurman, 1992*

T **85. *Rainbow Inn 10a**
Start: 10' left of Pussyfied. Climb a brown face past a bolt to anchors. 30' *FA: Glenn Ritter, 1991*

T **86. *Sampson's Gym 11a/b**
Start: 30' left of Rainbow Inn. Climb a shallow corner with thin cracks, then hike up ledges to the top. 60' *FA: Glenn Ritter and Tony Robinson, 1991*

T **87. Americus 9**
Start: 20' left of Sampson's Gym. From atop the aforementioned flakes, move right and follow a hand crack above roof to the top. 60'

T **88. Harrison's Ford 9**
Start: Same as Americus. From atop huge flakes, continue up a steep, blocky face to the top. 60'

S **89. Abe's Lincoln 10a**
Start: 10' left of Harrison's Ford. Climb a short face over a bolt to anchors. 30' *FA: Tony Robinson, 1991*

S **90. Freddie's Mercury 9+**
Start: Same as Abe's Lincoln. Climb a short arete over a bolt, to anchors. 30' *FA: Glenn Ritter, 1991*

T **91. Boys Of Argon 8**
Start: 30' left of Freddie's Mercury. Climb a face over small overhangs to the top. 50' *FA: Glenn Ritter, 1991*

T **92. Off Yer Rocker 10b/c**
Start: 10' left of Boys Of Argon. Climb a scrappy corner; through a roof slot and continue to the top. 50' *FA: Ron Davis, 1990*

S **93. *Dance Of The Vampires 11a**
Start: 150' left of Off Yer Rocker. (4 bolts, anchors) 40' *FA: Tim Roberts, 1992*

🅣 94. *Spider Tropic 10c/d
Start: 10' left of Dance. Climb up a short, left-facing dihedral over a small roof, then follow a thin seam over a bulge to the top. 40' *FA: Fritz Lovingood, 1988*

🅣 95. *Coral Methane 10c/d
Start: 10' left of Spider Tropic. Climb past a large flake and meander to the top. 40' *FA: Fritz Lovingood, 1988*

🅣 96. *Reception 8
Start: 15' left of Coral Methane. Climb a right-facing corner over a small roof. 40' *FA: Ron Davis, 1988*

🅣 97. Peacocks And Hemlocks 7
Start: 30' left of Reception. Climb a corner for a few moves, then step left and up the face to the top. 40' *FA: Fritz Lovingood, 1989*

🅢 98. Stained Glass (Project)
Start: Scramble on top of a block, 20' left of Peacocks. Pull lip of large roof, then up and right past more bolts to the top. 50'

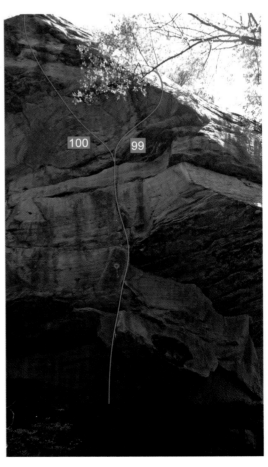

🅢 99. ***Au Naturale 13b/c
As Jeff so mildly put it, "Au Naturale starts on Pieta, but avoids the issue". Still hard.
Start: 30' left of Stained Glass, on an impressive buttress. Power over the roof and up to the horizontal. Break right and up steep ground to anchors. (7 bolts) *FA: Jeff Gruenberg, 1989*

🅢 100. ***Pieta 14a
One of the first 5.14's in the South. Seldom repeated.
Start: Same as for Au Naturale. Follow a line of bolts over a low roof and up to an obvious horizontal. Continue over a smooth, sweeping overhang and up to anchors. (7 bolts, anchors) *FA: Jeff Gruenberg, 1989*

🅢 101. ***Fantasia 12a
Start: 20' left of Pieta. Follow bolts up a pocketed orange face to the top. *FA: Chris Chesnutt, 1988*

🅣 102. *Refrigerator Crack 12a
Start: 15' left of Fantasia. Follow a hand crack in a flaring corner. 50' *FA: Chris Chesnutt, 1989*

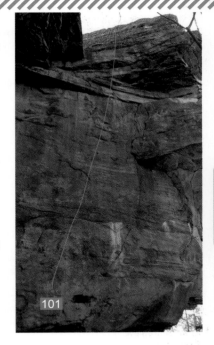

🪨 103. ***Sweat This 12b/c
Start: 15' left of Refrigerator Crack, on the left wall of a recessed alcove. Climb an overhanging flake, over a bulge to anchors. 40' *FA: Ron Davis, 1988*

🪨 104. Praise Ye Jah! 13c
Short and stout. (3 bolts, anchor) *FA: Anthony Meeks*

🪨 105. The Drill Sergeant 12c
Controversial because of manufactured pockets. Nonetheless a nice arete.
Start: Just left of Sweat This. Climb the arete, step left and up to the top. 40' *FA: Ron Davis, 1989*

🪧 106. Formula Rock 11b
Start: 30' left of Drill Sargeant, 20' right of the old ladder downclimb. Climb past a bolt, pull a roof to anchors. 35' *FA: Glenn Ritter, 1991*

To the left is the old ladder access, which is all but completely unusable at this point. The following routes are located to the left.

🪧 107. **Scandalous Intentions 10d
A bulgy wall leads to roofs. 45'

T **108. Shirley's Temple 9**
Start: 15' left of Scandalous Intentions. Angle left past a bolt and pull a small roof to anchors. 45' *FA: Glenn Ritter, 1991*

T **109. Fox's Earth 10d**
Start: At the right side of a tan face, 10' left of Shirley's Temple. Climb a ledgy arete. 40'

S **110. *Royal Flesh 10d**
Start: 100' left of Fox's Earth. Four bolts to anchors. 30' *FA: Glenn Ritter, 1991*

S **111. Sand Dollars 9**
Start: 25' left of Royal Flesh. Climb a face, over several bolts, to anchors. 30' *FA: Tony Robinson, 1991*

T **112. Sonic Boom 9**
Start: 5' left of Sand Dollars. Blast up a face, over roofs, to the top. 30'

THE BOULDER

The Boulder lies down in the woods, directly below Pieta/Au Naturale. The following nine routes are on the backside of The Boulder and are listed from right to left.

S **113. Beefaroni 10d**
Start: At the right end of the boulder. Climb the arete. 25' *FA: Tony Robinson, 1991*

S **114. Conan The Vegetarian 10d**
Start: Just left of Beefaroni. Climb past a bolt, trend left and up to overlap. Continue to anchors. 25' *FA: Tony Robinson, 1991*

S **115. Defpotec 11c**
Start: Just left of Conan. Follow a few bolts. 25' *FA: Tony Robinson, 1991*

S **116. Geekis Khan 11b**
Start: At center of the wall, just left of Defpotec. Clip a bolt, proceed to a crack and anchors. 25' *FA: Tony Robinson, 1991*

S **117. Atilla The Nun 11a/b**
Start: Just left of Geekis Khan. Climb past a left-facing corner to anchors. 20' *FA: Tony Robinson, 1992*

S **118. Jack The Stripper 10d**
Start: Same as Atilla The Nun. Climb to anchors. 20' *FA: Glenn Ritter, 1992*

The next three routes are on the west side of the boulder:

S **119. Vols And Chains 8**
Bolts and a cold shut anchor. 20' *FA: Tony Robinson, 1991*

S **120. Vols To The Wall 8**
Bolts and cold shuts. 20' *FA: Tony Robinson, 1991*

S **121. Have A Vol Tonight 8**
Bolts and cold shuts. 20' *FA: Tony Robinson, 1991*

Buzzard Point – Far Left (west) End and Boulder

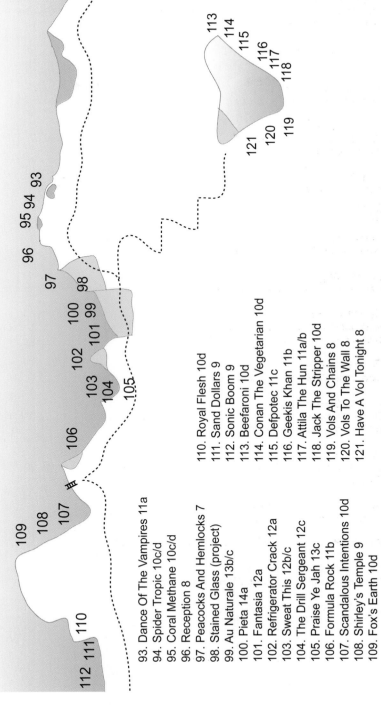

93. Dance Of The Vampires 11a
94. Spider Tropic 10c/d
95. Coral Methane 10c/d
96. Reception 8
97. Peacocks And Hemlocks 7
98. Stained Glass (project)
99. Au Naturale 13b/c
100. Pieta 14a
101. Fantasia 12a
102. Refrigerator Crack 12a
103. Sweat This 12b/c
104. The Drill Sergeant 12c
105. Praise Ye Jah 13c
106. Formula Rock 11b
107. Scandalous Intentions 10d
108. Shirley's Temple 9
109. Fox's Earth 10d

110. Royal Flesh 10d
111. Sand Dollars 9
112. Sonic Boom 9
113. Beefaroni 10d
114. Conan The Vegetarian 10d
115. Defpotec 11c
116. Geekis Khan 11b
117. Attila The Hun 11a/b
118. Jack The Stripper 10d
119. Vols And Chains 8
120. Vols To The Wall 8
121. Have A Vol Tonight 8

Laurel Falls
Photo: Charles Sutherland

PARKING   WEATHER

Laurel Falls is the "other" crag in the Laurel/Snow Wilderness, having basked in the shadow of it's better known neighbor, Buzzard Point, for many years. This may no longer be the case for two reasons: Buzzard is now more difficult to get to, and second, Laurel has become quite popular lately as a bouldering area. Laurel Falls is one of those cliffs that everyone should visit at least once. The setting is spectacular, the hike in is gorgeous (one of the prettiest in the region) and the rock is some of the best quality sandstone anywhere: super hard and smooth, with an almost granite-like feel. The lengthy, but beautiful approach (one hour at a leisurely pace or 45 minutes at "climbers pace") is balanced by a high concentration of three star routes, all in the higher grades. Laurel Falls is mostly a sport climbing area, so a rack of quicks is all that's required, nevertheless, there are a few stellar traditional cracks and corners. South facing, it can be hot in the summer, but the waterfall may make things a bit more bearable. In winter, Laurel Falls is bathed in warm sunshine.

History

A handful of climbers visited Laurel through the 80's, but because the rock is smooth and featureless, few natural lines existed, and the cliff lay dormant for many years. Chris Chesnutt, Eddie Whittemore and Porter Jarrard put up most of the routes at the Falls Area, and in the early 90's, Glenn Ritter, Tony Robinson and Kelly Brown concentrated on the Powerline Area. Surprisingly, there were a few outstanding crack lines that fell to Shannon Stegg in 1993. In recent years, locals have ferreted out an extensive amount of bouldering, mostly in the creek and along the hillsides.

Location and Directions

From Dayton, Tennessee, take Walnut Grove Road, located at the north end of town at the 8th traffic signal. Follow Walnut Grove for 1.4 miles (it will become Back Valley Road) and look for the entrance to the Laurel Snow Wilderness Area, at a gravel road on the right. Continue .8 miles to the picnic area/trailhead. The trail follows Richland Creek and crosses an old wooden bridge. After about a mile, the trail cuts uphill and right, crosses a metal footbridge, continues through a boulderfield beside the creek to a fork. Bear right and follow it to the cliff. Where the trail intersects the cliff, it is possible to follow a steep gully to the top. This trail crosses Laurel Creek above the falls, then continues to Snake Head Point (Bryan Overlook) along an old logging road.
Yes, the rumors are true, there is a top drive-in for Laurel Falls, but you'll need to do a little

exploring and be resourceful. The top access follows a four-wheel drive road that branches off the Evensville Mountain Road, from the town of Evensville, just north of Dayton. Hint: Check out the Evensville and Morgan Springs USGS quad sheets, Google Earth or similar. This is a 4 wheel drive road in the best conditions and impassable in the worst conditions. Bring a tow rope.

Camping

Camping used to be unrestricted at Laurel Snow, but that is no longer the case. Backcountry camping permits are required. To obtain a permit, call (423) 566-2229 or visit http://cumberlandtrail.org/laurel.html. Should you choose to camp near the parking area or along Richland Creek, be aware of posted fire restrictions and stay only in designated areas.

Rules and Regulations

The area is closed from sunset to sunrise and the gate is locked. This is strictly enforced. Camping is in designated spots only and registration is required. Currently, no new route development is allowed at Laurel Snow, insofar as bolted sport routes go. Anchor management and replacement are allowed however. This is especially enforced at the lower cliffs close to the parking area and along the first part of the hiking trail.

Luxuries

Groceries, gas and restaurants can be found in Dayton - anything more and you'll have to venture south to Chattanooga.

Emergency Services

Dayton Police Department	(423) 775 - 3876
Rhea County Sheriff's Department	(423) 775 - 2442
Rhea County Medical Center	(423) 775 – 1121

Cliff Layout

Upon departing from the parking area, you will soon come to the old mine opening beside the trail, and some mining ruins above. A faint trail leads up beside the ruins to a short cliff up in the woods, with a sport route or two, and a popular bouldering cave/hangout spot.

Continuing on, follow the well blazed trail leading to the falls. The trail intersects the cliff and everything to the right is the Falls Area, while everything to the left is the Powerline Area. Please see the accompanying topos and route pics.

Laurel Snow Wilderness Trail Map

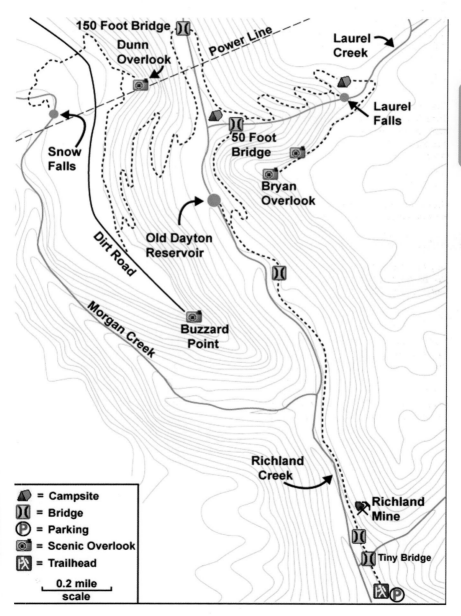

150 Foot Bridge

Dunn Overlook

Power Line

Laurel Creek

Snow Falls

Laurel Falls

50 Foot Bridge

Bryan Overlook

Dirt Road

Old Dayton Reservoir

Morgan Creek

Buzzard Point

Richland Creek

Richland Mine

Tiny Bridge

= Campsite
= Bridge
= Parking
= Scenic Overlook
= Trailhead

0.2 mile
scale

Laurel Falls

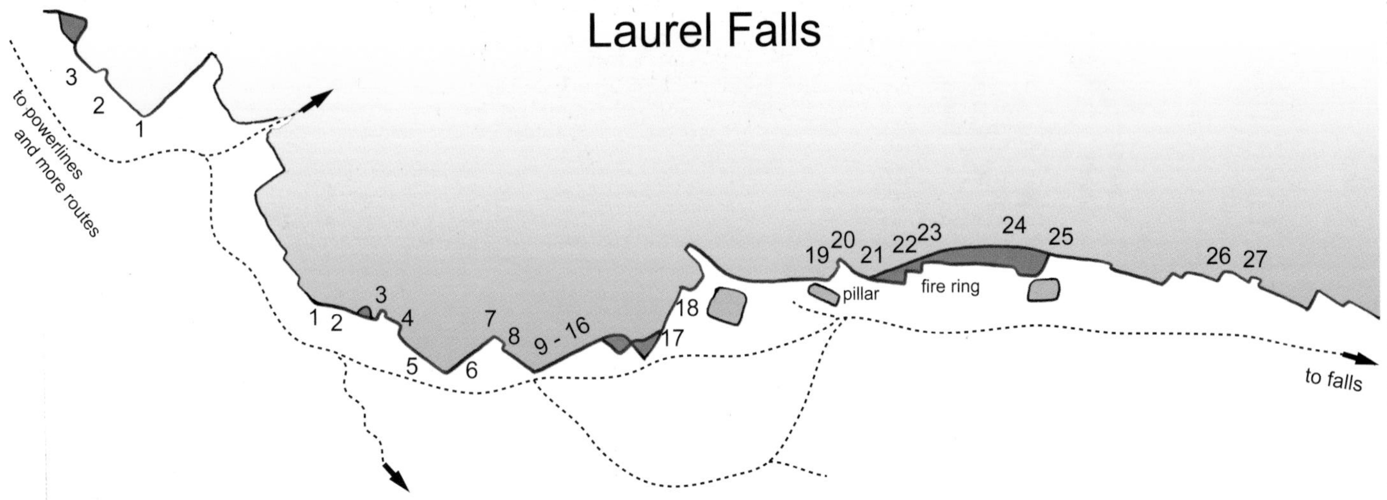

to falls

to powerlines
and more routes

fire ring

pillar

1. Ritter's Arete 5.10c
2. Super Slick Slick Seam
3. Man With The Blue Guitar 5.8

1. Vanishing Breed 5.12a
2. Cracker Jack Kid 5.13a/b
3. Classical Crack 5.11c
4. Cyclops' Belly 5.13a
5. The Jackal (project)
6. Darwinism 5.11b
7. Knoxville Boys 5.8

8. Visions of Jesus Freaks 5.8
9. Leap Of Faith 5.12c
10. Annie Sprinkle's Christmas 5.12c/d
11. Evolution Number Nine 5.12c
12. Origin of Species 5.12a
13. Monkey Boy 5.12a
14. Arms Control 5.12c/d
15. The Next To The Last Boy Scout 5.12c/d
16. The Last Boy Scout 5.12b
17. Unknown Mixed Route
18. Attic Toys 5.12a

19. Webs We Weave 5.12b
20. Tooth, Fang and Claw 5.11a
21. Coolio 5.13b/c
22. Live And Let Dihedral 5.11b/c
23. Shallow Water 5.12b
24. New Sport Route
25. Brown Book 5.12a
26. Gideon's Corner 5.10b/c
27. Tradland 5.9

This is the area to the right of where the trail intersects the cliff line, if you approach from the bottom.

🔲 1. Vanishing Breed 12a
Start: In a shallow, left-facing corner over a bulge, then move right over a blank face to the top. 60' *FA: Shannon Stegg, 1993.*

🔺 2. **Cracker Jack Kid 13a/b
Start: Where the trail meets the wall, just right of Vanishing Breed. Follow six bolts up a bulgy, brown wall to anchors. 60' *FA: Jerry Roberts, 1996*

🔲 3. ***Classical Crack 11c
Start: 25' right of Cracker Jack Kid. Difficult moves lead to a perfect hand/finger crack. Follow this to a rappel tree/ledge. 70' *FA: Shannon Stegg and Greg Allen, 1992.*

ⓈＳ 4. **Cyclops' Belly 13a
Start:10' right of Classical Crack.
Follow five bolts up a short corner,
over a roof to anchors. 65' *FA: Jerry
Roberts, 1996.*

ⓈＳ 5. The Jackal (project)
Start: 10' right of Cyclops' Belly. A
bolted but unclimbed face to anchors.

Continue walking right around a
corner, and look for a tree that has
grown against the rock just right of
an arete. The next route lies near the
middle of the wall, just right of the
tree.

🅃Ｔ 6. Darwinism 11b
Start: 50' right of The Jackal on a tall
lichen-covered face. Trend up and left
to a vertical crack system and follow
it to the top. 60' *FA: Shannon Stegg,
1992*

🅃Ｔ 7. Knoxville Boys 8
Start: 10' right of Darwinism. Climb a
prominent crack/corner. 60' *FA: Kelly
Brown and friends, 1992.*

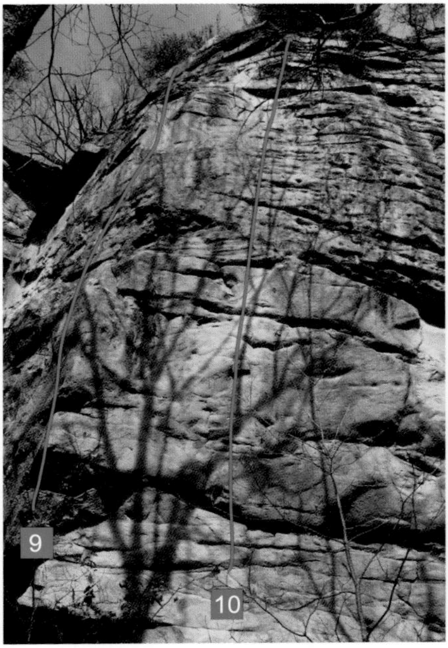

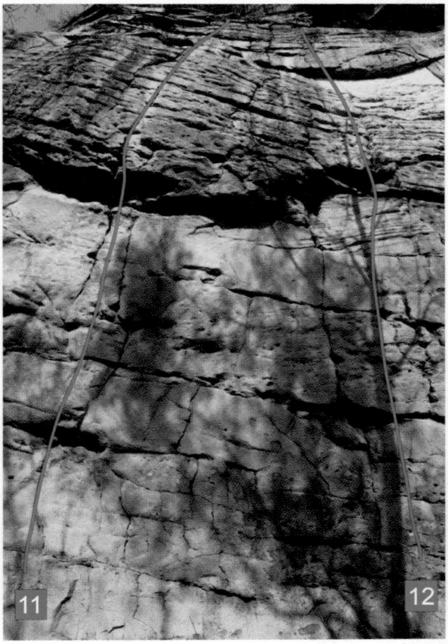

8. Visions of Jesus Freaks 8
Start: 10' right of Darwinism. Climb a shallow, left-facing dihedral and face to the top. 60' *FA: Kelly Brown and friends, 1992.*

9. **Leap Of Faith 12b/c
Start: 30' right of Visions of Jesus Freaks. A striking, blunt arete. 60' *FA: Lance Brock, Jerry Roberts, Travis Eiseman*

10. ***Annie Sprinkle's Christmas 12c/d
Start: 10' right of Leap Of Faith. Follow five bolts up steep ground to anchors. 60' *FA: Porter Jarrard, 1990.*

11. ***Evolution Number Nine 12c
Start: 10' right of Annie Sprinkle's Christmas. Follow eight bolts to an anchor. 60' *FA: Porter Jarrard, 1990.*

12. ***Origin of Species 12a
Start: 15' right of Evolution Number Nine. Follow a crack/water groove to the top. 60' *FA: Shannon Stegg, 1992*

13. ***Monkey Boy 12a
The easiest route on the wall.
Start: 10' right of Origin Of Species. Follow a line of gray, red and beige hangers to anchors. 60' *FA: Chris Chesnutt, 1990*

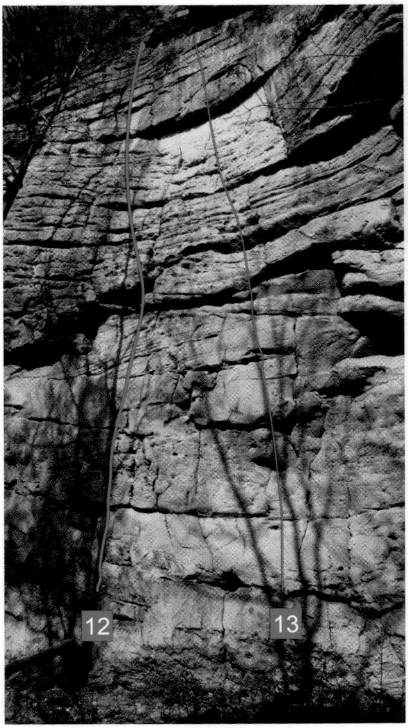

⑤ 14. **Arms Control 12c/d
Start: 15' right of Monkey Boy. Follow gray and beige hangers to anchors. 60' *FA: Porter Jarrard, 1990.*

⑤ 15. **The Next To The Last Boy Scout 12c/d
Start: 20' right of Arms Control. Follow gray, orange and beige hangers to an anchor. 60'
FA: Porter Jarrard, 1990.

⑤ 16. ***The Last Boy Scout 12b
Start: Same as for The Next To The Last Boy Scout. Break right from Next To The Last Boy Scout, over a roof, to anchors. 60' *FA: Porter Jarrard, 1990*

🅣 17. Unknown Mixed Route
Starts just right, around the corner. Paw and claw out the low roof on slopers past a couple of bolts, to gain the face.

🅣 18. Attic Toys 12a
Start: 10' right of previous route at a tree growing next to the rock. Climb past fixed pins, and up the steep headwall above, to the top. 60' *FA: Shannon Stegg and Kevin Cantwell, 1992.*

Continue walking right about 100', to a prominent, boot-shaped pillar next to the cliff.

🅣 19. **Webs We Weave 12b
Start: On an arete behind the boot-shaped pillar, 100' right of Attic Toys. Follow a hand and finger crack through roofs to a tree. 60' *FA: Shannon Stegg and Wade Gilbert, 1992.*

🅣 20. Tooth, Fang and Claw 11a
Start: 10' right of Webs We Weave. Climb a wide crack over a roof, and finish on Webs We Weave. 70' *FA: Shannon Stegg, 1992.*

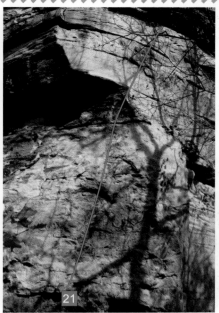

Ⓢ 21. Coolio 13b/c
Start: 25' right of Tooth, Fang and Claw. Follow eight bolts up an arete/bulge to anchors. 60'
FA: Jerry Roberts, 1996.

Ⓣ 22. *Live And Let Dihedral 11b/c
Start: 15' right of Coolio. Climb a crack
in a striking, white corner to an obvious
horizontal. 30' *FA: Arno Ilgner, 1991.*

Ⓢ 23. **Shallow Water 12b
Start: 20' right of Live And Let Live
Dihedral. Follow six bolts up a shallow,
right facing corner and headwall to an
anchor. 60' *FA: Porter Jarrard, 1990*

Ⓢ 24. ***New Route
Starts 25' right of Shallow Water. A nice
steep white face with six bolts and rings.

Ⓣ 25. Brown Book 12a
Start: 50' right of Shallow Water. Climb
a prominent, right-facing dihedral to a
ledge. Rappel off or continue to the top.
60' *FA: Arno Ilgner and Glenn Ritter,
1990.*

Ⓣ 26. Gideon's Corner 10b/c
Start: Just right of a wet, seeping wall, 30'
right of Brown Book. Follow a right-facing
dihedral over bulges to the top. 60' *FA:
Shannon Stegg, 1992.*

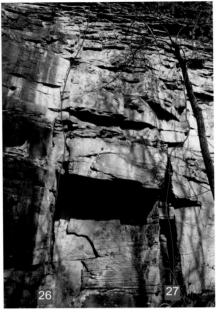

T **27. Tradland 9**
Start: 10' right of Gideon's Corner. Unpleasant mountaineering leads to a chimney. Move right onto a ledge, up to a right facing dihedral, and then to the top. 65' *FA: Shannon Stegg and Wade Gilbert, 1992.*

THE POWER LINE AREA

This section of the cliff lies to the left of where the trail meets the cliffline. Walk left towards the power lines.

T **1. *Ritter's Arete 10c**
Start: About 70' left of where the trail meets the cliff line. Climb a steep, blunt arete, past fixed pins, to the top. *FA: Shannon Stegg, 1998.*

2. Super Slick Slick Seam
Start: 10' left of Ritter's Arete. An unclimbed steep face featuring a slick, vertical seam. 65'

T **3. Man With The Blue Guitar 8**
Start: 15' left of Super Slick Seam. Climb a large crack and skirt left around the blocky overhang up high. 65' *FA: Kelly Brown, 1992.*

Continue walking left to a recessed alcove...

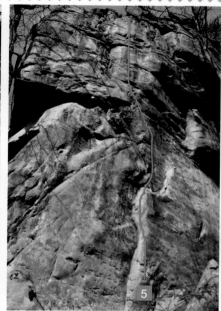

4. Turtle Route
Start at the right side of the alcove. Toprope a steep, concave face with a turtle-shell shaped feature midway up.

🔺 5. Unknown Route
Starts on a right-facing steep wall, 150' left of Turtle Route. Begin in a narrow left-facing dihedral and follow a steep wall past four bolts to a bail biner or topout.

🅣 6. Line Drive 7
Start: 150' left of Man With The Blue Guitar. Mantle on to the low ramp and follow overlapping bulges and slopers to the top. 60' *FA: Tony Robinson, 1991*

The trail continues toward the powerlines, and the cliff gets much lower in height. Just past the powerlines, there is a cave with tiered roofs. There are two routes here...

7. Power Tropic 11c
Start: At the right side of the cave, 200' left of Line Drive. Toprope a bulgy roof/arete, on good holds, to the top. 60'

🅣 8. Low Self Opinion 9+
Finger crack to ledge with tree. Continue along a flaring handcrack through a small roof and finish up the upper face. *FA: Tony Sykes and John Dean, 1994*

🅢 9. **Cave Route 12c
Start: Just left of Low Self Opinion. Jug out roof, past five bolts, to an anchor. 50' Note: May have a fixed wire near the lip. *FA: Porter Jarrard, 1990.*

🅢 10. **Dubstep Polka 9
Start: 100' left of Cave Route. Navigate a flaring slot down low. A bucket ladder leads up to and over a roof. (7 bolts, anchor) *FA: Micah Gentry, Richard Parks and Blane Andrews.*

🅢 11. ***Harder 10b/c
Start: 100' left of the Cave Route. Follow bolts up a pretty, orange face, to anchors. 60' *FA: Kelly Brown, 1991*

🅢 12. **Laurel 9
Start: 10' left of Harder. Climb past bolts to anchors. 60' *FA: Kelly Brown, 1991*

Laurel Snow Bouldering

In recent years, Laurel Snow has become a popular bouldering spot, and for good reason - the hillsides and creekbed of Richland Creek are lined with boulders of all sizes. One of the more popular features is the Dayton Roof (or Honeycomb Roof), a flat horizontal low cave at the base of the cliff above the old mine. To get there, hike a few minutes along the main roadbed. Just before reaching the old mine tunnel entrance, a faint trail cuts uphill to an obvious cliffband. There's a nice sport route on the left end, and the roof can be found to the right.

Torpedo, Dayton Roof
Photo: Wes Powell

Old mine entrance along the approach trail to Lautrel Falls

Louis Rumanes on The Turret
Photo: Rene Pirolt

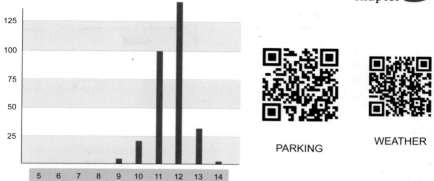

PARKING

WEATHER

The white sandstone buttress of Castle Rock stands above the town of Jasper, Tennessee like a sentinel – hard to miss for those traveling up TN150/41 on the way up the Plateau to Foster Falls. Developed largely in the late 80's and early 90's by such stalwarts as Chris Chesnutt, Jeff Gruenberg, Ron Davis, Travis Eiseman and Jerry Roberts, the cliff plays host to some of the highest quality sandstone sport climbing in the Deep South. Unfortunately, sampling this abundance of great routes was impossible for many years, as it is on private land, and was closed for most of the past decade. Assembling this chapter was extremely tedious and difficult, as the cliff has seen several "eras" of development. Many of the routes were bold trad or mixed routes with different names. Most have been retrobolted and renamed, with updated grades.

In the fall of 2004, The Southeastern Climbers Coalition representatives Brad McLeod and Kirk Brode began negotiations with the landowners to open access to this area. In 2005, a verbal commitment was reached, a lease was signed and with help from the Access Fund and dozens of volunteers, the cliff was re-opened. The SCC manages the property and hosts trail days throughout the year. Chattanooga locals Luis Rodriguez, Steve Deweese, Micah Gentry and several others have been hard at work in recent years replacing bolts and anchors, as well as establishing new routes.

The cliff itself is approximately 1/2 mile long, averages 80' to 120' in height and is comprised of bullet sandstone. With a current route inventory of over 50 sport and traditional routes, there should be plenty to whet the appetite of climbers of all skill levels, though most of the routes are in the higher grades, including Jerry Robert's Apes on Acid (13d), one of the hardest routes in Tennessee. There is no easy toproping here, so if you visit, you gotta tie into the sharp end.

A word from the SCC website: "Castle Rock is located on private land and currently leased by The SCC. If you have a chance to attend a fundraiser like the one held at TBA Gym on Halloween then throw a few dollars in the jar to help donate to pay the lease. If you can't donate cash then show up at a trail day or help repair anchors. Any donation of time or energy will help. The long range goal for Castle Rock is to eventually purchase the cliff and allow the climbing public to utilize this tract in the same open manner that we operate Kings Bluff, Boat Rock and Jamestown."

Parking Area Coordinates

35° 07'00.63"N
85° 37'52.77"W

Location And Directions

From Chattanooga, Tennessee: Take I-24 West towards Nashville. Drive about 20 miles, crossing over the Tennessee River at Nickajack Lake. After passing the huge fireworks store in the highway median (!), exit on to Hwy. 28 and proceed north a couple of miles to the off ramp for Jasper and Hwy. 41. Go left and under the bridge, passing a Dairy Queen on your right and into downtown Jasper. Take a right at the light by the courthouse onto Hwy. 41 heading towards Tracy City. Drive 1.2 miles and veer left (staying on Hwy. 41) at the light and follow it up the mountain, with a nice view of Castle Rock to the right.

From here, there are two parking options. (1) At press time, representatives from the SCC are working on a new option of parking at the bottom. As you are driving up Hwy 41 (Castle Rock lies to the right) turn right into a development marked Greystone on the right. Follow this drive as it winds along the hillside and look for a parking pulloff before the rock yard. A trail will be built that departs from this point. Where it will intersect the cliff base is uncertain at this time. **(2)** The longstanding parking is accessed via the following directions. Follow 41 to the top of the mountain and turn right on Sequatchie Mountain Road (the old Mountain Mart stone building is on the left at this turn). Drive about 2.5 miles and you will see an old dirt road and open area on your right. Turn right into dirt area and park. Park and walk the jeep trail (30 minute hike) towards the Castle Rock point. The old jeep trail will lead to a powerline. Walk left along the powerline for a ways, crossing a small stream and heading into the woods once again, towards the point. The trail will end on top of the point, so check out the view. The descent trail goes off to the right before the point, trending downhill and into a gully/corridor to the base. The routes Rocks Are For Climbing and Dickel's For Drinking are in this corridor.

Camping

Camping is not allowed at Castle Rock. The closest camping is at Foster Falls, a bit further up TN 41.

Luxuries

Jasper is a pleasant little town with gas. Groceries and a few restaurants. The Roy Acuff Inn, at the intersection of I-24 and Hwy 28 is a nice, clean, inexpensive hotel, with a Golden Corral restaurant.

Emergency Assistance

Dial 911

Regulations

Remember that while visiting Castle Rock, you are guests on private land. Act accordingly. Pack out all trash, including your own. Do not camp or build fires.

Cliff Layout

Upon descending through the entry corridor, turn right to check out the less developed North End of the cliff or turn to the left for the bulk of the routes. See photo.

CHAPTER 9

Castle Rock Overview Map

Powerlines

Main Trail

Upper Parking/Trailhead

Lower Parking Trailhead

Sequatchie Mountain Road

N

Powerlines

Apes Wall

Bonny and
Clyde Wall

Predator
Wall

Main Trail

Point

Entry Corridor

Lower Parking
Trailhead

North End

Castle Rock Overview Map

Castle Rock Overview Map

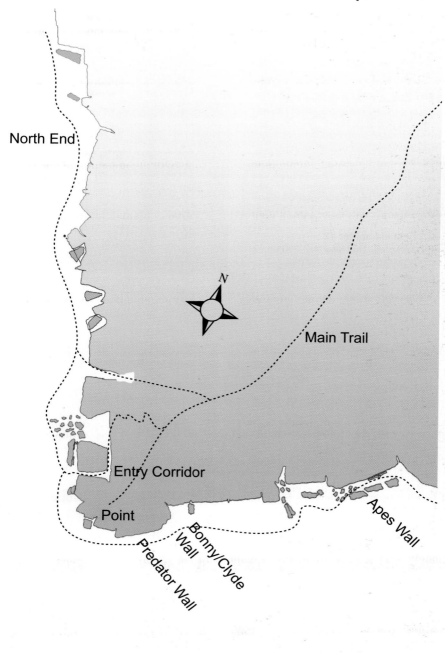

North End

N

Main Trail

Entry Corridor

Point

Predator Wall

Bonny/Clyde Wall

Apes Wall

CHAPTER 9

In the main entry corridor, there are several short trad lines, the most notable is:

🅣 1. Rocks Are For Climbing 9
Trad line on the right hand wall that ends at a pair of shuts.

🅣 2. Dickel's For Drinking 11
This is a mixed line to the left of Rocks, with a couple of bolts.

Turning right at the bottom of the corridor…

🅢 3. **Lone Justice 12
Follows the arête past a bulgy overlap midway.

🅢 4. **Glue Sniffer 12
Starts just left. Thin face climbing gives way to easier moves up above.

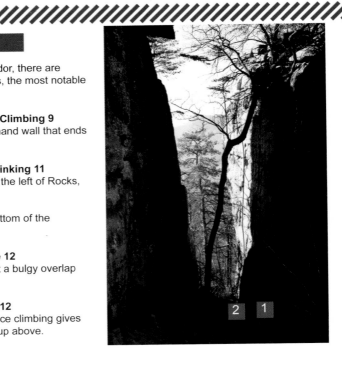

After reaching the bottom of the main access corridor…

🅣 5. Castle Arete 9+/10
Wander up the long pretty arête. Top out or finish at Turret anchors.

🅢 6. **The Turret 11a
Starts just right of the arête. Stick clip. *FA: Chris Watford, 1998*

🅢 7. **Lemoine 11b
Starts just right. Nice pretty face. (6 bolts, ring anchor) *FA: Brandon Lemoine*

🅣 8. Corners 10+
Follows shallow left-facing flakes and corners to top.

🅣 9. Dihedral 8
Follows the corner crack to top.

T **10. Wild Man 11d/12a X**
Climbs the blunt arête with scooped huecos, to top.

T **11. Trad Face**
Starts on a low slab and then past a steeper orange face to top.

T **12. Corner 10**
Follows a nice vague corner that gets more defined near the top.

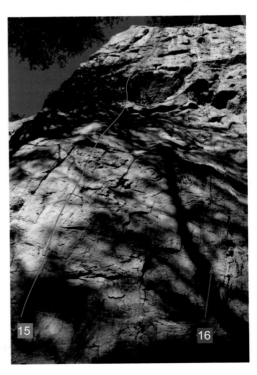

S **13. Optional Ethics 10b**
Starts off a block, in a small finger crack to vertical wall above. (6,7 bolts to ring anchors) *FA: Micah Gentry and Heston Mercer*

T **14. Arete**
incomplete, 2 bolts down low for now.

S **15. Swindled 11a**
Steep face that starts right of arête. (8 bolts, ring anchors) *FA: Luis Rodriguez*

T **16. Unnamed Mixed Line 11d**
Starts just right of Swindled. Climbs past a fixed pin up high in the roof.

T **17. Unknown Mixed Route**
Starts on Natty Light (see below). Breaks off after 3rd bolt and trends left.

S **18. Natty Light 11a**
Begins at a large block in a dead end corridor/gully, on a left-facing arête. Trends right over a short overhang at the 3rd bolt, then continues up to a facing arête to the top. (7 bolts, open shuts) *FA: Luis Rodriguez*

S **19. Unknown Route**
Hidden back inside the corridor on a high narrow yellow wall in an alcove.

T **20. Castle Corner 9+**
Starts up behind a block and follows a broken corner system.

S **21. High Road 8**
Starts just left of a wide crack/chimney. Blocky start to a high first bolt. Rings at top.

T **22. Chimney 7**
Follow obvious crack through wide slot.

S **23. Sleepless Nights 9+**
Starts just right of chimney. Passes a cave 20' up. (7 bolts, silver shuts)

S **24. Another Year Gone 9**
Climb up the slab to a right-facing corner and through a roof. Ends at shuts.

S **25. *Lucky Streak 9+**
Starts just left of a small right-facing corner. Negotiate a tricky bouldery move at the 1st bolt, then enjoy immaculate stone to the top. (7 bolts, anchors) *FA: Luis Rodriguez*

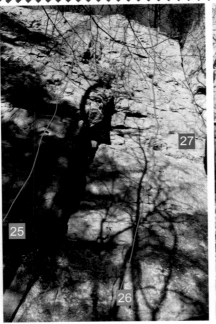

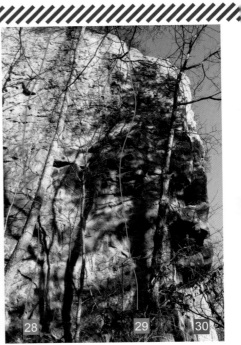

26. ***Orange Peel 10a
Starts just right of the small corner. A great route for the grade. (6 bolts, anchor) *FA: Luis Rodriguez*

27. Wide Corner 7
Follows a wide unpleasant corner. Best done when it's soaking wet or choked with ice.

Continue walking right around the corner for about 80' to an obvious prominent wall.

28. ***Brown Streak 10+
Starts just right of corner. Has high first bolt. Tall face. *FA: Luis Rodriguez*

29. ***Streaker 11a
Starts just to the right. Has high first bolt. Tall, technical face climbing. *FA: Luis Rodriguez*

30. Hueco Arete
Mixed line, arête with hueco

31. ***El Che 12b
Starts 15' right of Hueco Arete. Tall face. High first bolt. Technical climbing to overhang. *FA: Luis Rodriguez*

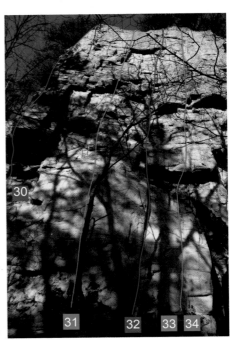

⑤ 32. **Wish (I Was Trad) 11b
Just right of El Che. High first bolt. Stick clip or carry a cam or two for the start. Ends at anchors.

⑤ 33. *Radline (Redline) 12d
Shares start with King Tong, just left of large chimney in right-facing dihedral. Pull overhangs to a sustained technical face up high. New anchors. *FA: Travis Eiseman*

⑤ 34. **King Tong 12+
Shares start with Radline. Split right after pulling last overhang halfway up the wall. *FA: Travis Eiseman*

🇹 35. Charlie Kable Solo Chimney 7

PREDATOR WALL

⑤ 36. **Cottonmouth 12a/b
Start just right of the chimney. Nice long face route. New bolts and anchors provided by Luis Rodriguez

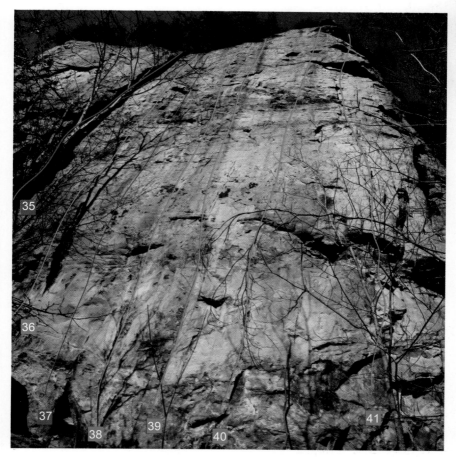

CHAPTER 9

⬛ 37. **Ricochet Rabbit 12+

A Jeff Gruenberg trad route, led on-sight, ground up. Named for an errant round of ammo fired from the valley that hit the wall during the first ascent. Originally graded 12-. Orange rock at start. Follows thin vertical crispy cracks and seams.

At press time, there appears to be an incomplete line with three bolts just to the right. It may be an alternate start that merges into either Ricochet Rabbit or Predator.

⑤ 38. *** Predator 12c

Long, airy and popular. (12 bolts, anchors) *FA: Jeff Gruenberg*

⑤ 39. ***Escapism 12d

Starts on left-facing corner feature, grey/orange rock. First hanger is gray, second is brown. *FA: Jeff Gruenberg and Ron Davis*

⑤ 40. ***Copperhead 13

More of the same. High stick clip. New bolts and anchors.

⑤ 41. Scarlet Begonias 12d

Begins on fractured rock down low and stays left of the wide rounded arete. New bolts and anchors. *FA: Jerry Roberts*

There are a couple of old trad lines to the right of Scarlet Begonias. Keep walking right, past an old junk car at the base. Scramble up along the trail to a shaded corner and a shorter cliff. To the left is a long slab to a ledge with a steep orange headwall at top.

BONNY AND CLYDE WALL

⑤ 42. Escalade Escapade 9

Starts on the slab to the right of the Predator Wall. Easy 5.6 slab to 5.9 finish at top. (5/6 bolts) *FA: Chris Seirzant*

Andrew Miller, Redline
Photo: Edward Yates

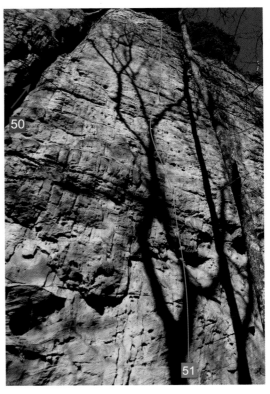

📷 43. Nuts and Bolts 9
Starts on the short wall directly above the car. Follows a right-facing corner feature down low. (5 bolts, anchor) *FA: Eric Pittman and Jason Painter*

📷 44. Chesnutt Sport 12b
Recently re-equipped by Luis Rodriguez.

📷 45. Rust Bucket 11c
The right-most route. (5 bolts, anchors) *FA: Luis Rodriguez*

Continue walking right...

🔲 46. Mixed Arête 9
Either mixed or unfinished. 2 bolts up high.

📷 47. *The Odor 12a
Starts just right of the wide chimney. (5/6 bolts, anchors)

📷 48. **Drifters 12
First hanger is red. Steep, featured orange wall with rills and flutes. (7/8 bolts, rings) *FA: Brent McDaniel*

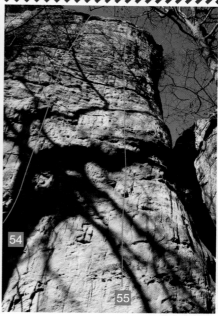

49. **Grifters (Deuces' Wild) 12c
Obvious crux mid route with a long reach (leaver biner) to two small pockets. Fixed biners at the anchors. *FA: Luis Rodriguez*

50. Crack 7
Obvious hand crack to top.

51. ***Psychospasm 13a
Boulder up to a distinctive mushroom horn at the first bolt. Grab a rest, 'cause it's the last one you'll get in the next 80'. (6 bolts, anchors) *FA: Jerry Roberts*

52. *Chesnutt Route12a
Starts just right of a short right-facing corner feature and passes a hole at the 2nd bolt. Often has a leaver biner on the 4th bolt. (6,7 bolts, anchors)

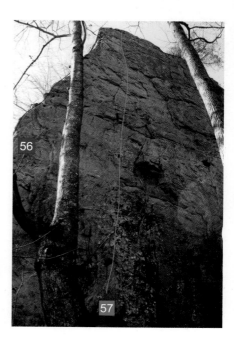

53. **Slingblade 12b
Starts in front of tree. Horns/jugs down low. (5 bolts, anchor)

54. New Route?
Starts to the right, on orange rock. Starts slightly left and trends right over first bolt. (5 bolts, anchor)

ⓢ 55. Chesnutt Arete 12b
Starts just left of arête at a horizontal row of pockets in orange rock. 10+/11a to the next to last bolt. Cruxy finish. (5,6 bolts, anchor)

Step around corner into a wet seep/spring area…

🅣 56. Aerobic Arete 9
A nice warmup. Toprope off the Mosaic anchors.

ⓢ 57. **Mosaic 11a
Starts above the stream. (6 bolts, anchors) Note: It's possible to deck clipping the 2nd bolt – be careful! *FA: Greg Kottkamp*

Walk on across the stream to a ledgy broken face. There are several decent trad lines and topropes here, as well as one notable route up the tallest part of the face…

🅣 58. *Lovingood Route 10-
Nice steep featured face with a fixed piece up high. *FA: Fritz Lovingood*

Continue walking right…

Steve Deweese, Escapism
Photo: Rene Pirolt

63

64

⑤ 59. Project
An open project up a steep arête.
Bolted by Chris Sierzant

⑤ 60. Catupult 12+
Starts to the right of a right-facing
corner, on brown and orange
fractured rock. (4,5 bolts, anchor)
FA: Chris Sierzant

⑤ 61. *Shart In Your Armor 9
Follows a broken vertical crack.
(4,5 bolts, anchor) *FA: Chris
Sierzant*

⑤ 62. **Evil Times 11c
Starts just to the right. Follows
vertical crack features. *FA: Chris
Sierzant*

⑤ 63. Double Feature 12a/b
Takes a line through brown/purple
rock, then out roofs up high.
Trends left. (7 bolts, anchor) *FA:
Travis Eiseman*

65

66

🅂 64. ***Creature Feature 13c/d
Scramble start, then up a shield of bullet rock and roofs up high. (9 bolts, anchors) *FA: Jerry Roberts*

🅂 65. ***Apes On Acid 13d/14a
One of the hardest routes in the state. More bullet hard steepness. Often has fixed draws on it. (6 bolts, anchors) *FA: Jerry Roberts*

🅂 66. La Bamba 13c
Starts to the right. (10/11 bolts, anchor) *FA: Anthony Meeks*

🅂 67. Escalade Crusade 12c
Starts slightly uphill to the right. Last route on the wall. (5 bolts, anchor) *FA: Chris Sierzant*

To the right, on the adjacent left-facing wall…

🅂 68. Project
Steep orange face to high roof. At press time, it's a James Webb project. (8 bolts, anchor)

🅃 69. Powerline Crack 11
The obvious vertical hand and finger crack.

🅂 70. **Holy Moly 12a
Goes up through two sizeable huecos down low. (5 bolts, anchor) *FA: Kelly Dalton and Mark Pelfrey*

This marks the end of the cliff. Intrepid boulderers might consider walking further to explore the large boulders in the powerline cut that descends down the mountain.

NORTH END

The North End is not nearly as consistent in quality as the main area, and development has been sporadic, nevertheless, it offers some quality routes in more moderate grades and a few surprising crack lines. From the access gully/downclimb, turn right. Continue past some tumbledown blocks and boulders, then on past a wide rocky gully. The next route is on a sharp formation with a low roof on the right end.

🅢 1. The Claw 12
Steep, technical face climbing. (4 bolts, anchor) *FA: Jeff Gruenberg*

Continuing on, there are several moderate trad routes up featured faces and arêtes.

Continue left to a somewhat wide gully leading to the top. At the bottom right side of this gully, look for a white hanging arete.

🅢 2. Arete (unclimbed at press time)
Steep start, working left out a low roof to a white arete. (5 bolts, anchor) *FA: Micah Gentry*

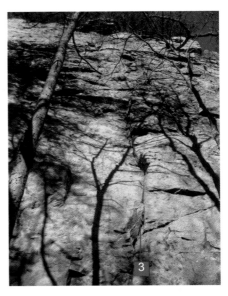

Continue left, to the next tall wall...

🆃 3. *Smokestack Crack 7
Nice vertical handcrack. *FA: Fritz Lovingood, cigarette in mouth)*

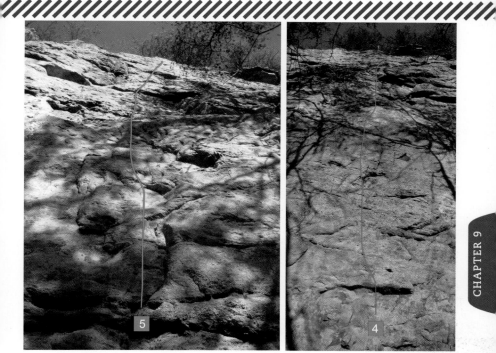

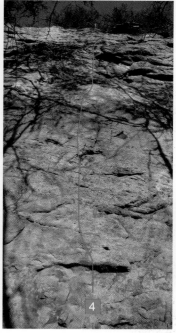

🅂 4. **Inga La Dinga 10b/c
High stick clip. Bouldery start gives way to easier climbing up high. (7 bolts, anchor) FA: Micah Gentry

🅂 5.***Tallboy 10a
Nice steep face to anchors below high roof block. (7 bolts, anchor) FA: Micah Gentry

🅂 6. ***Gentry Route 10d
Steep face. Thin at 2nd/3rd bolt in orange rock. (7 bolts, anchor) FA: Micah Gentry

Continue left, to where it is necessary to scramble behind and over, or around a sizeable boulder. Continue on...

🆃 7. **White Corner 9
Nice crack in a white dihedral. FA: The Ancients

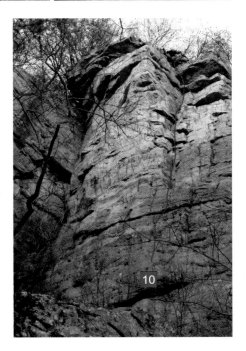

T **8. Unknown Route**
Starts further left around the corner, right of a prominent flake. Has 3 or 4 fixed pins.

T **9. *Flake Right 10**
Follow the right edge of the right-facing flake, past a bulge to the upper face. Step right and on to the top.

T **10. *Honey Corner 10**
Follow the right edge of the right-facing flake, past a bulge to the upper face. Step right and on to the top. *FA: Jeff Gruenberg*

Continue walking about 100 yards or so, to a corridor formed by a large boulder against the wall. Scramble back into this corridor to the furthest route on the left hand face.

$ **11. Fragile Holdings 10d**
Move past a left-facing corner down low and past a cave up high. *FA: Micah Gentry*

🪨 12. Easy Enough 9
Next route to the left. Nice vertical face.
FA: Micah Gentry

🪨 13. Machete Mayhem 10d
Move up through nice rock in a vague
scoop/trough. *FA: Micah Gentry*

🪨 14. *Land Of The Long 9
Steep-ish start to nice upper face. *FA:
Micah Gentry*

🪨 15. Gnash And Grab 11c
Just outside the corridor. Follows a blunt
white arete. *FA: Micah Gentry*

🔳 16. Bent 11c/d
Follow a clean white face on thin gear to
a roof. Pull this to top or move right and
out a weakness**.** *FA: Jeff Gruenberg*

🔳 17. Unnamed project/TR 11c
Follow a clean white face, on thin gear to
a roof. Pull this to top**.** *FA: Jerry Roberts*

The cliff continues northward, with more
routes scattered throughout and more
route potential, though the rock is not as
consistent as the main area. Perhaps the
gaps will get filled in as time goes by.

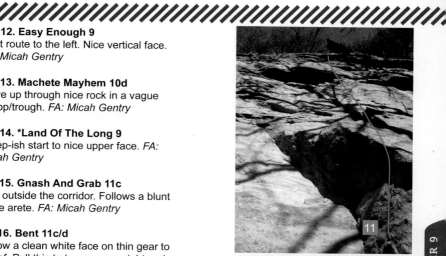

Foster Falls, surely one of the best swimming holes around!
Photo: Lori Walden

FOSTER FALLS 10
chapter

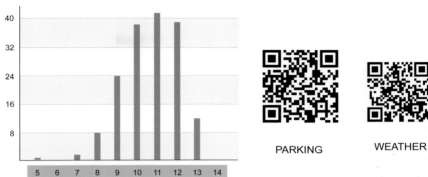

PARKING   WEATHER

There is no doubt that Foster Falls is one of the premier destinations in the region! This scenic and pristine cliff plays host to some of the most difficult sport climbing in the Sandstone Belt, since the steep, compact rock is tailor- made for pumpy, technical routes. The cliffline begins at Foster Falls, and runs downstream for nearly two miles, following the curving contour of Little Gizzard Creek. The cliff primarily faces south, so it is drenched in sun for most of the day. The Right Bunker and the Darkie Cave offer some shade, and of course, a cold dip into the pool below the falls is heartily recommended. Foster Falls is almost entirely a sport climbing area, so a rack of quickdraws is all that's necessary. A 60 meter rope is useful for several routes, but is not required.

History

Although a handful of Chattanooga climbers, including Steve Goins and Forrest Gardner, put up a few natural lines at Fiery Gizzard in the mid 1980's, the cliff lay dormant for a number of years. In 1990, prolific Nashville climber Eddie Whittemore recognized the area's vast potential for steep, strenuous sport routes. Putting himself to the task, he, along with Paul Sloan, Craig Estes, and Zack Jones, began developing the area, snapping up plum lines at a rapid pace. Other route developers included Porter Jarrard, Doug Reed, Steve Jones, Chris Watford and Steve Deweese. There are still new routes being done at Foster Falls, most notably on the newly purchased tract downstream from the Red Light District and further along past Dog Boy's Village.

Location and Directions

From Nashville, take I-24 East and exit at Monteagle (U.S. 41, TN 150). Continue through Tracy City toward Jasper, Tennessee, for about eight miles to the Foster Falls entrance on the right.

From Chattanooga, take I-24 West, over Nickajack Lake, toward Jasper. Exit onto TN 28 (exit#155), then exit again into the town of Jasper proper. Follow signs for TN 150 / US 41 toward Tracy City. Follow TN 150 to the top of the plateau, passing the now closed Mountain Mart on the left. Proceed for three miles to the Foster Falls entrance on the left.

The trail begins at the parking lot and passes under the dining pavilion. At this point, the trail splits and a choice must be made:
For a stunning view of Foster Falls, as well as easier access to the farthest climbing areas,

then go right along the top of the falls, to cross a metal foot bridge. (This is the Fiery Gizzard Trail, which goes to Grundy Forest State Natural Area.) Continue along the trail, following white blazes, past the falls overlook, for about 5 minutes or so, to Climber Access Trail #1. This trail intersects the cliff between the Dihedrals and Jimmywood. Continue further to Climber Trail #2, which intersects the cliff between the Rehab Slab and the Snatch Wall.

Alternately, from the parking lot, walk past the pavilion and bear left along the powerline cut, for about 200 yards, passing a wooden overlook. Look for a sign directing you to the base of the falls and a set of wooden steps. Continue down to the creek, cross a footbridge, and bear left to the cliff base. Continue along the base under a low roof to the first route.

Camping

There is a "first come, first served" campsite at Foster Falls, complete with tables and clean bathrooms. Registration is required and there is a nominal fee. This campsite is open mid -April through mid -October. There are also primitive camping opportunities available year round, along the Fiery Gizzard Trail. The most popular is the Father Adamz Campsite, near the falls overlook. Call (423) 942 5759 for campground info and reservations.

Luxuries

Jasper has gas, groceries, the Acuff Hotel and Ridley's Restaurant (Fantastic southern homestyle fare and beer!) Tracy City is home to the regionally famous Dutch Maid Bakery (there is also a location in downtown Jasper) offering a selection of phenomenal "training pastries" and other treats! Chattanooga is about 25 minutes away.

Emergency Assistance

Marion County Sheriff's Department   (423) 942-2525
Jasper Police Department   (423) 942-5667

Regulations

Please use existing fire rings and do not cut trees for firewood. Alcohol is not permitted in the park.

FYI

Foster Falls Recreation Area was established by the Tennessee Valley Authority as part of its Small Wilds Program. In 1994, the gorge came under the threat of potential logging by Mead Containerboard, who owned the timber rights. Jim Prince, a supporter, benefactor and activist on behalf of the area, began long and protracted negotiations with Mead, the TVA, and the State Of Tennessee. His hope was to transfer his tract of land into the Small Wilds Area, and turn the whole parcel over to the State. Massive support from the Southeastern Climber's Coalition, The Access Fund, the Friends Of The South Cumberland Recreation Area and the Conservation Alliance resulted in a stunning victory for climbers, hikers and others who enjoy outdoor recreation. Sadly Jim Prince lost a long battle with cancer in 1997, but his legacy lives on. The story of Foster Falls is, in reality, a story of one man, and his unflagging determination and hard work. Our thanks go out to Jim Prince and also Park Manager John Christof, who made (and make) Foster Falls what it is today. Note: The Friends of the South Cumberland can be reached at www.friendsofscsra.org.

A Bit Of Trivia

According to Russ Manning's excellent book, "The Historic Cumberland Plateau – An Explorer's Guide", the name Fiery Gizzard can be traced to several different stories. The first maintains that Davy Crockett, or an Indian companion, burned their tongues on a hot turkey gizzard while camped nearby. An alternative tale claims that an Indian chief threw the gizzard from a freshly killed turkey into a fire to get the attention of white explorers, who had come for a peace talk. "The Historic Cumberland Plateau – An Explorer's Guide" is available from Mountain Laurel Place P.O. Box 3001 Norris, TN 37828

Foster Falls is a linear cliffline, divided into separate, individual crags. They are presented in downstream order, from the waterfall all the way down to Dog Boy's Village and The Battery. See the accompanying diagram and topos.

The mission of the Friends of South Cumberland is to support the Park, preserve and protect it, and to serve as a mechanism to reach out to individuals to become involved. http://www.friendsofscsra.org

Who We Are & What We Do

The Friends of South Cumberland is a group of volunteer citizens dedicated to supporting the South Cumberland State Recreation Area, Tennessee's largest state wilderness park. Some of our goals are:

•To educate the public about the unique qualities of the Park
•To promote the use of the Park as an environmental, wilderness and biodiversity resource
•To encourage the development of the Park to meet the recreational needs of park visitors and area residents
•To work with the Park to develop and implement plans to protect and preserve the unique wilderness and recreational resource that the South Cumberland State Recreation Area represents, including the acquisition of property and conservation easements
•To preserve biodiversity and a true wilderness experience for current and future generations

As a non-profit membership corporation Friends of South Cumberland funding is derived from individual and corporate memberships and from private donations. We are a 501(c)3 non profit public benefit corporation and your membership and donations are Federal tax deductible..

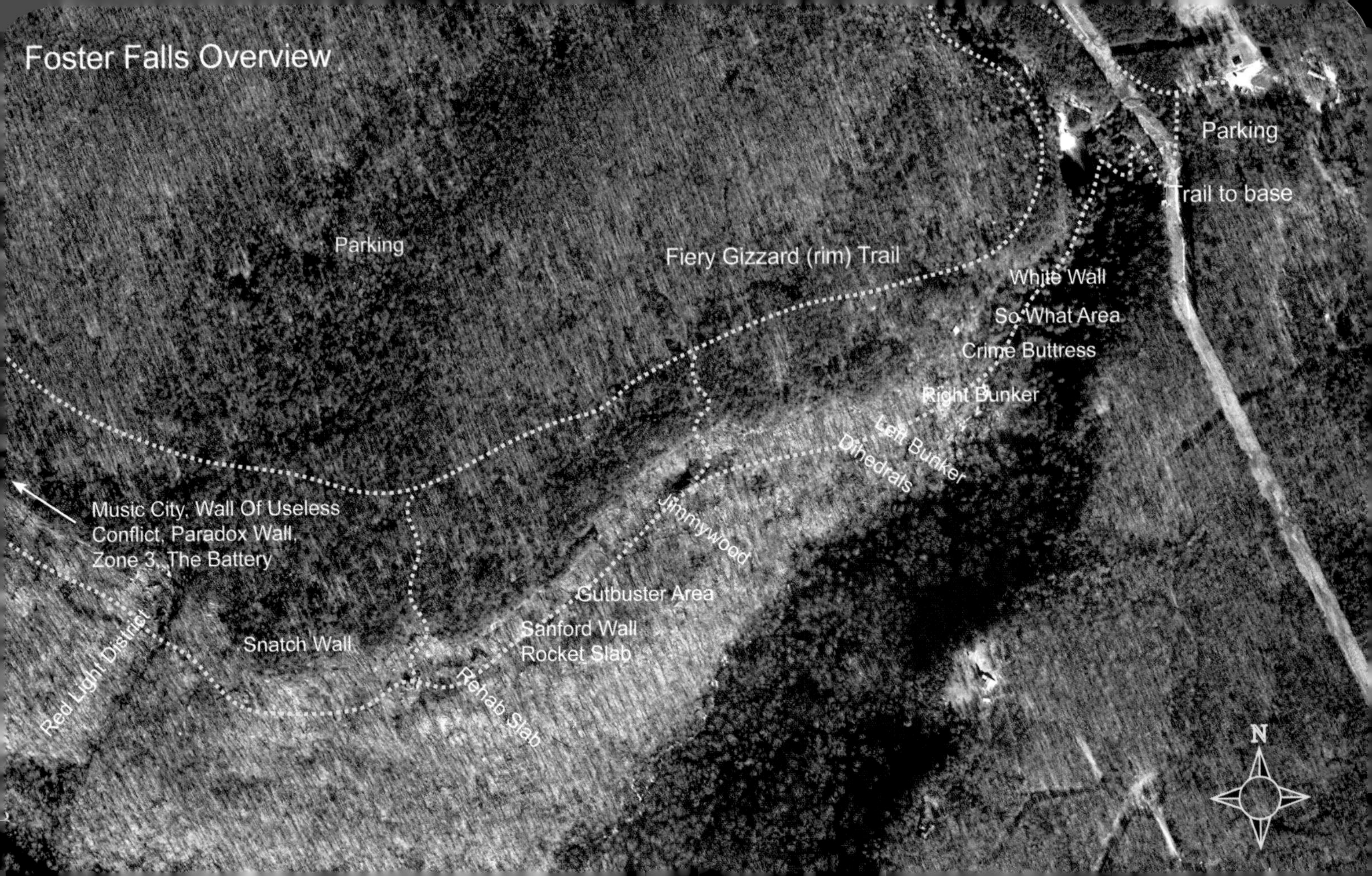

Foster Falls Overview

Parking

Trail to base

N

White Wall

So'What Area

Crime Buttress

Right Bunker

Left Bunker

Dihedrals

Fiery Gizzard (rim) Trail

Jimmywood

Gulbuster Area

Sanford Wall

Rocket Slab

Rehab Slab

Parking

Snatch Wall

Music City, Wall Of Useless
Conflict, Paradox Wall
Zone 3, The Battery

Red Light District

SOUTH CUMBERLAND VISITOR CENTER

The South Cumberland Recreation Area is a group of 10 seperate park areas managed [a]s a single park. Totaling over 16,000 total acr[e]age, the units ar[e] located thr[o]ughout a 100-[s]quare-mile region within Grundy, Sequatchie, Franklin, and Marion counties. The park head[qu]arters and Visitor Center is loca[t]ed on U.S. 41 between Monteagle and Tracy City just 4 [mil]es from Interst[at]e 24.

A monthly schedule of free public p[r]o[g]rams and guided hikes is provided [b]y park staff [an]d volunteers. A copy of the schedule can be obtained at the Visitor Center. Anyone inter[est]ed in helping maintain the trail system or other v[o]lunteer activity with the park is encour[ag]ed to contact the park office.

GRUNDY LAKES S[T]ATE PARK

Grundy Lakes was donated to the Sta[t]e of Tennessee in the 1930's f[o]r a Civilian Cons[er]vation Corps recreation proj-ect. Famous for its mines, prison labor, re[v]olts, and the Lone Rock Coke O[v]ens, the whole area is on the Na[t]ional Historic Register. The Lone Rock Trail winds through woods [ar]ound the main lake and leads y[o]u alongside the coke o[v]ens. This tr[ai]l has much scenic beauty in addition to its historic sites. Total length of the tr[ai]l is appr[o]ximately 1.3 miles, but many shor[t]er walks are possible since it cr[o]sses sev[er]al picnic areas and has num[er]ous road crossings.

GRUNDY FORES[T] STATE NATURAL AREA

This 233-acr[e] natural area was donated by a group of local citizens in Tracy City who acquired it by subscription in 1935. The group asked that the tr[ac]t become a sta[t]e forest suitable f[o]r accommodating Civilian Cons[er]vation Corps Camp S-67. A tr[ai]l was built down to the Fruit B Bowl, and a picnic shelter was constructed b[y] 1937. The area soon became one of the most popular sc[e]nic a[t]tr[a]ctions of the r[e]gion.

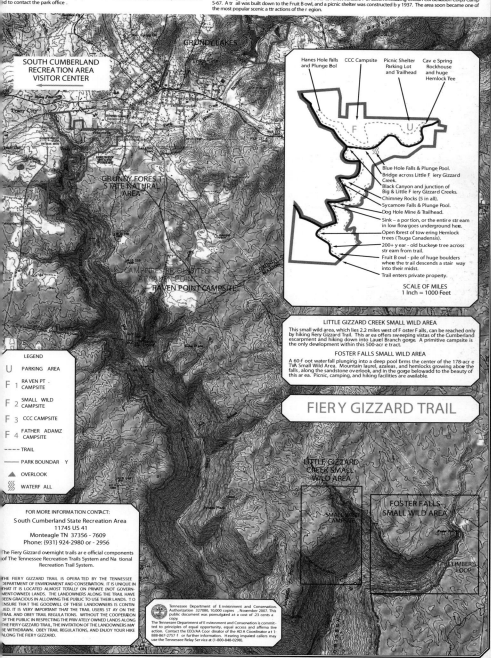

Map labels (top right detail map):
Hanes Hole Falls and Plunge Bo[w]l
CCC Campsite
Picnic Shelter Parking Lot and Trailhead
Cav[e] Spring Rockhouse and huge Hemlock T[r]ee

Blue Hole Falls & Plunge Pool.
Bridge across Little F[i]ery Gizzard Creek.
Black Canyon and junction of Big & Little F[i]ery Gizzard Creeks.
Chimney Rocks (5 in all).
Sycamore Falls & Plunge Pool.
Dog Hole Mine & Trailhead.
Sink – a por[t]ion, or the entir[e] str[e]am in low flow goes underground h[e]re.
Open forest of tow[e]ring Hemlock trees (Tsuga Canadensis).
200+ y[e]ar - old buckeye tree across str[e]am from trail.
Fruit B Bowl - pile of huge boulders wh[e]re the tr[ai]l descends a stair[w]ay into their midst.
Trail enters private property.

SCALE OF MILES
1 Inch = 1000 Feet

LITTLE GIZZARD CREEK SMALL WILD AREA

This small wild area, which lies 2.2 miles west of F[o]ster Falls, can be reached only by hiking [Fi]ery Gizzard Trail. This ar[e]a offers sweeping vistas of the Cumberland escarpment and hiking down into Laur[e]l Branch gorge. A primitive campsite is the only development within this 500-acr[e] t[r]act.

FOSTER FALLS SMALL WILD AREA

A 60-f[o]ot waterfall plunging into a deep pool [fo]rms the center of the 178-acr[e] TVA Small Wild Area. Mountain laurel, azaleas, and hemlocks growing abo[v]e the falls, along the sandstone overlook, and in the gorge belo[w] add to the beauty of this ar[e]a. Picnic, camping, and hiking facilities are available.

FIE[R]Y GIZZARD TRAIL

Map labels:
SOUTH CUMBERLAND RECREA[T]ION AREA VISITOR CENTER
GRUNDY LAKES
GRUNDY FOREST STATE NATURAL AREA
RAVEN POINT CAMPSITE
LITTLE GIZZARD CREEK SMALL WILD AREA
FOSTER FALLS SMALL WILD AREA
SMALL WILD CAMPSITE
[CL]IMBER'S LOOP

LEGEND
Symbol	Description
U	PARKING AREA
F 1	RA[V]EN PT. CAMPSITE
F 2	SMALL WILD CAMPSITE
F 3	CCC CAMPSITE
F 4	FATHER ADAMZ CAMPSITE
----	TRAIL
——	PARK BOUNDAR[Y]
▲	OVERLOOK
〰	WATERF[A]LL

FOR MORE INFORMATION CONTACT:
South Cumberland State Recreation Area
11745 US 41
Monteagle TN 37356 - 7609
Phone: (931) 924-2980 or - 2956

[Th]e Fiery Gizzard overnight trails ar[e] official components [o]f The Tennessee Recreation Trails System and Na[t]ional Recreation Trail System.

James Pullum beatin' the heat at Foster Falls
Photo: Laurel Graefe

From where the lower access trail meets the cliff, walk left (downstream), about 60 feet. There are two short routes:

ⓢ 1. Pond Scum 10d
A short warm up. (3,bolts, ring anchors)

ⓢ 2. Skipper 9
Start: Just left of Pond Scum. (4 bolts, anchors)

Continue left...

ⓢ 3. Crawdaddy 10a
Start: 100 yards left of Skipper. Climb past a hanging dihedral. (4 bolts, rings) *FA: Eddie Whittemore, 1998*

ⓢ 4. Tea And Strumpets 10a
Start: 15' left of Crawdaddy (5 bolts, ring anchors) *FA: Brent McDaniel*

THE WHITE WALL

Continue walking left (downstream) about 100 yards, to the first tall wall. This is the White Wall, and offers some of the best routes at Foster Falls on clean, hard sandstone. In 2002, Steve Deweese and Amy Brooks took on the task of replacing most of the rusty bolts and improving the anchors.

ⓢ 5. Bottom Feeder 12a/b
Start: At the extreme right end of the wall. Follow 6 bolts up an arching corner and steep face to a chain anchor. Note: Staying in the crack/corner a few more moves reportedly lowers the overall grade to 11a. *FA: Eddie Whittemore, 1996*

ⓢ 6. Saab Story 12d
Start: Just left of Bottom Feeder. (6 bolts, chain anchor) *FA: Hassan Saab and Chris Chesnutt, 1992*

🅢 7. ***Satisfaction 12a/b

Start: 10' left of Saab Story. Follow 6 bolts up a thin finger crack to the Wristlet ring anchors. *FA: Hidetaka Suzuki, mid 1980's.*

🅢 8. ***Wristlets 11c

Start: 20' left of Satisfaction. Climb up and right over 7 bolts to ring anchors. *FA: Eddie Whittemore, 1990*

🅢 9. **Handcuffed 11c/d   *Flash*

Start: Same as for Wristlets. Follow a plumb line over 7 bolts to anchors. *FA: Eddie Whittemore, 1990*

🅢 10. Tom And Jerry 12d

Start: On Wristlets/Handcuffed. Follows a plumb line just left of Handcuffed. *FA: Jerry Roberts*

🅢 11. *Gun Bunny 12b/c

Start: Same as for Handcuffed/Wristlets. Start on Handcuffed, then trend left and up, to an anchor. Sometimes wet at the start. (9 bolts, anchor) *FA: Eddie Whittemore, 1991*

🅢 12. **First Offense 12a   *Very Cool*

Start: At the top of the White Wall, above Handcuffed. Climb Handcuffed, then proceed up the overhanging prow, past 3 bolts, to an anchor. Note: Use a 60 meter rope to do Handcuffed and First Offense as one pitch. *FA: Louie Rumanes and Paula Bindrich, 1993*

🅢 13. *The Big Bopper 12c

Start: 20' left of Handcuffed. Climb Acquittal for three bolts, then up and right to the Gun Bunny anchors. (9 bolts, anchors) *FA: Eddie Whittemore, 1991*

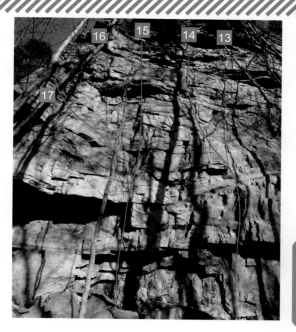

⑤ 14. **The Acquittal 11b/c
Start: Same as for The Big Bopper. Climb through a vertical hand jam slot. Start is often damp. (8 bolts, cold shuts) *FA: Eddie Whittemore, 1991*

A directional bolt has been placed down and right from the Acquittal anchors, making it possible to toprope a 12b direct route straight up from the 4th bolt on Acquittal (avoiding the hand crack).

⑤ 15. Filthy Pig 12b/c
Start: Just left of Acquittal. Share the start for Stun Gun, then trend slightly up and right. Start is often damp. (8 bolts, anchors) *FA: Eddie Whittemore, 1991*

⑤ 16. **Stun Gun 12a
Start: Same as for Filthy Pig. (7 bolts, anchors) *FA: Eddie Whittemore, 1990*

⑤ 17. Ground Strike 11c/d
Start: Start on Stun Gun, then head left on wavy rock to a chain anchor (5 bolts, anchors) *FA: Eddie Whittemore, 1994*

⑤ 18. Grand Larceny 12a
Start: Just left of Ground Strike, under the hanging arete. Stick clip. Negotiate a flat roof and follow the steep arete to the Ground Strike chains (5 bolts, chains) *FA: Eddie Whittemore, 1998*

⑤ 19. Hammerhead 11c/d
Start: Around the corner from Grand Larceny, in a left-facing dihedral. Pass an awkward, blocky roof and up steep face. Originally 11a until something broke. (6 bolts, chain anchors) *FA: Eddie Whittemore and Charlie Collins, 1992*

There is a crappy 10 just 20' uphill and left of Hammerhead. Skip it.

Amy Deweese, Handcuffed
Photo: Scott Perkins

SO WHAT AREA

Essentially the extreme right end of the Crime Buttress, this area offers a cluster of four short routes.

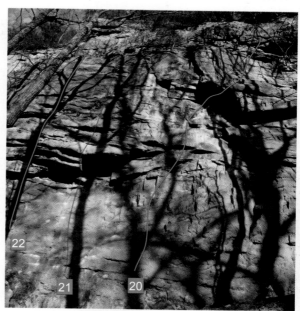

⑤ 20. Moving Target 9
Start: At the right edge of the wall. Climb up and slightly right across left-facing flakes and corners. Note: Because of the extreme angling nature of this route, it's best to toprope it to clean it safely. (6 bolts, rings) *FA: Eddie Whittemore, 1998*

⑤ 21. **So What 11b
Start: Near the center of the wall. Has an old rusty bolt at the start. Climb past an overlap to anchors (6 bolts, anchors) *FA: Eddie Whittemore, 1991*

⑤ 22. **The Hoosier 11c
Start: Just left of So What. Breaks left over a small roof to tweaks on a brown face. (4 bolts, anchors) *FA: Jason Guynes, 1992*

⑤ 23. Reach 12a/b
Start: Same as for The Hoosier. Trend left up super thin, painful holds (4 bolts, old cold shuts) *FA: Eddie Whittemore, 1990*

CRIME BUTTRESS

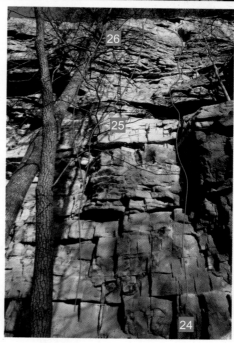

⑤ 24. ***Standing Room Only 11a/b
Start: 20' left of Reach. Follow a system of corners and bulges to the top (9 bolts, anchors) *FA: Chris Watford, 1992*

⑤ 25. *Liars 12c
Start: 10' left of Standing Room Only. Climb slightly left past 8 bolts to anchors. *FA: Eddie Whittemore, 1990*

⑤ 26. **Thieves 12a/b
Shares the first 3 bolts with Liars, then breaks left. (8 bolts, anchors) *FA: Eddie Whittemore, 1990*

David Paulete searchin' for a Heart Of Gol
Photo: Scott Perkins

⛰ 27. Street Crime 11d
Start: 10' left of Thieves. Climb to a ledge and up a steep headwall (9 bolts, anchor) *FA: Porter Jarrard, 1990*

⛰ 28. *If I Had A Shotgun 11d
Climb Street Crime to the ledge, move left and finish on Framed (8 bolts, anchors) *FA: Eddie Whittemore, 1990*

⛰ 29. ***Framed 12a
Start: Just left of If I Had A Shotgun. Stick clip. Follow the arete to the roof, finish on steep, rounded jugs (7 bolts, anchors) *FA: Eddie Whittemore, 1990's.*

⛰ 30. **Looters 12a
Start: 10' left of Framed, around the corner. Stick clip. Pull opening moves, trend right over a ledge and up rounded holds, then crimps, to anchors (10 bolts, anchors) *FA: Eddie Whittemore, 1990*

⛰ 31. **Greed 11d
Start on Looters, trend left into a shallow dihedral. Continue to anchors (10 bolts, anchors) *FA: Doug Reed, 1990*

⛰ 32. *Iron Buns 12a
Start: 15' left of Greed. 9 bolts to anchors. *FA: Paul Sloan and Charlie Collins, 1991*

⛰ 33. **Heart of Gold 12a
Follow Iron Buns for 4 bolts, trend left up steeper rock to a chain anchor (8 bolts, anchor) *FA: Steve Deweese, 1998*

Amy Deweese, Bottled Up Warrior
Photo: Scott Perkins

THE RIGHT BUNKER

ⓢ 34. Lynn's Route 11b/c
Start: On the face at the upper right end of the Right Bunker next to a tree. Climb the face, vaguely following the edge of the arete (8 bolts, double biner anchor) *FA: Jerry Roberts, 1998*

ⓢ 35. ***Kill Or Be Killed 13c
Features a never-ending onslaught of tiered roofs.
Start: 100' left of Heart of Gold, at the right edge of the Right Bunker (13 bolts, anchors) *FA: Eddie Whittemore, 1993*

ⓢ 36. **Ethnic Cleansing 12b
Start: 15' left of Kill Or Be Killed. (6 bolts, chain anchor) *FA: Eddie Whittemore, 1993*

ⓢ 37. The Conflict 13d
Climb Ethnic Cleansing to the last bolt, traverse hard left to finish on Gas Chamber (10 bolts, anchors) *FA: Jerry Roberts, 1997*

ⓢ 38. **Gas Chamber 13a
Start: 30' left of Ethnic Cleansing. Steep rock leads through a shoulder-wrecking dihedral and roofs to a chain anchor. (10 bolts, anchors) Note: There's an alternate (and better?) finish to this route that avoids the dihedral by climbing on crimps just to the left. Also, there is a chipped extension of this route, dubbed Turbo Dog. It follows Gas Chamber up to the dihedral, then traverses right on some natural and unnatural pockets. Ends randomly on Kill or Be Killed. *FA: Eddie Whittemore, 1991*

ⓢ 39. *Abacus 13a
Start: On the steep lower face and follow a thin finger crack in the roof (8 bolts, anchor) *FA: Eddie Whittemore, 1997*

Laurel Graefe on Abacus, Right Bunker
Photo: James Pullum

🪨 40. ***Bottled Up Warrior 12b/c

Start: On Abacus or Gas Chamber. Climb ever-steepening rock, through roofs and up a beautiful white headwall. Sports a new start just to the right of the original start that helps alleviate the congestion. (8 bolts, anchors) *FA: Eddie Whittemore, 1991.* Note: Moving left at the lip of the roof lowers the grade to 12a/b.

🪨 41. **Dumkopf 11c/d

Start: At the left end of the Right Bunker, 10' left of Bottled Up Warrior. Climb easy ground, over a block, and up a steep face (7 bolts, anchors) *FA: Eddie Whittemore, 1991*

🪨 42. **Something's Always Wrong 10d

Start: On Dumkopf. Climb the first five bolts of Dumkopf, then trend left to anchors (8 bolts, shuts) *FA: Eddie Whittemore, 1996*

Continuing left, there is a yellow/gold wall high above the trail, atop a ledge, with a series of short corners. The leftmost is a right-facing corner with a fixed webbing anchor. No details.

Carry on…

THE LEFT BUNKER (aka: The Darkie Cave)

Lying about 100' left of the Right Bunker, the Left Bunker offers the steepest routes at Foster Falls. Don't assume that they will always be dry after a rainy spell, as they tend to seep a little. Like most caves, where space is tight and bolting difficult, there are all sorts of link ups, often facilitated with an extra bolt here and there.

CHAPTER 10

Nico Brown lost in The Big Empty, Second Bunker
Photo: Andrew Kornylak

💲 43. **Cock the Hammer 12d
Start: At the far right end of the Left Bunker, on a steep, blunt shield. Stick clip. Follow 4 bolts to link up with the last moves of Darkie The Bum Beast (4 bolts, anchor) *FA: Eddie Whittemore, 1993*

💲 44. ***Squeeze The Trigga 13a
Start: On Cock The Hammer. A link up of Cock The Hammer and Eclipse. Clip the first 3 bolts of Cock The Hammer, clip a solitary link-up bolt, and finish on the last 5 bolts of Eclipse to a double chain anchor (9 bolts, anchor) *FA: Eddie Whittemore, 1994*

💲 45. **Darkie the Bum Beast 12d
Start: 20' left of Cock The Hammer.
Follow 5 bolts, trending right, out the roof to an anchor at the lip, same as for Cock The Hammer. Note: There is (or was) a pitch that continues up the smooth upper face, past 3 bolts to anchors (11c/d) *FA: Hassan Saab and Chris Chestnutt, 1993*

💲 46. After Dark 13a/b
Starts on Darkie, then breaks up and right, along a higher set of holds, to the Darkie/Hammer anchor.

💲 47. ***Eclipse 12d
Clip the first two bolts on Darkie, then head left to chain anchor (7 bolts, chain anchor) *FA: Eddie Whittemore, 1993*.

💲 48. Fire In The Hole 14a
Climb the first 2 bolts of Darkie et al and then go hard left, following the line of bolts to the right of The Big Empty. Finishes on the Eclipse,/Big Empty anchors.

💲 49. ***The Big Empty 13b
Start: 20' left of Darkie. Stick clip. Climb out steepest part of cave, past 6 bolts, to chain anchors on Eclipse (6 bolts, anchor) *FA: Eddie Whittemore, 1997*

💲 50. Premarital Drilling 10b
Start: At the left end of the Left Bunker. (4 bolts, Fixe ring anchor) *FA: Jared Jenkins*

💲 51. New Route 11d/12a
Slab route that starts 15' left or Premarital Drilling. Easy ground leads to some cool slab moves. Ends under the roof. (6 bolts, anchors)

🗒 52. Dirty Corner 8
Climb the wide crack to hidden anchors at the top of the block.

THE DIHEDRALS

A popular and sometimes congested area.

💲 53. *Long Slab 8
Sure to be popular, this new route climbs a slab past a ledge and upper face. Seeps a bit at top. (9 bolts, anchors)

💲 54. ***Pillsbury 11a
Start: 30' left of The Left Bunker. Climb a flake/chimney to a steep face. Difficult third clip (5 bolts, anchors) Note: Dave Shewell once climbed this thing in a pair of Koflach plastic mountaineering boots. Can't get better edging shoes than those! A bit sandbagged. *FA: Eddie Whittemore and Chris Watford, 1993*

🅢 55. Crimp Knob 12d/13a

This longstanding toprope goes up just left of Pillsbury. Now has orange hangers, courtesy of Darryl Bornhop. Awaiting the send as of press time.

🅢 56. **Kids With Guns 12d

Start: 8' left of Crimp Knob, just right of the arete. Follow bolts up a steep, technical face (6 bolts, anchor) *FA: Louie Rumanes, 1998*

🅢 57. ***Twist And Shout 9+

Pretty arete, fun climbing.
Start: 20' left of Pillsbury. Follow an arete past 6 bolts to an anchor. *FA: Paul Sloan and Eddie Whittemore, 1991*

🅢 58. ***Ankles Away 9

Start: 5' left of Twist And Shout. Climb a face, past 6 bolts, to an anchor. *FA: Eddie Whittemore and Paul Sloan, 1991*

🅣 59. *Dihedral 9

Start: 10' left of Ankles Away. Climb the corner to an anchor? or top out. *FA: Roger Marlowe and Tom Kenny, 1992*

🅢 60. ***Narcissism 10b

Start: 10' left of Dihedral. Follow 7 bolts up a bulgy face to an anchor. *FA: Zack Jones and Craig Estes, 1992*

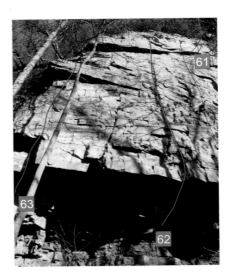

🅢 61. *Atrophy 11b/c

Start: 8' left of Narcissism. Stick clip first bolt at lip of roof and continue to anchors (7 bolts, anchors). *FA: Craig Estes, 1996.* Note: The direct start to the first bolt is 12a.

🅢 62. Sponge 12d

Start: Just left of Atrophy. Pull the roof to a steep, technical face (7 bolts, shuts) *FA: Eddie Whittemore, 1996*

🅢 63. Foster Child 10d
Start: 25' left of Sponge. Crank a low, awkward roof/corner and continue up a steep face (5 bolts, anchors) *FA: Jeff Noffsinger, 1993*

JIMMYWOOD

Walking left from The Dihedrals, the cliff breaks down a bit. After about 300 yards or so, the next prominent buttress will appear. An access trail from the top comes down in this vicinity. Look for a narrow, white face in the woods above the trail, and several routes that start from a large ledge to the left.

🅢 64. *Snake Charmer 11a
Start: 50' uphill, behind .38 Special on a short face. Follow 6 bolts over a roof and face to anchors. *FA: Craig Estes and Paul Sloan, 1992*

🅢 65. .38 Special 10a
Start: Above the trail at the right end of the ledge on the main formation. Climb a steep white face, over a roof, to chains (4 bolts, anchor) Note: The bolting job on this one is a little wierd, so be comfortable at the grade. *FA: Paul Sloan, 1992*

🅢 66. **Bear Mountain Picnic 8+
Start: 10' left of .38 Special. Climb the obvious, juggy arete (6 bolts, anchor) *FA: Paul Sloan, 1992*

🅢 67. *La Pistola 12a
Start: From the ledge, 10' left of Bear Mountain Picnic. Pull a low roof and a short face (4 bolts, anchor) *FA: Eddie Whittemore and Chris Watford, 1993*

🅢 68. *That Orange Hat 10b
Start: At the left end of the ledge system, 10' left of La Pistola. Pull the low roof to a face and good holds (4 bolts, anchor) *FA: Eddie Whittemore, 1993*

🅢 69. Earflaps 10b
Clip the first 2 bolts on That Orange Hat, then move right to the La Pistola anchors (4 bolts, anchors) *FA: Eddie Whittemore, 1993*

Drop back down to the main trail and continue walking left about 100 yards to a cluster of popular routes…

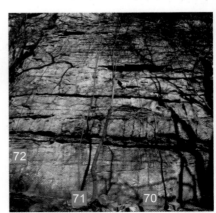

🅢 70. *Miss Prissy 9
Start: About 100' left of Earflaps. Climb up to and lunge over a roof (4 bolts, anchor) *FA: Steve Jones and Cathy Crooks, 1998*

Nathalie DuPre enjoys a Bear Mountain Picnic
Photo: Jim Putnam

71. **Miss Scarlet 9+

Start: Just left of Miss Prissy. Climb a steep featured face. (4 bolts, rings) *FA: Eddie Whittemore and Paul Sloan, 1993*

72. **Diamond Cutter 10b/c

Start: 10' left of Miss Scarlett, on the left side of the tree. Follow 3 bolts to a ring anchor. *FA: Steve Jones, 1993*

73. **Mammy 9

Start: Just left of a wide crack. Climb past 3 bolts to rings. *FA: Eddie Whittemore and Paul Sloan, 1993*

74. *Arete Butler 9+

Start: On a ledge above Mammy. Climb Miss Scarlett or Mammy to gain the ledge. Follow the obvious green and orange arete above, to an anchor. Note: Staying strictly on the arete, not stemming, ups the grade to 11+. *FA: Paul Sloan, 1992*

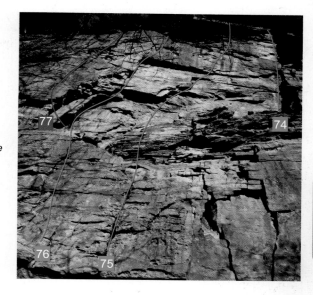

75. Carpet Bagger 11c

Start: 20' left of Arete Butler.
P1: Follow a short finger crack (gear required) to the top of a pedestal/ledge.
P2: Continue up a series of shallow right-facing corners. Pull past a small overlap. Proceed up and out a 6' roof to anchors. Note: Be careful when moving around on the loose ledge system above Pitch 1. *FA: Steve Jones, 1998*

76. *Story Of My Life 11b

Start: Just left of CarpetBagger.
P1: Follow four bolts to a ledge, then left to a belay. (7)
P2: Step up and right on loose rock along ledges. Continue past a vertical crack and roof to anchors (6 bolts, shuts). (11 b) Note: Can be done in one pitch with a 60m rope. *FA: Eddie Whittemore and Jody Rozin, 1999*

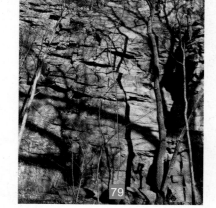

77. Saved By Zeroes 10c/d

Start: Same as Story Of My Life. Follow the obvious lightning bolt crack system to the left.

78. Flim Flam 8

Start: 10' left of Saved By Zeroes. Mountaineer up unpleasant rock and follow a crack to a tree ledge. *FA: Paul Sloan and Roger Fleming, early 1990's*

Kirk Brode enthralled on Finger Puppets
Photo: Nathalie DuPre

79. *Finger Puppets 11a

Start: 100' left of Flim Flam, around the corner. Stick clip the first bolt and climb up a delicate orange slab and roof to anchors (6 bolts, anchors) *FA: Chris Watford and Steve Deweese, 1993*

80. Wet Willie 9

Start: 50' left of Finger Puppets, from a low rock bench/ledge. A series of hidden holds leads to the route's namesake. Has recently been extended to top of cliff. (12 bolts, anchors) *FA: Steve Jones and Cathy Crooks*

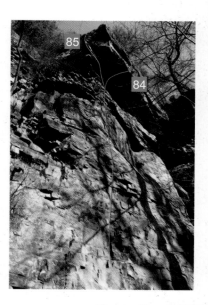

81. Wedgie 10b/c

Start: 5' left of Wet Willie. Follow 3 bolts to a chain anchor. *FA: Steve Jones and Cathy Crooks, 1993.* Note: Veering left of the bolts reduces the grade to 9

GUTBUSTER AREA

82. It's All Good 9+

Start 100' left of Wedgie. Follow 4 or 5 bolts to an anchor. *FA: Spencer Turrentine and Steve Jones*

83. Moonscape 10b

Start: 25' left of It's All Good. Climb a short arete (4 bolts, cold shut anchor) *FA: Eddie Whittemore, 1991*

CHAPTER 10

⑤ 84. *Crunch Junkie 13a/b
Start: 20' left of Moonscape. Climb a steep and chossy face to a roof. Trend right out roof and headwall (9 bolts, anchor). *FA: Eddie Whittemore, 1992*

⑤ 85. Gutbuster 12a/b
Start: Same as Crunch Junkie. Move left at the sixth bolt to anchors (8 bolts, anchor) *FA: Eddie Whittemore, 1992*

⑤ 86. Sport Puppy 9
Start: 30' left of Gutbuster. Climb up blocky rock past 4 bolts to a tree. *FA: Jody Jacobs and Mike Crowder, 1993*

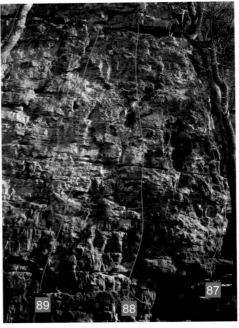

THE SANFORD WALL

This orange colored, gently overhanging wall is about 20' left of Sport Puppy, and offers six nice routes of varying difficulty.

⑤ 87. Grey Matter 9
Start: At the right edge of the wall, next to a tree. Climb the awkward arete. Features a somewhat dangerous clip for the novice leader (3 bolts, rings) Note: The first hanger is gone. Best to stick clip the 2nd bolt. *FA: Eddie Whittemore, 1992*

⑤ 88. Junkyard 11a
Start: 10' left of Grey Matter. Follow 4 bolts to rings. *FA: Eddie Whittemore, 1992*

⑤ 89. *Rollo 11a
Start: 8' left of Junkyard. Follow 4 bolts to rings. Chain on the 3rd bolt. *FA: Eddie Whittemore, 1992*

⑤ 90. *The Big One 11c
Start: 8' left of Rollo. Climb past 3 bolts to rings. *FA: Eddie Whittemore, 1992*

⑤ 91. **You Big Dummy 11d/12a
Start: 10' left of The Big One. Climb past a few cruxes to anchor (5 bolts, shuts) *FA: Eddie Whittemore, 1992*

⑤ 92. *Fish-Eyed Fool 10b
Start: 10' left of You Big Dummy, at the left edge of the wall. Follow 5 bolts to the Dummy rings. *FA: Eddie Whittemore, 1992*

CHAPTER 10

Andy Voss and another bored friend put up the Sanford Wall Traverse, which starts on the 1st bolt of Junk Yard, to the 1st bolt of Rollo, to the 2nd bolt of The Big One, to the 2nd bolt of You Big Dummy then finishes on You Big Dummy. It is 12c.

ROCKET SLAB

Offers a few slabby routes and is a popular spot for beginners.

ⓢ 93. *Gravity Boots 7
Start: About 60' uphill and left of the Sanford Wall. Climb the right side of a slab (3 bolts, anchor) *FA: Paul Sloan and Eddie Whittemore, 1992*

ⓢ 94. Afterburner 5
Start: 10' left of Gravity Boots. Climb past 3 bolts to an anchor. *FA: Paul Sloan, 1992*

ⓢ 95. Witchy Woman 10c
Start: 10' left of Afterburner. Begin on sloping, awkward moves and continue to anchors (3 bolts, anchor) *FA: Jody Jacobs, 1993*

ⓢ 96. *Launch Pad 12b/c
Start: 25' left of Witchy Woman. Climb a steep arete, past 4 bolts to shuts. *FA: Eddie Whittemore, 1992*

⑤ 97. Rode Hard, Put Away Wet 10b
Start: 50' left of Launch Pad. Climb a face, over a roof, to chain anchors (6 bolts, anchor).
Note: The direct start is 11a. *FA: Steve Jones, 1993*

REHAB SLAB

The Rehab Slab is located 150' left, around the corner from Launch Pad. It offers three
routes...

⑤ 98. *Rolffed 9+
Start: The right most route on the face. Amble up the face, over a juggy roof, finish on
Therapist (6 bolts, shuts) *FA: Eddie Whittemore, 1992*

⑤ 99. *Therapist 9+
Start: 5' left of Rolffed. Climb the center of the face (5 bolts, anchor) *FA: Eddie Whittemore
and Paul Sloan, 1992*

⑤ 100. *Rehab 10a
Start: 5' left of Therapist. Climb a face, over a roof, to anchors (5 bolts, anchors) *FA: Paul
Sloan and Zack Jones, 1992*

To the left of the Rehab Slab is a wooden access staircase to/from the top. (Climber Access
#2)

SNATCH WALL

This prominent, tall buttress lies approximately 100 yards left of Rehab Slab, and offers four
airy and intimidating routes.

Gail Vaughn busts up Mammmplitude
Photo: Jonathan Hollada

ⓢ 101. The Confederate 11a
Start: The right-most route. Unpleasant gruntaneering leads to a bolt. Continue up through a slot/roof (6 bolts, anchors) *FA: Eddie Whittemore, 1992*

ⓢ 102. **Snatch 13b
Start: 25' left of The Confederate. Climb the steep wall to, and out, the roof up high (13 bolts, anchor) *FA: Eddie Whittemore, 1992*

ⓢ 103. **Reptile 12a
Follow Snatch to the first bolt in the high roof, then trend left and up to anchors (12 bolts, anchors) *FA: Eddie Whittemore, 1992*

ⓢ 104. Glory 12a
Start: Same as for Snatch/Reptile. Climb to the second bolt of Snatch, bear left and up past the headwall (10 bolts, anchors) *FA: Eddie Whittemore, 1992*

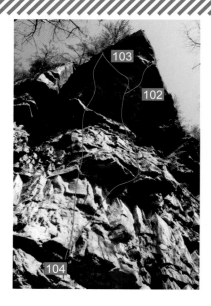

THE RED LIGHT DISTRICT

This prominent "box-like" formation is located about 100 yards left of the Snatch Wall. The next nine routes start on an obvious ledge above the trail, on the right side of an orange wall.

ⓢ 105. Turnin' Tricks 10c
Start: The right most route on the aforementioned ledge. Climb the orange wall past 5 bolts to an anchor. *FA: Eddie Whittemore, 1992*

ⓢ 106. *Timeless Christian Values 9
Start: 15' left of Turnin' Tricks. Climb gently overhanging rock past 4 bolts to anchors. *FA: Eddie Whittemore and Craig Estes, 1992*

ⓢ 107. The Young and the Restless 9
Start: 5' left of Timeless Christian Values. Climb past 4 bolts to shuts. *FA: Eddie Whittemore, 1998*

ⓢ 108. *Mammplitude 10a
Start: 5' left of The Young and the Restless, at a fallen pine tree. Climb over 3 bolts to anchors. *FA: Paul Sloan, 1992*

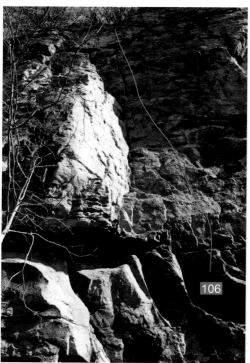

🅢 109. **Dutch Maiden 10b

Start: 10' left of Mammplitude. Climb past 3 bolts to anchors. *FA: Paul Sloan, 1992*

🆃 110. Cornered Market 8

Start: 20' left of Dutch Maiden. Climb a dirty corner. *FA: Paul McNabb, 1991*

🆃 111. On The Side 8

A crack system 10' left of Cornered Market. *FA: Eddie Whittemore and Paul Sloan, 1992*

🅢 112. Quickie 11b

Start: 10' left of On The Side. Climb a pocketed face, over 3 bolts to shuts. *FA: Eddie Whittemore, 1992*

🅢 113. **Cold Shoulder 10c

Start: 25' left of On The Side. Climb the beautiful arete (5 bolts, anchors) *FA: Eddie Whittemore and Paul Sloan, 1992*

🅢 114. **Butt Trumpet 12d

Start: 10' left of Cold Shoulder, back down on the trail. Tweaker face climbing (6 bolts, anchor) *FA: Eddie Whittemore, 1997*

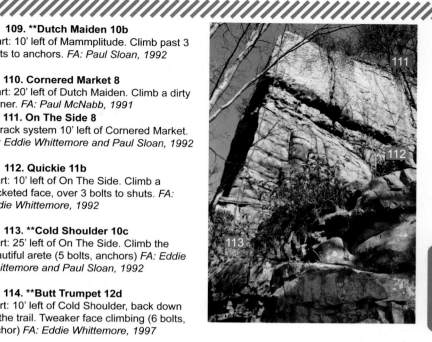

Ryan Nichols on Katana
Photo: Nathalie DuPre'

⑤ 115. Guest Appearance 13a/b
Start: 10' left of Butt Trumpet. Follows a plumb line up a steep, technical face (8 bolts, anchor) *FA: Eddie Whittemore, 1997*

⑤ 116. ***Proposition #One 12c
Start: On Guest Appearance. Clip the first 3 bolts on Guest Appearance, trend out left and up (8 bolts, anchors) *FA: Eddie Whittemore, 1997*

⑤ 117. **Autocratic For The People 13b
Start: 15' left of Proposition #1.Climb the steep face, just right of the Vapor Lock arete (10 bolts, shuts) *FA: Eddie Whittemore, 1998*

⑤ 118. **Vapor Lock 12a
Start: Same as for Autocratic for the People. Crank past the opening moves of Autocratic, then trend left and up the stunning arete (8 bolts, shuts) *FA: Eddie Whittemore, 1992*

⑤ 119. **Mrs. Treated 11a
Start: 10' left of Vapor Lock. Climb the steep face with a corner and mantle move up high (7 bolts, shuts) *FA: Paul Sloan and Eddie Whittemore, 1992*

🅣 120. MILF 9
Trad corner to the left of Mrs. Treated with a two-bolt station at the top.

⑤ 121. *One Hand In My Pocket And The Other On A Stout 11b
Climbs a nice steep face to a crimpy, smooth headwall. (7 bolts, rings) *FA: Michael Moore and Darryl Bornhop*

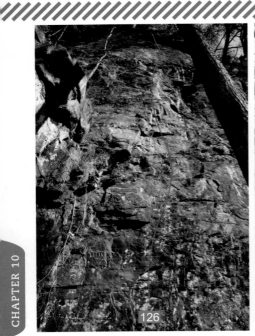

🅢 122. *Size Matters 10b
Starts just left of Stout. Climbs a nice steep face. (7 bolts, rings) *FA: Michael Moore and Darryl Bornhop*

🅢 123. Sweet Feet 10d
Start: 60' left of Size Matters. Climb a short left-facing corner. Step right out a roof and up the face, passing a suspect "diving board" flake, to anchors. (5 bolts, anchors) *FA: Steve Jones, 1998*
Continue left…

🅢 124. Pocket Pool 9
Start: About 100' left of Sweet Feet, on an obvious orange buttress. Follow 5 bolts to an anchor. *FA: Steve Jones, 1997*

🅢 125. Jacob's Ladder 8
Start: 6' left of Pocket Pool. Climb a leaning blocky corner to anchors (5/6 bolts, anchors) *FA: Jody Jacobs, 1993*

There is an unofficial climb out gully to the left of Jacob's Ladder, leading to the top. From Jacob's Ladder, follow a faint trail to the left for 150 yards (about 10 minutes). Stay on the lower trail to pass the waterfall or it will lead to a dead end. After passing the waterfall…

MUSIC CITY

These are new routes and there may still be loose holds. All routes are bolted with anchors and some are more sandbagged than others. All routes require a 60 meter rope.

S 126. ***All the Way to Heaven 11a/b
Starts about 50' past (left of) the waterfall. Intricate face climbing on bullet gray sandstone, to small roof. Climb is in the shade and seeps after a rain. Gets winter sun. *FA: Darryl Bornhop and Steve Jones, 2008*

Walk a bit left from All The Way To Heaven, past a large detached boulder, to where it is possible to scramble up onto a ledge above the trail. Carefully move right across a tenuous step-across (perhaps rope up?) to a ledge below an orange face. The next route starts here…

S 127. **Katana 12a
Stick clip, then climb the low orange face on crimps, to a large ledge. From here, trend out left over roof (crux), then up an amazing white, hanging arête. Top out around the corner for the 12a, or continue straight up (currently unclimbed) (9/10 bolts and anchors) *FA: Jim Putnam, 2010*

S 128. Sweet Surrender 8
Slab climbing to moderate vertical face. A nice warmup. *FA: Steve Jones and Brenda Korte, 2008*

⑤ 129. Elephant Ears 9
Vertical face to slab to more vertical face. Tricky sequence at crux. Not the best route, but has some interestingly complex moves. *FA: Steve Jones and Brenda Korte, 2008*

⑤ 130. *Lay Lady Lay 10a
Tricky face moves on the start, eases off towards the top. *FA: Steve Jones, 2007*

⑤ 131. ***Crash into Me 11b
Desperate face climbing leads past a moderate mid-section. Finishes to a beautiful orange arête. *FA: Darryl Bornhop, 2007*

🅣 132. **Hips Don't Lie 11c
Starts in a small alcove. Fight through the hand crack, then trend up and right to ledge. Continue over the second roof via a thin crack, then pass a final roof straight to ring anchors. *FA: Jason Reynolds*

⑤ 133. Stairway to Heaven (Project)
Series of tiers to face. Bolting not complete.

Continue left…

WALL OF USELESS CONFLICT

These routes are listed from right to left and all require a 60 meter rope. Route grades are estimates that need confirmation. Bolt counts are needed.

⑤ 134. Humane Bomb 11a
Starts about 60 yards left of Stairway To heaven. An easy start in a short left-facing corner leads to a waltz across a ramp, then to a steep, kindly face. Culminates in a compassionate crux. *FA: Darryl Bornhop, 2006*

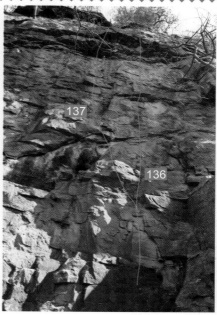

🪝 135. Tit For Tat 10c/d
Starts just left of Humane Bomb. A boulder start leads to a ledge/cave. Fun moves lead up the left margin of the cave and on to another ledge. Finishes via a tricky short roof/bulge and thin face. The top is a little sandbagged - might be 11a. *FA: Steve Jones, 2006*

🪝 136. Right Hook 11d
Start: In a shallow left-facing corner. Climb an ever-steepening face to a coldshut anchor (5 bolts, shuts) *FA: Eddie Whittemore and Chris Watford, 1995*

🪝 137. Left Hook 11a
Share the first bolt and opening moves of Right Hook, then trend left up a gently overhanging face (5 bolts, shuts) *FA: Eddie Whittemore, 1995*

🪝 138. **Shock And Awe 11b/c
Starts just left of Left Hook. The name says it all. Finish over the big roof. (12/13 bolts, rings) *FA: Darryl Bornhop, 2006*

139. **Holy War 9

Starts just left of Shock And Awe and right of a seasonal waterfall. Crusade to the ledge, then jihad to the top. (11/12 bolts, rings) *FA: Steve Jones, 2006*

140. Mitch's Bitch 10c/d

Don't get her too excited when moving through the slot and before turning the corner. Avoid the big roof by climbing up and out over the arête before face climbing to the anchors. *FA: Mitch Toomey 2006?*

141. Sucker Punch 11a

Start left of Mitch's Bitch . Stick clip the first bolt and follow ever-diminishing holds to a hard move before the anchors (8 or 9 bolts, anchors) *FA: Eddie Whittemore and Chris Watford, 1995*

142. Smear, Queer and Fear 11b

Just left of Sucker Punch. Thin face climbing to the right leads to small roof followed by face climbing to another overhang. *FA: Darryl Bornhop, 2006*

143. Good vs Evil 10c/d

Wander up the easy low face to a short roof/corner 40' up. Fun climbing up the headwall to finish. *FA Steve Jones, 2006*

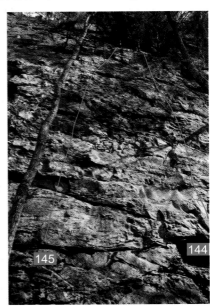

144. He Said, She Said (9- to the ledge, 10c to the top)
Just left of Good vs Evil. This route serves as the second warm-up or can be continued from the ledge to the top (10c) by climbing quality rock on interesting traversing moves. *FA: Steve Jones, 2006*

145. Sibling Rivalry (7+ to ledge/anchors, 9 to the top)
Left of He Said, She Said. Rap from the anchors or traverse the ledge left to a belay bolt and continue to the top climbing beautiful brown rock (9). *FA: Heather Andrews, 2006*

146. Panty Raid 10
Starts in a shallow alcove left of Sibling Rivalry. Trends up and slightly left from the ledge. Slightly overhanging face to arête. Alternatively, climb the face above the belay bolt of Sibling Rivalry. Can be some loose rock on the first part - belayer should stand to the side. *FA: Heather Andrews, 2006*

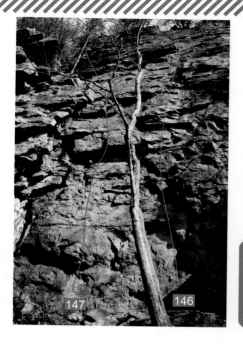

147. Puss and Boots 11a.
Boulder up the steep low face to a ledge. Climb the bulges off of the ledge and move up and slightly left across several cruxes on the varnished face. *FA: Michael Moore and Darryl Bornhop, 2011*

These next routes are accessed by climbing Sibling Rivalry et al and traversing left along the ledge to the platform, then down climbing a bit to the start. The routes are behind the huge flake.

148. Midnight Plowboy 10b
Starts just below the ledge 50 feet left of Panty Raid and behind the flake. *FA: Steve Jones, 2007*

149. Brokeback Mountain 11b/c
Start at the bottom of the face and take the ride to the top. *FA: Darryl Bornhop, 2007*

PARADOX WALL AREA

Nice tall face routes, all requiring a 60 meter rope. Route grades are estimates that need confirmation.

155 154 153 152

150. See the Egress 7
Starts off a ledge with tree anchor 25 yards right of Vividly Grey. Fun exit route. Face to arete. Not a beginner lead route and probably not good for setting a toprope. *FA: Heather Andrews, 2004*

151. Vividly Grey 9+/10
Starts right of two large downed trees. Named in memoriam for Professor Grey who passed away after climbing a nearby route. Note: 5.9 leaders should stick clip the first bolt. *FA: Steve Jones, 2005*

152. Hidden in Plain Sight 10a
A hidden hold before the ledge and a stimulating clip going over the roof. *FA: Heather Andrews, 2005*

153. The Three Gs (Guns, Gays and God) **11b/c**
You have to be rabidly in favor of 2 out of the 3 to get elected. Power up the start, prance through the middle and pray you don't blow it at the end. *FA: Darryl Bornhop, 2006*

154. Hurts So Good 10b
Starts at low roof. Tight little crimps at the tail end. *FA: Steve Jones, 2005*

156 157 158

155. Girly Man 11a/b
Have you ever been spanked by a girly man? *FA: Darryl Bornhop, 2004*

156. Bad Girls are Good 10b
Bad girls can be heart breakers in the end or they can just be good. Chain anchors. *FA: Steve Jones, 2004.*

157. Republican Conservationist 10c
Paradoxical moves at the crux. *FA: Spencer Turrentine, 2005*

158. Republican Give-Away-Program 10d/11a
Easy if you are already strong. Face climb to a traverse, turn the roof and climb the face. From the ledge stay left through the face to the splitter, then face climb to the anchors. *FA: Darryl Bornhop, 2006*

ZONE 3 (DOG BOY'S VILLAGE)

This area lies at the far end of Foster Falls and boasts the newest route development. Unfortunately, Dog Boy's Village is really easy to identify now, since there has been some kind of bulldozing going on and a road comes up right behind the cliff face, destroying the serene and spiritual feeling of the area. You can still get a good view of the intertwining valleys at the top of the 140' cliff face. The climbs are listed from right to left

159. RJ Cam 8
Follow a hand crack that trends left at the top. Ends at the anchors of Secret Passage. *FA: James Moore, 2001*

160. **Secret Passage 12a
Starts on gray rock and leads to a gold face. It's just left of a crack in a left-facing dihedral. (4 bolts, anchors) 50' *FA: James Moore, 2001*

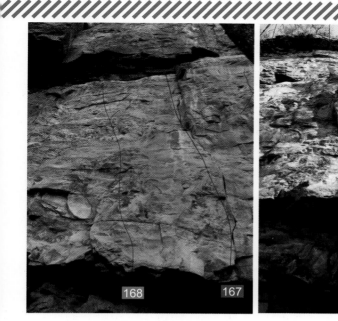

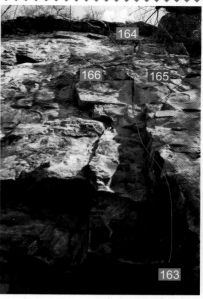

🇹 161. The Ruff And Nasty 8
Follow a crack in a left-facing dihedral between Secret Passage and Cave Man. It can be done in one pitch but it isn't recommended. This nasty crack leads over bushes and nasty rock and has no anchors. *FA: James Moore and Steve Jones*

162. Cave Man 11
30' left of Ruff And Nasty, an inverted staircase leads to a shallow chimney. Climb the left side of the rock breakage. Not yet bolted, though it does have anchors

🇸 163. **Half Man 10c
This beautiful face climb is not to be missed. Start: Approximately 40' left of Cave Man. Begins in a dihedral split by a finger crack and an arête and can be linked with Half Beast into one long pitch. The first pitch leads to the large ledge that splits the large face in half. Stop here or continue on to the second set of anchors at 100ft. The first pitch has 6 bolts. *FA: Steve Jones, 2001*

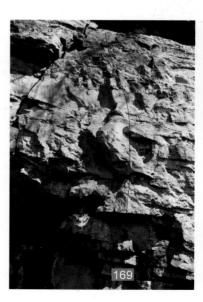

🇸 164. ***Half Beast 11a
The second pitch of Half Man. Intricate and sustained climbing leads to a left-facing dihedral. *FA: Steve Jones, 2001* Note: 60m rope required for linking pitches. If you're into adventure climbing there is a third set of anchors at the top past the roof. This last 40' is protected by only 1 bolt and requires 2 ropes to rap down.

T 165. *Horseshoe 10a
Just right of the 2nd pitch of Half Man/Half Beast, look for a single bolt at the base of a left-facing dihedral, with a crack running from the ground to the top of the cliff. *FA: Eddie Whittemore and Mark Cartwright*

S 166. **Prison Of The Mind 12c/d
From the ledge of Half Beast is another bolted line just to the left. It starts just right of a loose jug and cranks up a variety of sustained lockoffs to the roof. (5 bolts, anchors) Note: Stick clip the first bolt. *FA: James Moore, 2002*

T 167. **Gold Finger 11a
Continue left from Half Man and look for an obvious finger/hand crack with an opening roof. Follow the crack to the top. *FA: Arno Ilgner, 2001*

S 168. **Golden Girl 10c
Start: Just left of Gold Finger. Pull a low roof lip and move left over a golden face to anchors (6 bolts, anchors) *FA: Steve Jones*

S 169. ***Everybody Knows Fire' 9+
This is a fun line that requires a variety of moves to keep it mellow (6 bolts, anchors) *FA: Steve Jones*

T 170. *Keeping It Straight 9+
Follows a crack at the left end of a cave, just right of the right-facing dihedral. The start is the same as Finding The Trust and can be a mixed route if the first bolt is used. At the roof, pull right to rap anchors. *FA: James Moore and Steve Jones, 2000*

S 171. *Finding the Trust 10d
Follow a right-facing dihedral with fun technical stemming, then move around the left side of the roof to a set of rap anchors (5 bolts, anchors) *FA: James Moore and Steve Jones, 2000*

172. **The Process 12a

Climb the thin face just left of Finding The Trust. Stay to the left except when necessary and throw in a few acrobatic moves and breeze to the anchor. Shares anchors with Trust. *FA: James Moore, 2000*

At this point, cut uphill and around the corner to a tall, steep left-facing wall. There are 3 routes here. Note: If you are going to skip these routes, then stay low on the trail and continue along...

173. Chesnutt's Route 12a/b

Start On a ledge around the corner from The Process. Follow approximately 8 or 9 bolts to an anchor. Note: 60m rope required. *FA: Chris Chesnutt, 1991*

174. *Dead Battery 12a

Start: 15' left of Chesnutt's Route. Climb discontinuous flakes and corners to an overhanging finish (9 bolts, anchors). Note: 60m rope required. *FA: Eddie Whittemore, Chris Watford, 1991*

175. Unknown New Route – no details

176. Sloppy When Wet 5

Starts to the left in a gully. Follow 2 bolts up a semi-technical face or stem the chimney to a set of anchors at the top. This minus 3 star route is more fun when wet. This is the exit route to get back to the main rim hiking trail. *FA: Steve Jones*

177. Pump Me 'Til I'm Goofy 10d

Follows a gently overhanging wall. (6 bolts, anchor)

Continue walking left through the talus for five minutes or so to an impressive cave called The Battery.

THE BATTERY

Characterized by a monster roof, this area sports the most recent new routes at Foster Falls. There are three short routes where the trail intersects the cliff. The two right hand routes are chossy, with no anchors, and at this point, not worth doing. The left-most route is:

178. Battery Warmup 11a/b

A nice warm up, though somewhat sandy and dirty. (5 bolts, anchor) *FA: Steve Jones*

Continue walking 100' left, under the massive roof...

179. Paradigm Shift 5.14? (project)

Equipped by Jim Putnam, who provides the following description: "Climb up and right towards the beautiful roof crack, past cruxes that keep doubling in difficulty until you hit the business. If you make it past the iron finger crux into the first hand jam, it's only a 12+ finish out a world class roof traverse".

180. Under Water Ninja Moves 13+? (project)

Climb Paradigm Shift past the first crux, then break left at the hand jam saddle rest. Work left along a horizontal until you're forced to clip. Dive backwards and begin the fun - long moves and multiple powerful cruxes through a monster roof. Equipped by Jim Putnam

According to Jim, "There are possibly other lines in The Battery that would have to move though chossy rock. There may be bolts on other lines in the cave, but if they are red tagged, please be respectful of loose flakes, some of which will break if not glued first. There may not be any more all natural lines out the cave proper but someone will have to aid out there first and find out."

There are probably a dozen or so more routes past the Battery, spread out along the cliffline for the next hundred yards or so, but the rock quality is spotty and the trail is often overgrown. For the adventurous, a five minute walk past The Battery leads to a steep scramble up a small hill. Locate the lone route the left side of a large corner.

🔺 181. **Tipsy Gypsies 11a
Follow a sparsely bolted face that wonders left towards the top. Hand drilled. *FA: Jim Putnam*

One of the helpful signs along the upper clifftop trail, clearly denoting the climber access gullies.

Wesley Caulkins on Kacee's Route
Photo: Nathan Brown

BIG SOUTH FORK **11**

chapter

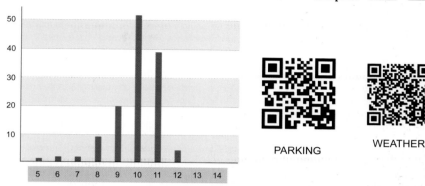

PARKING WEATHER

The Big South Fork National River and Recreation Area lies on the Cumberland Plateau, where the Big South Fork of the Cumberland River flows north into Kentucky, and in the words of author Russ Manning, contains "some of the most primitive and isolated lands in the eastern United States." Recognition of the wilderness character of the area led to a long and protracted effort to create a protected national park, which was finally accomplished in 1991, after many years of being managed by the Army Corps Of Engineers. Currently encompassing 123,000 acres, the BFSNRRA is vast. Deep isolated river gorges, natural stone arches, caves, rock shelters, waterfalls and miles of cliff line make the area a virtually unexplored rock climbing destination.

Although mainly known for its extensive backpacking trails and white water rivers, the sheer quantity of rock in the Big South Fork is mind-boggling - more rock in one area than anywhere else in the southeast! Designated as a recreation area, it offers almost unlimited climbing potential, though most of the cliffs are extremely remote and difficult to get to, and a sizeable portion of them are either off limits due to park regulations or are too chossy and loose to be viable. There are few good trails to the cliffs, and most of the rock is undeveloped. Don't expect a "Popular Crag" feel, as the Fork lends itself to the true adventurer.

History

Climbing history at the Big South Fork likely goes back several decades. It's a remote, wild place and I'm sure that over the years, intrepid climbers from Tennessee, Kentucky and North Carolina explored the cliffs looking for some adventure. It's a safe bet that most of the obvious crack lines, if they are reasonably close to road access, have probably been done. There are records of climbing and rappelling in the gorge dating back to the 1960's and more than one university professor probably brought students there for a bit of high-angle academics. Documenting history and first ascent information has been a daunting task, since the area seems to have been developed largely by small, independent groups of people without any direct contact and sharing of information with each other. It is entirely possible, and probable, that an entire cliff could be developed by one group, while a few miles away, another group labored away on their own little chunk of Shangri-La.

The first known climbing history in the BSF started back in the mid-eighties, when river guide and climber Bob Wheeley moved to the South Fork to start a rafting service. While running the river, he noticed the enormous sandstone walls looming above. He contacted his partner Phil Barkesdale, and they pioneered such gorge classics as the Original Route on the O&W Wall, and The Nose in the Nose Area. Phil told kayaker/climber Terry Smith from Chattanooga of his exploits, and Terry, in turn, told his friend and climbing partner Jeff Noffsinger about a fabled three pitch 5.9 route. Several years later, on Thanksgiving Day in 1990, Jeff and Patrick Turner went searching for the elusive route. After talking with rangers and scouring maps, the pair found a four wheel drive road that led in to the top of the O&W Wall, where they were greeted by a stunning view of the massive gorge, giant sandstone walls, and the incredible whitewater river below. Not knowing how to hike to the bottom of the wall, they rappelled down, pulling their ropes the whole way, assuming they would have little difficulty climbing back out. From the base of the wall, there was only one main weakness-a soaring corner capped by large roofs, with nice ledges in between. Once atop the second pitch, the infamous third pitch, a gnarly off width chimney, presented itself and the pair opted for a low angled face to the left. This decision added a new variation to the route, and was topped out in sleet and rain. Totally stoked about the new area, the pair have continued to pioneer routes ever since. Frank Jackson and Jeff Dopp have made their mark as well. The Main Gorge is only one small area in the park, offering everything from big multi-pitch routes, to shorter cragging walls and unlimited bouldering. There are many other areas in the park, and some will be noted in this book. More information on other areas will certainly be available in the years to come. Although climbing history dates back to 1985, the potential for the Big South Fork is just now coming to light.

For the most part, first ascent information for Blue Heron has not been kept or provided, even for the more recently developed sport climbs, since most of the trad routes were probably done a long time ago. Further, many bolted lines may have been toproped. The route name chosen by the first known ascent party has been maintained. For the record, climbers who have recently helped develop Blue Heron are: Keel Coleman, Scott Hubbs, Paul Jakus, Mark Kominiak, Ian McAlexander, Lenore McAlexander, Chris Petty, Kelly Brown and Matthew Shallbetter. Jeff Noffsinger, along with Patrick Turner and various other partners, has almost singlehandedly developed the "outback" areas at Big South Fork. Jeff graciously provided his route information and topos for Pine Creek, the Main Gorge and No Business Creek. Jeff has mostly focused on the tall multi-pitch cliffs, establishing some of the best adventure routes in Tennessee, but has included some single pitch crags as well. Mark Dew and Kelly Brown also were kind enough to share their information. Perhaps over the years, a more complete guide can be done for the Big South Fork.

Location and Directions

The Big South Fork National River and Recreation Area lies on the Cumberland Plateau west of I-75 between Lexington, Kentucky and Knoxville, Tennessee. The park actually spans the border of Tennessee and Kentucky and is most easily reached by car. These are general directions for accessing the park. Specific climbing area directions are included below.

From I-75 southbound, exit at Mt. Vernon and take KY461 south to KY80, take KY80 southwest to Somerset. Turn south on US27, to Oneida and follow TN297 west into the park.

From I-75 northbound, exit for Huntsville and Oneida and take TN63 west to US27, take 27 north to Oneida and follow TN297 west into the park.

From I-40 westbound, exit at US27, travel north to Oneida and follow TN297 west into the park.

From I-40 eastbound, exit at Monterey on TN62. Follow this east to intersect with US127. Travel north to TN154, take TN154 north to TN 297 and follow TN297 east into the park.

There are two Park Service visitor centers. One is in the community of Stearns, Kentucky and serves the northern part of the park. The other is the Bandy Creek Visitors Center off of TN297 where it crosses the river just west of Oneida.

It is recommended that the first time visitor get a copy of a Tennessee state map, or preferably a Tennessee Gazetteer, which is an invaluable resource for adventurers.

From Nashville, take I-40 East to exit #300 for Monterey. Go left, then take a right on Hwy 62. Follow this to intersect Hwy 127. (Hwy 127 is also the way you would come if driving in from Chattanooga). Go north on Hwy 127 through Jamestown and look for signs leading towards Pickett State Park and Big South Fork National River and Recreation Area. Take a right onto Hwy 154. Continue on Hwy 154, and look for another BSF sign at the intersection of Hwy 297. If you end up in Pickett State Park, you've gone too far. Follow Hwy 297 into the BSF and down to the Leatherwood Ford area. Continue up the other side of the gorge and drive out of the park. Keep driving until you see Terry & Terry Market on the left. Go right at the stop sign, which is still Hwy 297. Go .6 miles and take the next right onto Toomey Road. There is usually no sign, but it is the first gravel road on the right after turning at the Market. Follow this, trend left at a house, then continue down a steep hill into the Gorge. Although not technically a four wheel drive road, good clearance is a must. If you are driving a low slung Cadillac, do not take the left onto Toomey Road; instead, continue on Hwy 297, and take a right on Verdun Road. If driving in from Knoxville, go to Oneida and take Hwy 297 towards the park, and look for Verdun Road on the left in about a mile or so. Take a left onto Verdun Road. As the road curves left, stay straight, follow this down and take a right at the bottom onto the Gorge Road. (Going left here will take you back into the town of Oneida.) Follow the Gorge Road to an old wooden bridge and look for another road going up hill to the right. This road is Toomey Road, mentioned above as the first way in when arriving from the west side of the park. Upon crossing the old wood bridge, reset your odometer and proceed 1.5 miles to a second wooden bridge. Both bridges cross over Pine Creek, leading into the Main Gorge. At 2.5 miles from the first bridge, look for the steep white sandstone of Pine Creek Wall on the left. Just past Pine Creek, drive through a rock road cut at 2.6 miles and into the gorge proper. At 2.9 miles, Lost City Wall is visible on the right, and at 3 miles you will be under the giant Box Car Roof. Just past the Box Car is the canyon known as The Crack House, and just past that is the Nose Area. At around 3.4 miles you will be under the 911 Wall, and if you continue a little further, you will be at the O&W Bridge, and under the O&W Wall.

Camping

The BSFNRRA has four campgrounds. The 190-site Bandy Creek Campground near the Bandy Creek Visitor Center has water and electric hookups. The 45-site Blue Heron Campground near Stearns at present has no utility hookups. Two new camps cater to horseback riders at Station Camp East in Tennessee and Bear Creek in Kentucky.

There is a permit required to camp in the gorge. It is only $5.00 for a group, and is available at the Bandy Creek visitor center, Kentucky visitor center, and the Blue Heron Complex. Call (423) 286-7275 for info. Permits can also be obtained at some of the stores and shops in the area. There is a great store on Hwy 297 called Willie Lee's General Store. They have a deli, a good selection of beer (No beer on Sunday), and backcountry permits. They can be contacted at (931) 879-6987 or (877) 255-0075. They are climber friendly, and will be glad to help you out with whatever you might need. They also have free coffee!

The best camping spot in the gorge is down by the O&W bridge. Just before crossing the bridge, trend right onto an old road bed, which leads down to the South Fork equivalent of Yosemite's Camp 4, Boulder Camp. Boulder Camp is named for the large boulder that rolled off the mountain and landed right in the middle of the road. This has been the meeting spot for climbers for years. It is right below the O&W Wall, and has great views from the bridge. There is a nice little beach below the bridge with good swimming, just don't get washed down the class IV rapids below! There are also other good spots across the bridge and downstream if Boulder Camp is full. Bring all the supplies you will need for camping, including water. You can always drive back into Oneida, but it's a bit of a haul.

There are other camping spots available all over and around the park. Try Laurel Creek Campground on Hwy 154, on the left coming from Jamestown, before reaching Hwy 297. Pickett State Park has camping and cabin rental. Bandy Creek Campground is in the park on Hwy 297. For Blue Heron, camp at the Park Service campground (all facilities, $12/ night), just inside the park, off Route 742.

Luxuries

The small towns of Jamestown, Stearns, Oneida and Revelo should have everything you might need in the way of gas, groceries and lodging. Hotels can be found in Jamestown and Oneida. Try the Galloway Inn in Oneida, just off Hwy 27, (423) 569-8835 or (423) 569-5999. They have clean rooms and you can sleep four for around $40.00. Charit Creek Lodge in the backcountry is the sole lodging in the recreation area. Hiking and horseback riding, or mountain biking, are the only ways to get there. You'll stay in bunk cabins or bunk rooms in the lodge, pioneer log structures. Breakfast and lunch provided. Reservations are needed (250 Apple Valley Road Sevierville, Tenn. 37862. (423) 429-5704. In addition to small motels in the surrounding communities, inns offer a night's stay. At Stearns, you'll find the Big South Fork Motor Lodge (606) 376-3156 and the Marcum-Porter House (606) 376-2242. A restoration of the nearby Barthell Mining Community will include lodging; check with the visitor center for the opening. On the southern boundary of the park lies Historic Rugby, an English colony founded in 1880 (P.O. Box 8, Rugby, Tenn. 37733. (423) 628-2441. You can stay at Newbury House or a cottage and have dinner at the Harrow Road Cafe. There's also the nearby Clear Fork Farm (423) 628-2967 and Grey Gables (423) 628-5252 bed and breakfasts, and the Bruno Gernt House (1-800-771-8940) in the old German community of Allardt. Tennessee's Pickett State Rustic Park on the west side of the recreation area has cabins and a campground (615) 879-5821. A new Big South Fork Wilderness Resort (423) 569-9847 on the east has cabins.

Emergency Assistance

Dial 911
BSF Park Headquarters (423) 569-9778
Bandy Creek Visitor's Center (423) 286-2275

Regulations

The Park Service is now in the process of developing a Climbing Management Plan for the park to help protect this precious resource for generations to come. Although Park management has a good relationship with climbers now, it will take all of us to help the park maintain climbing areas, and uphold the new CMP. There have been instances in the past that tarnished the park's view of climbers. Cutting trees to build ladders, grid-bolting with power drills, and climbing in areas that are not designated for climbing are all prohibited. Created with input from climbers, the CMP will likely be modeled after the plan used at the nearby Obed River National Park unit, which provides for limited use of fixed anchors by permit. Ranger Chris Stubbs provided the following basic rules and regulations:

1. All routes must be located at least 30 feet from a maintained USNPS trail.
2. No climbing within 100 feet of an established (named) overlook.
3. No climbing on arches.
4. Sport routes must be 20 feet apart.
5. The first bolt should be at least 10 feet off the deck.

6. All hardware must be camouflaged with dark paint.

7. New routes should have lowering stations to protect rim ecology.

8. Damage to vegetation should be minimized. Do not scrub a white streak up the rock! Simply clean the holds you need and let climbing traffic do the rest.

The area that has been developed thus far allows the use of power drills by permit only. Still, the plan is tentative and could change at any time. Power drills are not allowed in wilderness areas of the Big South Fork. Roughly speaking, these are areas where hunting is permitted. Let's not ruin a good thing. Please keep your power drills holstered until the CMP is finalized. Have fun, and enjoy the Southeast's new climbing mecca!

Varmints, Critters and Rock Fall

From Jeff Noffsinger - "Bears, spiders, scorpions, wild boar, copperheads, lots of rattlesnakes. Did I mention lots and lots of rattlesnakes? And of course there is also the notorious Big South Fork Devil Bug, a wild insect seemingly crossbred with aliens or something. It looks like a giant preying mantis, except that it has huge anodized mandibles. It waits until you are cozy in your lawn chair and then swoops down out of the woods and rips your eyes out. Believe me, this bug is real, and for some reason they are very aggressive. I have met locals who didn't even know they existed. Then there are the Star Trek slugs that seem to go for the ears of those who choose to bivy in the open. We think these may be the larvae of the Devil Bug. Look before you leap!"

Rockfall wise, the Big South Fork is a very volatile area. I have climbed a route, and come back a week later to find hundreds of pounds of rock that fell off the summit. It actually shaved all the branches off half a pine tree, and left the other side untouched. This is rare, and could be caused by freeze/thaw or pine beetle damage and erosion, but then again the large boulder in the road at Boulder Camp might prove otherwise. One would think nothing that big ever cuts loose, but this last fall another giant boulder rolled off the mountainside below 911 Wall and landed in the middle of the Gorge Road, and has only recently been dynamited and removed. Most routes were cleaned on the first ascent, but on routes this big that are rarely climbed, there will be some loose stuff, especially on ledges. Be careful, protect the belayer, and wear a helmet."

FYI

The best place to start any visit to the Big South Fork is the Bandy Creek Visitor's Center, where you'll find an information center as well as books and maps. The Bandy Creek Center also has a campground with electricity, RV hookups, stables, picnic areas and a swimming pool. There are tons of other recreational opportunities in the Big South Fork: horseback riding, fly fishing, hiking, mountain/road biking, caving, camping, backcountry lodging and paddling. Check out two excellent books by noted Tennessee author Russ Manning, "An Outdoor Guide To The Big South Fork" (Mountaineers Books) and "Trails Of The Big South Fork" (Mountain Laurel Place). Both are available at local bookstores or outfitting shops.

A Word About Grades

The route grades were given after doing the first ascent. Subsequent ascents, fixed gear, and beta all seem to change route grades eventually. The grades given are only a general idea of what you might encounter, so be careful not to get in over your head. All of the Gorge routes were put in ground up and hand drilled, in keeping with the tradition of the backcountry, adventure climbing ethos. Assume that all of the grades are old school. Aid ratings are not new wave, and even though a route is given an aid rating, it probably goes clean unless noted. A2 routes generally have decent gear, but could be very steep and strenuous. A3 routes have some body weight placements, where a fall will probably seriously injure the leader. Most pitons are left fixed to help preserve the rock. Please don't remove fixed gear, and replace pitons when needed. Most routes do not have fixed anchors, so make sure you know how to build gear belays. Unfortunately, the South Fork has been hit hard by pine beetle infestation, rendering many of the stout trees unusable. Efforts will soon be under way to begin retro fitting routes with anchors, but for now, use your best judgment and be extra careful.

Prolific Big South Fork route developer Jeff Noffsinger airing it out high above the Cumberland River.

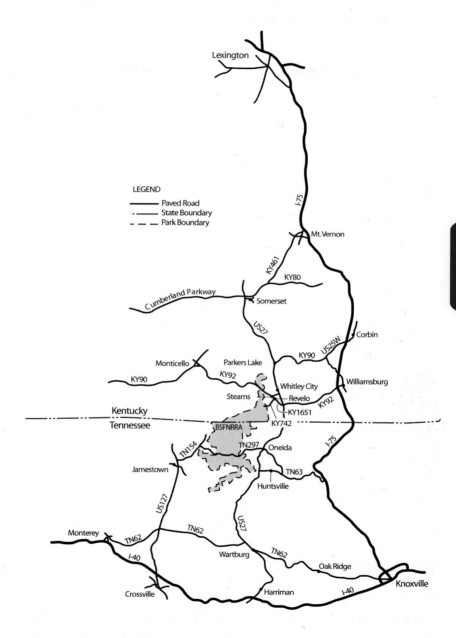

LEGEND
— Paved Road
·–· State Boundary
– – Park Boundary

Lexington

I-75

Mt. Vernon

KY461

KY80

Cumberland Parkway

Somerset

US27

KY90

US25W

Corbin

Monticello

Parkers Lake

KY92

KY90

Whitley City

Stearns

Revelo

Williamsburg

KY1651

KY92

Kentucky

Tennessee

BSFNRRA

KY742

TN297

Oneida

I-75

Jamestown

TN154

TN63

Huntsville

US127

TN62

Monterey

TN62

TN62

US27

I-40

Wartburg

Oak Ridge

Crossville

Harriman

I-40

Knoxville

Getting to the Big South Fork

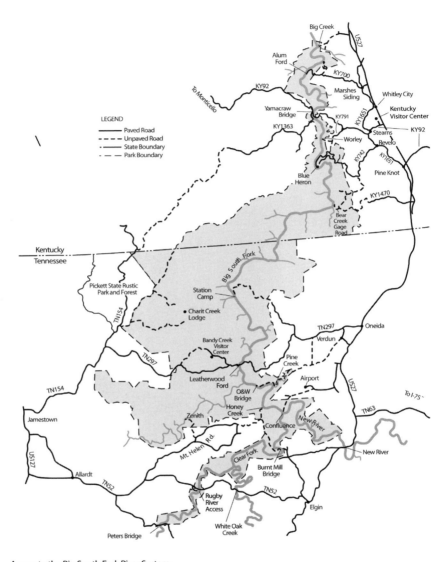

LEGEND

— Paved Road
- - - Unpaved Road
—— State Boundary
- · — Park Boundary

Big Creek

Alum
Ford

KY700

US27

KY92

Marshes
Siding

Whitley City

Yamacraw
Bridge

KY791

KY1651

Kentucky
Visitor Center

KY1363

Worley

Stearns
Revelo

KY92

To Monticello

KY742

KY1651

Blue
Heron

Pine Knot

KY1470

Bear
Creek
Gage
Road

Kentucky
Tennessee

Big South Fork

Pickett State Rustic
Park and Forest

TN154

Station
Camp

Charit Creek
Lodge

TN297

Oneida

Verdun

TN297

Bandy Creek
Visitor
Center

Pine
Creek

Leatherwood
Ford

Airport

TN154

O&W
Bridge

US27

Jamestown

Honey
Creek

Zenith

Mt. Helen Rd.

Confluence

New River

To I-75

TN63

US127

Clear Fork

New River

Allardt

TN52

Burnt Mill
Bridge

Rugby
River
Access

TN52

Elgin

Peters Bridge

White Oak
Creek

Access to the Big South Fork River System

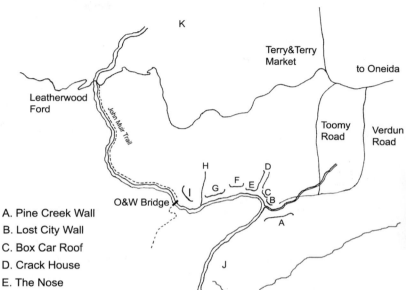

A. Pine Creek Wall
B. Lost City Wall
C. Box Car Roof
D. Crack House
E. The Nose
F. Hidden Ledge
G. 911 Wall
H. Twin Falls Wall
I. O&W Wall
J. Honey Creek
K. Mill Creek

The Big South Fork

Climbing Area Overview

Big South Fork Main Gorge Overview

N

Crack House

Boxcar Roof

Lost City

Pine Creek Wall

The Nose

Hidden Ledge

911 Wall

Twin Falls Wall

O&W Wall

O&W Bridge

White Oak Creek

Big South Fork - Upper Gorge

Photo: Jeff Noffsinger

Lost City

Box Car Roof

Nose

Crack House

Hidden Ledge

911

Note: While putting together this chapter it occurred to me that it made little sense to include the detailed route information and topos for the long multi-pitch routes in the Gorge. Nobody doing these routes will want to bring the book along. Consequently, for this edition, I have produced separate single page route topo sheets for the long routes that can be downloaded at www.dixiecragger.com. In this book, the routes will be listed and brief information given, but the details will be on the downloadable topos.

PINE CREEK

Pine Creek is one of the finest cliffs in the Big South Fork, and is the first big wall visible on the left when first entering the gorge. Facing northwest, the imposing white sandstone of Pine Creek is shady in the morning, but catches sun in the afternoon. At nearly 200' in height, Pine Creek offers the experienced trad climber the unique opportunity to climb multi pitch routes, many of which are possible even in the pouring rain due to the steep angle and massive roofs high on the cliff.

To get there, take TN297 west from Oneida, for 1.7 miles. Turn left (south) on Verdun Road. After .6 miles, turn right onto the O&W railroad bed, which turns to gravel in half a mile. Continue down toward the O&W Bridge, which is at 7.6 miles. The pulloff for Pine Creek is a mile before the Bridge, at roughly 6.6 miles. Alternately, if you are traveling east on TN297, turn right at the Terry and Terry Store, and then at .6 miles, turn right onto Toomey Road (unmarked), which descends to join the O&W railroad bed after 3 miles. Bear right and continue 4.2 miles to the bridge. There is a popular camp spot near the bridge called Boulder Camp. Continue another mile to Pine Creek.

To get oriented, it may be best to do a recon from the road to pick out a few of the main features that can be used as reference points. The cliff is broken by two main ledge systems, so it is possible to "mix and match" different routes. There are two sharp corners three-quarters of the way up the wall. The left-facing corner on the left is the third pitch of Captain Hook. The right-facing corner on the right is the second pitch of the Cave Route. They both lead to the Cave Of Despair, about 150' up, where there is a bolted rappel station. (Incidentally, this rappel is the third pitch of Solar System). There are two main ledge systems on the wall, both of which are roughly 75' off the ground. Left Ledge is accessed by hiking left up a gully, then back right to the ledge. Right Ledge is accessed by scrambling right and then stepping back left to the ledge. Each ledge provides access to three routes. Got it?

The approach to Pine Creek is no easy task. The way is steep and requires crossing a Class VI creek. From the parking area at the rock road cut, hike back along the road to a point roughly even with the center of the cliff. Look for a faint climber's trail (The Borneo Slide) Drop straight down, grabbing trees to slow your descent, toward the creek and a sandy beach with big boulders. Jeff and his comrades have sussed out the only reliable way across the creek and here it is: Climb up and left atop a large boulder with a waterfall under it. From here, slide down to another boulder lying in the water. There will be a 20' drop to the right and a boiling waterfall to the left. Work across the creek, wading and bouldering up the opposite bank. Caution: Do not attempt this in high water! Once across, climb up and right through some rocks, where a good trail leads to the base. Good luck!

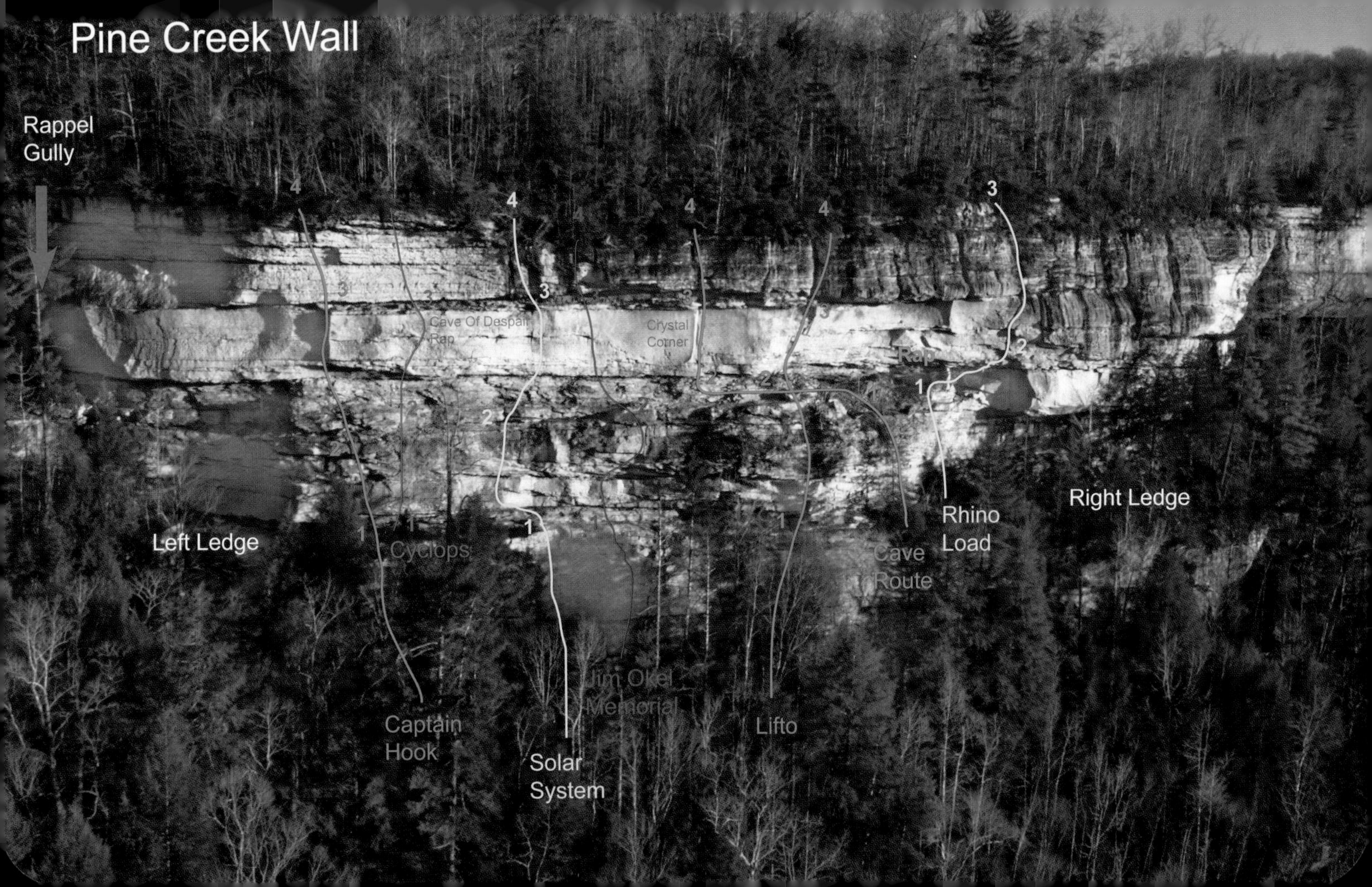

Pine Creek Wall

Rappel Gully

Right Ledge

Rhino
Load

Cave
Route

Lifto

Crystal
Corner

...in Ore...
...Memorial

Solar
System

Cave Of Despair

Cyclops

Captain
Hook

Left Ledge

3
2
1
4

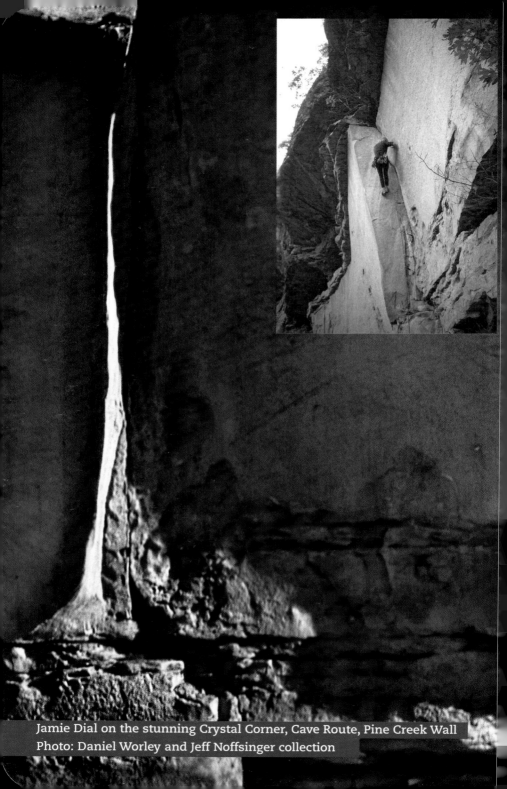

Jamie Dial on the stunning Crystal Corner, Cave Route, Pine Creek Wall
Photo: Daniel Worley and Jeff Noffsinger collection

T 1. *Captain Hook 11 A3+

Steep, thin and dangerous, with some hooking on the third pitch and ledge fall potential. The third pitch belay is bad, but hopefully bolts will be added in the near future.
FA: Jeff Noffsinger and Patrick Turner, 1995
Please refer to topo available at: www.dixiecragger.com.

T 2. **Cyclops 11 A2+/3

A fine route with varied climbing and cool features.
FA: Jeff Noffsinger and Patrick Turner, 2006
Please refer to topo available at: www.dixiecragger.com.

T 3. Solar System 11c A2+

This fantastic route was the first one at Pine Creek, and is characterized by a splitter finger crack on the third pitch. Great free climbing with adequate gear in an exposed position.
FA: Jeff Noffsinger and Patrick Turner, 1996
Please refer to topo available at: www.dixiecragger.com.

T 4. Jim Okel Memorial

The newest route at Pine Creek. No details yet. *FA: Wayne Roy and Shannon Stegg.*
Please refer to topo available at: www.dixiecragger.com.

T 5. **Cave Route 11+

This fun route stays dry and provides an easy way to access the middle portion of the wall.
FA: Jamie Dial, Patrick Turner and Jeff Noffsinger, 1995
Please refer to topo available at: www.dixiecragger.com.

T 6. ***Lifto 11 A3

By far, one of the best routes at BSF! Unrelentingly steep and sustained with good ledges and quality rock. *FA: Jeff Noffsinger and Patrick Turner, 2006*
Please refer to topo available at: www.dixiecragger.com.

T 7. ***Rhino Load 10+ A2

Pure adventure! Steep, with good ledges.
FA: Jeff Dopp and Jeff Noffsiinger, 2001
Please refer to topo available at: www.dixiecragger.com.

BOX CAR ROOF

Named by river guide and climber Bob Wheeley, Box Car Roof looms above "The Narrows" portion of the Big South Fork, and is easy to spot from the main road or from the river. At nearly 175' in height and facing south, the Box Car heats up in the summer but is rather comfortable in winter. Although the cliff was not climbed successfully until 1997, an old piton and descending ring provide evidence of at least one early attempt. There are two major lines on the wall, one on either side of the roof. Incidentally, the Box Car lies between two other areas-the Crack House to the left and Lost City to the right.

After passing the tall and shady Pine Creek Wall, continue through a road cut. Lost City Wall lies to the right and almost overhangs the road. Box Car is easy to spot a little further down the road. The Crack House lies to the left, as you approach the cliff, in the vicinity of a major creek/gully on the right. Park here and hike steeply up the right side of the creek with no trail, trending up and right to the cliff base. Head right and scramble up onto a ledge below the roof. Runaway Train is the obvious line on the left and Box Car Willies is the imposing line to the right.

🅣 1. ***Runaway Train 10+ A2
FA: Arno Ilgner, Jeff Noffsinger and Patrick Turner, 1997
Please refer to topo available at: www.dixiecragger.com.

🅣 2. **Box Car Willies 11 A3
One of the steepest lines in the gorge and not for the faint of heart.
FA: Jeff Noffsinger, Curt Johnson, Patrick Turner, 2003
Please refer to topo available at: www.dixiecragger.com.

THE CRACK HOUSE

The Crack House offers some of the only single pitch climbing in the Main Gorge, and offers a mix of sport and trad routes. Essentially a narrow side canyon or cleft, the Crack House features an east side (west facing) and a west side (east facing). The east side begins at the left edge of the Box Car Roof, while the west side starts at the right end of the 911 Wall. I know, seems confusing until you get there. To get there, follow the driving directions described at the head of the chapter, which is the parking for Boxcar Roof and the Crack House. The Crack House is a side canyon with a creek flowing down through the middle and has an east and west side. For the east side, a faint trail leads up the right side of the creek and intersects the wall somewhere in the vicinity of the route Pro And Go. Before reaching the rock, another faint trail would have taken off left across the creek to the west side. You can also cross the creek wherever possible and bushwhack to the base of the west side. Another approach for the west side of the Crack House involves approaching the same as for the 911 Wall/Nose Area and continuing around to the right into the Crack House.

Crack House East Side

The East Side of the Crack House faces west, so it gets shade for most of the day - great for summer but quite cold in the winter. Though the trail intersects the middle of the wall, I have chosen to describe the routes in one direction - right to left, from the entrance to the canyon leftwards to the back of the canyon. Make sense?

🅣 1. Wide Corner A1
A 50' corner with a wide roof crack start. This offwidth beast could go free at hard 11 or 12. Nut anchor at ledge. *FA: Wesley Calkins, Nathan Brown*

🅣 2. ***Honeycomb 11b/c
This is a fantastically overhanging pocket fest that is well worth climbing if you've got the guns. Unfortunately, the start has a large blank roof and requires use of the flimsy tree or possibly a trolley-start, but it's well worth the trouble.
Starts left of the Unnamed Corner. Climb the flimsy tree to the first bolt just above the roof. From here, stand high and gain a horizontal (#2 or #3 camalot). Climb steep rock past another cam placement to a bolt and a move onto a ledge. A good knee bar rest or lie down rest can be had here. Once ready, fire up the overhanging wall on amazing pockets past bolts to the 2 bolt chain anchor lower off (fixed with biners). *FA: Nathan Brown*

3. Next Corner 9+

Climb a nice left-facing corner to ledge. *FA: Wayne Roy, Shannon Stegg*

4. **Kacee's Route 9

The next corner to the left. Climb corner and underclimb out roof. Follow stacked corners and roofs. Rap from top. *FA: Wayne and Patrick Roy*

5. **Pro Or Go 11a

This route is 50' right of where the trail comes up at and is about 40' left of Kacee's Route. Climb past a short vertical seam and continue past horizontals to a thin section. Look for a good but shallow horizontal 2.5 friend placement in pocket. There is a hard to place RP above, right in the middle of the business. Either Pro or go... There is a 2 bolt anchor on the ledge. (55') *FA: Nathan Brown*

6. **Unnamed 10a

Starts 20' left of Pro Or Go. Rap from bolts. *FA: Jeff's Friends*

7. **Classic Corner 8

Starts 10' left of previous route.
P1: Climb the corner to an anchor. *FA: Jim Okel and Shannon Stegg*
P2: Climb past a bolt to the top. *FA: Patrick Roy, Shannon Stegg and Wayne Roy*

8. *Carpet Bagger 11-

Start 20' left of Classic Corner. Start above a boulder and crank the bouldery seam to easier ground. It is possible to bail off right (onto pitch 2 of Classic Corner), but instead continue up the blunt arete past horizontals to a 2 bolt anchor. *FA: Nathan Brown, Jon Foster and Wayne Roy, 2005*

9. Soulshine 11b

Start 20' left of Carpet Bagger and 15' right of Birthday Route, under a small overhanging start. Climb past 5 bolts and a medium sized cam (between bolt 1-2) to a 2 bolt anchor. *FA: Nathan Brown*

10. Birthday Route 11c/d

Starts about 50 yards left of where the trail meets the cliff, on a small ledge just left of Soulshine. Climb past gear and 2 bolts. Continue up and left through an overhanging wall with some wide horizontals to a 2 bolt anchor. *FA: Nathan Brown, rope solo, 2005 FFA: Nathan Brown and Wayne Roy*

11. The Vine Line 11

Start just left of Birthday Route. Climbs short bouldery right-facing corner to ledge and new 2 bolt anchor (the old tricam and nut were severely weathered). Gear: Light rack. *FA: Nathan Brown, Wayne Roy and Jon Foster 2005*

12. Pocket Pool 11c

Start on ledge 3' up. Climb the steep face right of Un-named past 3 bolts (1/2 hilti) to the shared anchor at top of ledge. Gear: Supplement bolts with a few small to medium cams. *FA: Nathan Brown 2012*

Crack House East

3   Next Corner 9+

4   Kacee's Route 9

5   Pro Or Go 11a

6   Unnamed 10a

Trail

7   Classic Corner 8

8   Carpet Bagger 11-

9   SoulShine 11b

10   Birthday Route 11c/d

11   Vine Line 11

12   Pocket Pool 11c

13   Quickie 10

Rain Delay Wall

🅣 13. Quickie 10
Climb up the face and a short left facing corner to a crux move gaining a small ledge. The gear is funky getting to here. Make a few more moves to the large ledge and a 2 bolt chain anchor. *FA: Nathan Brown rope solo, 2005*

🅣 14. Explorer Route A1
The pair aided from the right to place the two bolt anchor at the top of the long thin crack. *FA: Shannon Stegg and Wayne Roy*

Continue walking left to the Rain Delay Wall - steeper, pocketed and the best bet for dry rock in case of rain.

🅣 15. Happy Ending 11-
This is the farthest right route in the Rain Delay area, just left of the seasonal waterfall. Start next to an unfinished bolted route and climb rightward along a crack and up to bolt. Climb to ledge and a bolt in the steep wall above. Crux past bolt to a huge patina/horn and up to base of a wide-ish crack. Climb crack to a chain anchor at 70'. *FA: Nathan Brown rope solo*

16. Project
Six bolts half way to top. *Wayne Roy and Patrick Roy*

🅣 17. Stegg Route grade unknown
Bolts lead to a two bolt anchor. *FA: Shannon Stegg and Wayne Roy*

🅢 18. Moral Dilemma 11c
Starts on the left end of the Rain Delay Wall. Finishes at an off width. *FA: Wayne Roy, Patrick Roy and Chris Watford, 2004*

🅢 19. Five Fun 11
Starts 10' left of Moral Dilemma. Stays dry. *FA: Wayne and Patrick Roy, 2004*

🅢 20. Scary Jerry 12
Start 10' left of Five Fun. Boulder up to the first bolt (stick clip?) *FA: Wayne Roy and Patrick Roy*

🅣 21. Git' R' Done 11b
Start just left of Scary Jerry. Boulder up into a steep right-facing corner with a bolt. Continue into pocketed terrain passing a hidden .5 Camalot slot. Follow this widening, but featured crack to a 2 bolt anchor near the top.

🅣 22. Unnamed Corner 9
Climbs a left-facing dirty corner to a small ledge with a single anchor bolt. *FA: Nathan Brown 2006*

🅣 23. Tricky Offwidth 10+
One bolt down low. Rap from tree. *FA: Nathan Brown and Jon Foster*

Crack House West Side

The West Side can be approached from the East Side by crossing the creek where possible. I have elected to describe the routes once again from the canyon mouth entrance rightwards to the back of the canyon, as if approaching from the 911 Wall/Nose pulloff.

Crack House Overview

Note: Route locations are not to scale.
Included to give the order of the routes.

Rain Delay Wall

Crack House West   **Crack House East**

Explorer Route
Quickie
Yeller Feller   Pocket Pool
Green Elbow   Vine Line
                          Birthday Route
                          SoulShine
Block Party   Carpet Bagger
                          Corner
Choss Corner
                          Unnamed 10a
Project   Pro Or Go
Just Another Corner   Kacee's Route
                          Next Corner
Uncle Pervy   Honeycomb
                          Wide Corner
Medicine Man
Slingblade   **BoxCar Roof**
The Nose

911 Wall

T **Sling Blade 10c**
On the very right edge of the 911 Wall, 50' right of the start for The Nose. Approach up the left (west) side of the Crack House as you would for the Nose route
P1: Start in an obvious, short left-facing dihedral. Climb about 15' until you can traverse left under a large loose block/roof to an arête. Continue on the arête past two fixed pins (crux) to a stance. Climb up and left and belay in a short right-facing corner.
P2: Climb up left out around the corner, then straight up and slightly right on plates and chicken heads to a classic belay on a giant horn/saddle (great position!)
P3: Climb chicken heads with sparse pro to the rim and a large tree. *FA: Frank Jackson and Jeff Dopp* Note: Bring a standard trad rack and plenty of runners for slinging horns

T **Medicine Man 10a**
At the entrance to the Crack House, on the west side. The climb follows the prominent right-leaning dihedral that can be seen clearly from the ground or the east side of the Canyon. Approach the same as the Nose.
P1: Climb an obvious V-shaped open chimney for 20' then move right to the base of the big dihedral.
P2: Climb jugs on a short, slightly overhanging wall directly below the dihedral then pull up onto a short slab split by a finger crack. Climb the obvious crack/dihedral for 80' to the ledge below a 20' roof. A #11 hex provides the anchor. *FA: Jeff Dopp and Frank Jackson*

T ****Climbing With Uncle Pervy 10+**
P1: Boulder into the right-facing corner. Continue up corner to a two bolt anchor 140'
P2: Follow crack/corner/chimney to top 80' (9+) *FA: Wayne Roy*

T **Just Another Corner 10+**
P1: Starts just right of Climbing With Uncle Pervy. Climb corner, then exit left to ledge with two bolt anchor.
P2: Crack and face climb to top (11?) Rap from tree. *FA: Wayne Roy, Nathan Brown*

The Nose Area

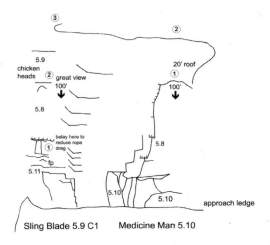

Sling Blade 5.9 C1   Medicine Man 5.10

CHAPTER 11

█

T **Unfinished project** - no details

T **Choss Corner**
Unfinished *FA: Nathan Brown and Wayne Roy, 2005*

T ****Block Party 10**
Starts left of Green Elbow, in a hard flared chimney that turns into a hand crack. Cool moves lead to atwo bolt anchor on ledge below a dripping chimney. Good warm up! 40' *FA: Nathan Brown and Wayne Roy, 2005*

T ****Green Elbow 11**
Starts in the middle of the cliff, above the right side of a ledge system.
P1: Climb the obvious steep pocketed crack on the right-hand side of main cliff. Ends on a ledge where a rightward traverse leads to a bolted belay.
P2: Climb past 2 bolts in pocketed wall, then right and to a steep off-width chimney. Gear: Standard rack including doubles on #1-3 Camalot, and # 4 and #5 Camalot. One 60 meter rope rap from tree at top of cliff will barely make the ground. *FA: Nathan Brown, Wayne Roy, Jon Foster 2005*

T *****Yeller Feller 11b**
Starts just right of Green Elbow. Climb up discontinuous crack/corner features past a couple of cam placements, then follow 5 bolts up very steep ground to the Green Elbow ledge and a 2 bolt anchor. The upper portion is very reminiscent of RRG style pocket pullin'. *FA: Nathan Brown*

THE NOSE

From the aforementioned parking pulloff for Box Car, hike up the left side of the creek to the base of the wall and a cave. Step around right into the Crack House and look to the left for a blocky chimney with a crack at the base.

T **1. **The Nose 9+/10a**
Fun, quick, tall and casual.
FA: Bob Wheeley, Phil Barkesdale, 1985
P1: Stem and lieback up the awkward crack to a stance, then follow the chimney to a tree. Sling the tree, step left onto the face and climb up and left to a good ledge. Belay off of a tree.
P2: Move the belay as far left as possible on the ledge to a tree. Power up a thin face, shooting for a prominent golden flake. Fish in some gear and negotiate a bouldery barndoor move, then step left to better holds. Run it out to good gear and easier climbing. Gain the good ledge and belay on gear or trees.
P3: Move left and climb the fun chimney to a good ledge. It is possible to climb the Roman Nose alternate (140', 5.10) from here. See topo.
P4: Short, bushy and not worth it except for reaching the top.
Descent: Move back right and rappel the Roman Nose back to the ledge on two ropes. Move back right and rappel the first pitch using the same belay tree. It is also possible to walk off from here by scrambling back up into the Crack House.

911 WALL

The 911 Wall is the second largest wall in the Big South Fork and one of the best. Soaring over 200', its sheer walls offer some of the best free climbing in the gorge. Facing mostly south, the face is clean and sunny, but broiling in the summer. Currently, there are only two established routes and one project. The route 911 lies to the left of the Nose Area, with the hard-to-spot Hidden Ledge between them. Hidden Ledge is a wild area reminiscent of a slot canyon in Utah, and contains a few short sport routes as well as a nice trad line on the

CHAPTER 11

Wayne Roy, Choss Corner, Crack House West
Photo: Nathan Brown

left called Gravity Slave. After passing the Box Car Roof, Crack House and the Nose Area, continue driving and look for the second major creek gully on the right. Park and hike back up the road a couple hundred feet or so and look for a cliff band up in the woods. Angle up to the base of the cliff and go left, gain a small ramp and continue up and left to the top. The massive 911 Wall will be easy to spot, dead ahead. Continue to a large cave. Salsa Del Diablo starts in the far right corner of the cave and 911 starts on top of the small rise to the right of the cave.

🔳 2. ***911 9+/10a R
One of the best free routes in the Gorge, offering three pitches of fun, varied climbing. Jeff Noffsinger claims that the name for the route comes from a group of Japanese businessmen who were broken down on one of the remote roads in the Gorge. Says Jeff, "We stopped to help, but all they could say was "You dial 911, you dial 911…""
FA: Jeff Noffsinger, Jamie Dial and Patrick Turner, 1995
Start: At a semi-detached pillar, up the slope to the right of the large cave, from a small ledge up off the trail.
P1: Climb the wide crack on large gear to a small stance. Follow a thin broken crack and face to the top of the pillar and a tree belay.
P2: Move onto a cool pocketed slab. Fun climbing leads up and right toward a left-facing corner. Get some good pro and yard left across some bushes to a small ledge. Belay on gear and small trees.
P3: This is a fantastic pitch, so flip a coin. From the belay, move up and right and along a funky ramp. Get some pro and continue right on sloping holds to a small stance. Carefully move up a bulge and run it out to finally reach good gear at the base of the Golden Corner. Climb the steep, well protected corner to the top.
Descent: Move back left above the first pitch tower. A 150' rappel reaches the tower and another 75' rappel reaches the ground.

🔳 3. **Salsa Del Diablo 10 A3
Super steep, with four good pitches and a bushwhack pitch.
FA: Patrick Turner, Jeff Noffsinger, 1996
Please refer to topo available at: www.dixiecragger.com.

🔳 4. Espresso Route 10
Starts at the far **left** end of the 911 Wall, at a stack of rocks.
P1: Head up the only break in the overhanging wall 120' to a cave-like ledge and a two bolt anchor to the right. (9)
P2: From the anchor, clip a bolt and exit roof to the left. Face climb (wires and small cams) angling left to the big tree ledge. Clip bolt just before ledge. (10)
P2b: From the bolt, pull roof to the left then step right. Climb to the large roof over a left facing corner. Follow corner, hand rail right under roof to a two bolt anchor (10) P3: Straight up from bolt to the top (8)
P3b: Up and left from anchor, then straight to the top (10+)
Rap from tree to P1 anchor, then to ground. *FA: Wayne Roy Mike Kirby and Patrick Roy*

🔳 5. First Responder 10+
P1: Start 40' right of Espresso Route. Start under fixed wire, climb to left side of ledge (10+)
P2: Out the left side straight to the top (10) *FA: Shannon Stegg Wayne And Patrick Roy*

O&W WALL

Facing southwest, the massive O&W Wall looms above the South Fork River and the old O&W Bridge, and at nearly 250' in height is likely one of the tallest walls in Tennessee. Long known by locals for its long freefall rappel, the cliff holds some great lines for climbers as well. First climbed by Bob Wheeley and Phil Barkesdale in the mid 80's, climbing didn't resume until the fall of 1990. Rumors of a three pitch 5.9 spread through the kayaking community and eventually reached the ears of climbers. Fortunately, the rumors proved to be true!

To get there, take TN297 west from Oneida, for 1.7 miles. Turn left (south) on Verdun Road. After .6 miles, turn right onto the O&W Railbed, which turns to gravel in half a mile. Continue 7.6 miles down to the O&W Bridge. Alternately, if you are traveling east on TN297, turn right at the Terry and Terry Store, and then at .6 miles, turn right onto Toomey Road, which descends to join the O&W Railbed after 3 miles. Bear right and continue 4.2 miles to the bridge. There is a popular camp spot at the east end of the bridge called Boulder Camp. Park here.

A quick walk out onto the O&W Bridge puts the wall into perspective. In the center lies the prominent dihedral of the Original Route. The obvious left-facing hanging dihedral of Tomb With A View is to the right and higher on the face. At the extreme left end, and following the break between gold and gray rock, is the long and steep Bushmaster. To approach the wall from Boulder Camp, there is no trail, so simply hike straight up the mountain. Upon reaching the base, look for a small base camp cave, which provides an excellent place to stow packs and gear. To the right of the cave is the start of Tomb With A View. Up the slope to the left is the start of the Original Route. To get to the routes, walk the old roadbed from Boulder Camp, past the obvious boulder, for about 50 yards. Cut uphill to the right to the cliff base.

🅣 1. Snake Charmer 8
FA: Shannon Stegg and Wayne Roy
Begin at far right end of cliff. Wander up under roofs into a right-facing block corner. When possible, traverse left acrodss top of block onto upper face. Moderate climbing leads to the huge ledge.

🅣 2. Under The Big Top 10a A0 or 12
Start 30' left of Snake Charmer. *FA: Shannon Stegg and Curt Johnson, 2004*
P1: Climb straight up below a low roof. Handrail right past roof over a knife edge arete. Finish at ledge with 2 bolts. (10a)
P2: Step up loose blocks and aid past a pin and 2 bolts (free?) to a ledge. Follow a shallow left-facing corner to another ledge, then free below a huge roof. Link up with Tomb at Boot Camp ledge.

🅣 3. **Dog And Pony Show 11-
Start: Just left of Big Top. *FA: Wayne Roy and Shannon Stegg, 2004*
P1: Start 5' left of Big Top. Angle left to to a roof and left-facing corner. Fixed pin. Up and left past two small roofs to finger crack to another roof. Belay at tree.
P2: Move right as far as possible until it is possible to traverse left to a horizontal (11) Continue right to a large hole. Tricky face moves lead to a left-facing corner. Rap from anchor or do P3 of Tomb.

🅣 4. **Tomb With A View 10+ A2 or 12a free
Features good ledges and tremendous exposure. *FA: Jeff Noffsinger, Terry Smith and Patrick Turner, 1996*
Start: Roughly 50' right of the cave where the trail intersects, at a small holly bush. Look for the obvious Red Roof above.
P1: Climb up behind the bush, plug some gear and move up and right (runout) towards a corner. Follow a short finger crack to a mantel, then up a larger crack to the roof. Traverse left under the roof on good gear to "Boot Camp Ledge".
P2: Work up through steep terrain on thin wires. Move up and right to sling a large flake. Free climb up better cracks until the face starts to slab out. Say your prayers, huck for the lip and belay on a good ledge.
P3: Climb stellar cracks up and right to a hanging corner. Follow corner to the top.
Descent: Two rappels lead back down to Boot Camp Ledge at the top of P1. Traverse left and rappel from a tree atop P1 of the Original Route.

Prolific BSF route developer Jeff Noffsinger doing the hard work of putting up new routes. Photos: Marc Seitzman and Daniel Worley

🎫 5. ***Suicide Direct 8 C2 or 11d/12a free

One of the best lines in the Gorge and a must do! Four fun pitches, all well protected and steep. *FA: Patrick Turner, Jeff Noffsinger, 1996. FFA: Kirk Brode, Tyler Stracker, 2009.*
Starts on the Original Route (see below) but breaks right at the top of P2. Hike uphill to the left of the base camp cave, to the top of the slope. Start on blocky, vegetated rock.
P1: (7) Follow a crack up and right then break left onto a small ledge. Climb a shallow dihedral up to a nasty fixed blade. Run it out up the corner to a good ledge. Don't underestimate the 5.7 rating on this pitch.
P2: Climb a nice corner up to a hanging belay on two bolts. Sustained with great protection.
P3: Climb out right and cross the awkward 10' roof free/aid. Above the lip, climb to the top of a right-facing corner. Move up and right across horizontals to a hook move, followed by a dicey TCU move to a hanging gear belay.
P4: Traverse left under a small roof to a 4' roof crack. Pull another awkward lip and free climb out left to a ledge.
Descent: A double rope rappel leads back to the top of P1. A short rappel leads to the ground.

🎫 6. **Original Route 9+

FA: Bob Wheeley and Phil Barkesdale, 1985
Start: Hike uphill to the left of base camp cave, to the top of the slope. Start on blocky, vegetated rock.
P1: Same as for Suicide Direct.
P2: Climb the giant corner until it gets wide and break out left along an escape ledge to access "Lunch Ledge" or continue up to bolted anchors in the Bat Cave and crawl over to the ledge. There are two rap ring anchors here.
P3: Climb a wide, gnarly off-width chimney to the top. This pitch has not been repeated as far as anyone knows.
Descent: Rappel back to Lunch Ledge. Crawl out into the Bat Cave and rap off the anchors. 130' back to the ground or a half rope back to the top of P1.

🎫 7. ***Suicide Blonde 8

The easiest multi-pitch route in the Gorge, though still not for the fledgling 5.8 leader.
P1, P2: Follow the Original Route up to Lunch Ledge.
P3: From the far left end of Lunch Ledge, follow an easy ramp up and left toward the top. Negotiate some steep ground and look for an anchor chain. Yard up to the top and belay at trees. Caution: Do not belay or rappel from the anchor chain! It is used simply to access the top. P3 traverses out over No Man's Land. If you lower from the chain, you will end up #%*& creek without an anchor!
Descent: Move right and rappel back to Lunch Ledge. Traverse right to the Bat Cave and use the bolted rap anchors. 130' to the ground or a half rope to the top of P1.

🎫 8. Suicide Hotline 10+/ 11? (new route in progress)

This route starts around 100' right of Vertigo.
P1: Climb your choice of easy cracks up to the ledge and gain a two bolt belay 5.6.
P2: Continue up a thin face on bolts, and negotiate around a large flake at the top to gain a ledge with a two bolt belay/rap station. 5.10+/11.
P3: Step right, and look for a bolt on a bulge. Climb straight on thin holds to gain lower angled terrain. Either continue up to bolted anchors under a small roof, or once on the slab, angle up and left to finish on the last pitch of Suicide Blonde. 5.10+/11.

Descent: You can rap back off the 3rd pitch anchors to the large ledge, then either rap off the top of the second pitch, or walk right to the rap station of the Original Route. Half ropes will get you down with multiple rappels. Or if you top out Suicide Blonde, walk right to a tree, then rap to the large ledge, and rappel from the other anchors.

O&W Wall - Left Side

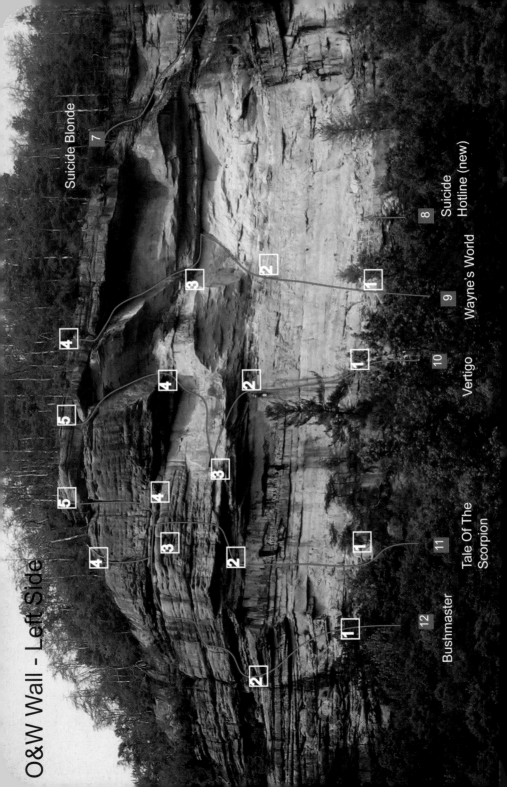

Suicide Blonde 7

8 Suicide Hotline (new)

9 Wayne's World

10 Vertigo

11 Tale Of The Scorpion

12 Bushmaster

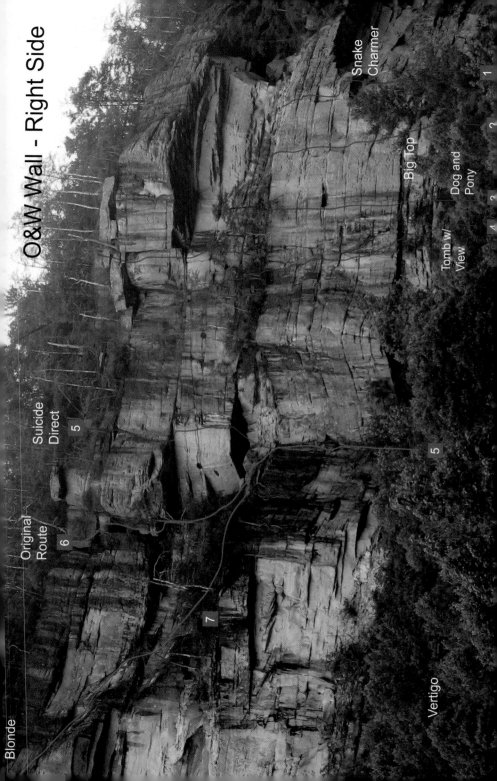

O&W Wall - Right Side

Blonde

Original Route
6

Suicide Direct
5

7

Snake Charmer

Big Top

Dog and Pony

Tomb w/ View

Vertigo

5

1

2

3

🔲 9. Wayne's World 11 A3

P1: Start 20' **right** of Vertigo under small pine. Climb out a right-angling ramp (9) to a belay.
P2: Go straight up from two bolt anchor, step in sling to blind hook placement to a jug. Free climb, passing one bolt (10+A2)
P3: Free climb the offwidth. Nail 6 or 8 knifeblades to the lip (A3)
P4: Pull a C1 aid move off the anchor (This pitch will go free at 12+?) then continue to top (10). Two raps reach the ground. *FA: Wayne Roy, Nathan Brown and Jon Foster*

🔲 10. ***Vertigo 10 A2 or 12++(?)

200' tall with over 300' of incredible mixed climbing, this unbelievably steep route goes straight up the center of the face to a stunning high corner, and is destined to become a classic. Established ground up, with no rappel inspection and hand drilled on lead, with belay/rappel stations at every belay. The route stays dry in all but the heaviest rains. A mind-numbing 200' free rappel drops you back to the deck. Woohoo!
FA: Jeff Noffsinger, Patrick Turner, Terry Smith, Mark Seitzman, Danny Hayes. 2004
Please refer to topo available at: www.dixiecragger.com.

🔲 11. Tale of the Scorpion 12+

A fun long route, that splits the left side of O&W wall. This route got its name from an irate scorpion that was found behind a loose block on the first ascent. Very steep, and sustained on the 2nd and 3rd pitches. 200' *FA: Jeff Noffsinger, Marc Seitzman, 2011, also help from Toyna Seitzman and Jerome Epstein*
Please refer to topo available at: www.dixiecragger.com.

🔲 12. ***Bushmaster 9 A3

The longest, and one of the steepest routes in the Gorge. Offers five pitches of awesome rock with only one protection bolt. This route is very committing - most parties should expect a very long day at the very least.
FA: Jeff Noffsinger, Terry Smith and Patrick Turner, 2000
Please refer to topo available at: www.dixiecragger.com.

OTHER CRAGGING AREAS

There are a lot of good shorter climbs for those wanting something with a little less commitment. Good cragging can be found all the way down the Gorge Road. There are short cliffs right on the road that haven't even been touched. The Crack House has some good short stuff, as well as Hidden Ledge, and Twin Falls Wall. The Boys Room on Hatfield Ridge has some steep sport routes as well.

THE BOY'S ROOM

To get to the Boy's Room, follow Hwy 154 past Hwy 297 towards Pickett State Park. Take a right at the sign for Twin Arches, then go left on Divide Road instead of driving towards the arches. Look for a road on the right with a sign that reads "Road Ends After A Mile" or something to that effect. Follow this road a short distance until it splits. Park and hike down the right split around 400' to 500' and look for a climber's trail on the right. This trail may be overgrown by now, but a little searching should yield rock.

STEPPING ROCK

Continuing out Divide Road towards Terry Cemetery and Maude's Crack, you will eventually come to a large gravel parking area. Park and follow a gated gravel road down the hill. At the third small creek crossing, trend up and right to find Vantage Point. This nice little crag, developed by Patrick Turner and Jeff Noffsinger, has some good lines and a two pitch A4 route. Hiking out to the end of the bluff yields a great view of No Business Creek. This large canyon is lined with rock, and only a few routes have been climbed. Stepping Rock is a large, 150' tall monolith. It is an incredible geological feature that can be a little hard to find. Hike past the gravel parking lot, and look for a four wheel drive road on the left. Follow this out until it ends. A vague hunting/deer trail leads out from here. Look for a branch to the right that leads out to a view of the rock. Down climb and hike over to the base. A topo map and compass are highly recommended. There are a few two pitch routes on Stepping Rock.

🆃 **South Face 10

P1: Climb up a face and gain a crack that angles up left. Look for a fixed piton in a pocket to start the route. Build a belay at large horizontal shelf.
P2: Trend up and right off the belay following good cracks to the top. *FA: Jeff Noffsinger and Patrick Turner*

🆃 *Smith & Wesson Oil 10+

Start: On the north face of the formation.
P1: Look for a wide short crack that is fairly steep. Climb this up to a belay ledge.
P2: Climb up the crack above, until it starts to get wide. Slap and grovel up the chimney to the top. *FA: Terry Smith and Jeff Noffsinger*

While on top, check out the secret cave. Hike around on top, and look for a small hole. Slide down this hole to end up inside Stepping Rock. There is a small room with a great view of No Business Creek!

LEATHERWOOD FORD

Bruce Burgess, Stuart Cowles and Bill Wilson reported what sounds like a fine route in this area. To get there, take TN297 West from Oneida, continue past the Park Headquarters and descend into the gorge. At approximately 2.2 miles from the park entrance and just before the bridge at Leatherwood Ford, turn right into the river access parking lot, where there are picnic tables, walking paths and restrooms. From here, hike north along the John Miur Trail for perhaps a little less than a half mile. The cliff is on the west side of the river and it is necessary to leave the trail and hike up into the woods. The route is an obvious 5.11 splitter crack! Mark Dew, Kelly Brown and Woody Loftis have done lots of other routes in this area, most are reported to be excellent 5.9 and 5.10 hand cracks and faces.

HONEY CREEK

Mark Dew graciously provided the following information on routes in the Honey Creek Gorge and the Mill Creek area. To get to Honey Creek, travel south from Oneida on Highway 27 to the Food Court with several fast food restaurants. Turn right, cross the railroad tracks then turn left on the road that runs parallel to the tracks. Take the next right on Airport Road and follow it for a mile or so, stay right at the split and continue past the Scott County Municipal Airport. Continue past a few cabins on the left and follow the road as it makes a hard ninety degree left turn. Continue another quarter mile or so past a cemetery to a large gravel turnaround/parking area. There is an old dirt road that continues down to the canoe hole, a popular boater's spot. Follow this a little ways, then duck right into the woods looking for a faint trail down a gully to the cliff base. There is some good bouldering in this area. Once at the base, walk downstream to the right.

🆃 **Crackhead 10

This is the first beautiful hand crack you come to. Climb the crack (40'), negotiate the crux mantel onto the ledge, then follow another easy crack to a pine tree belay and an easy rappel. *FA: Mark Dew and Woody Loftis*

🆃 Easy Eight 8

Just right of Harrison's Crack is a nice right-facing flake that ends at the same ledge.

T *Harrison's Crack 9
This 40' crack is 200' east of Crybaby Crack. Look for three crack/flake routes that end at a ledge with fixed rappel gear. *FA: Harrison Shull and Mark Dew*

T *Blade Runner 10
Starts 30' left of Harrison's Crack and finishes at the same ledge. 40' *FA: Kelly Brown and CJ Drews*

T ***Crybaby Crack 10
A bit of Indian Creek in east Tennessee!
This crack lies a good ways past Crackhead, directly across from the Honey Creek Overlook on the opposite rim. Climb the appallingly good crack for 60' or so, then pull a cruxy finish out right onto a ledge. Look for one bolt at the finish to lower from. *FA: Woody Loftis and Mark Dew*

T *** Hidden Jewel 10
A phenomenal splitter crack in gray rock 50' left of Crybaby Crack. *FA: Mark Dew and Harrison Shull*

T ***Vulgarian Crack (aka: Burl) 11b/c
This beautiful left-facing dihedral lies 50' left of Hidden Jewel. 90' *FA: Kelly Brown and CJ Drews*

These last three routes alone are reportedly well worth the hike in! Go find out.

MILL CREEK

To get to Mill Creek, follow Highway 297 west from Oneida for a few miles, to the point where 297 makes a sharp left turn into the gorge at the Terry and Terry Store. At this point, stay to the right on Station Camp Road, and set your odometer. This is where the directions get a little cryptic. After approximately 4.4 miles, look for the Station Camp East Trailhead. Somewhere in this vicinity, on the left, will be a faint gravel road. Travel down this as far as possible. There are often downed trees and undergrowth that may prevent driving very far. At any rate, either via a truck or stout legs, follow this road down to the rim overlooking the Mill Creek drainage. The climbing is on the north rim (south facing) side of the cove. Poke around a little to find the access gully/downclimb.

Note: After passing the Station Camp East trailhead at 4.4 miles, continue on another 2.6 miles or so (7 miles from the 297 turnoff) and look for a parking area for The Chimneys. Two of these interesting rock formations are located on the left side of the road and there are more in the immediate vicinity. For a swim, continue on down the road until it dead ends at the river at the 8 mile mark.

T ***Guillotine 10
This is the first route at the bottom of the walkdown. Climb a crack to a face with water groove/crack features. Move slightly right to top out. 100' *FA: Mark Dew and Kelly Brown*

T **Southern Pride 10c
Starts 30' right of Guillotine and follows a crack and face. A little runout at the top. 100' *FA: Anthony ? and Woody Loftis*

T *Ice House 8
Climbs a crack on the left side of a detached pillar. Currently ends at the top of the pillar. No top out and no rappel anchors. *FA: Woody Loftis and Ken Kolesar*

T **Project**
Proposes to follow the right edge of a steep arete. Has two bolts and is currently unfinished.

T *** **Campfire Crack 10c**
Climb a beautiful 40' finger crack on the right side of a small recessd alcove. *FA: CJ Drews and Mark Dew*

T ** **Hemophiliac 10**
Start 50' left of Moon Ledge. Follow crack and face to top. *FA: Mark Dew and CJ Drews*

Continue walking right to Moon Ledge, a prominent ledge 50' off the ground.

T **Anthony's Face 10**
Climb the obvious fat chimney/dihedral that accesses Moon Ledge on the left side. 50' *FA: Anthony ? and Woody Loftis*

T **Ride The Comet 10c/d**
Starts on the left side of Moon Ledge. Climb the face to a water groove to finish. 80'

T *****Bad Moon Rising 11a R**
Climb the left crack under the "crescent moon" feature, then move left and finish on Ride The Comet. 80' *FA: Mark Dew and Kelly Brown*

The South Face of Stepping Rock

T ****Half Moon 10c**
Start just right of Bad Moon Rising and climb out right of the crescent moon. 80' *FA: Mark Dew and Kelly Brown*

T ****Heaven's Gate 10c/d**
Starts on Moon Ledge and follows a beautiful crack system up to a big steep roof. 70' *FA: Woody Loftis and Mark Dew*

T **** Moon Dance 9**
Start from the ground below Moon Ledge and climb a nice right-facing dihedral that accesses the ledge. 50' *FA: CJ Drews and Mark Dew*

T **Ain't No Skin Off My Back 9+**
No details available.

T ****Kelly's Arete 10c**
Start: 150 yards right of the previous route. Climb a prominent arete. 70' *FA: Kelly Brown and Mark Dew*

T **** Tree Route 10**
Climb a tree to start the route. Follows a water groove to the top. 90' *FA: Mark Dew and Woody Loftis*

MUIR BUTTRESS

Towering 125' tall above Massey Branch sits the Muir Buttress. One of the newest discovered walls in the park, it has seen little development as of now. There are a few moderate crack routes at the base, and some very steep rock to be developed. Facing west, it gets afternoon sun, and has great exposure high on the wall. This wall was found by Jeff Noffsinger and Kory Hall on a rainy afternoon, and shows you what a little exploring and some good luck can produce in the park.

Directions: Drive north on Divide road towards Kentucky. Before you cross the state line, you will come to a parking area on the right, which is where the John Muir trail crosses the road. Hike west, to your left, down the trail until you come to a T intersection with the Rock Creek loop trail. Go right/north following an old railroad bed. There is some decent looking east facing rock on down up above the trail, that probably has not been climbed. You will be looking right from the trail, until you see the towering Muir Buttress on the other side of the creek. You cannot miss this wall. It's the first good looking rock on the right side hiking in. Position yourself directly across from the wall, then cut down across the creek and march back up the other side to gain the rock. The whole hike is maybe around a mile and half, and should take you around 30 minutes.

Live Action! 7
This fun route is short at around 35' to 40', but offers very fun, well protected crack climbing. Mostly #1, #2, and #3 camalots protect the climb. Follow the very obvious crack up and left to an awkward stance below the final steep section. Pull through to a good ledge, and either gear belay in a large horizontal using #4 camalots, or protect the second and continue right along a brushy ledge to finally gain solid ground, and a tree belay. *FA: Jeff Noffsinger and Marc Seitzman, January 2012.*

LAST CHANCE CLIFF

Head north on Hwy 154 through Pickett State Park. Right after you cross into Kentucky and start to drop down into the big valley off the mountain, look up to your left, and you will notice some rock right above the road. As you drive down the hill, look on your left for a dirt road pulloff area. Park here, then hike back south up an old logging road. When it feels like the road is starting to go west, head up the very steep hillside to gain the cliff. You will be pretty much parallel with the road at this point. There has only been a little bit of climbing done here. As you approach the cliff, you will see a large boulder with a flake behind it on the wall, which leads to a pretty cool roof. It goes at around 5.7+/5.8? Just poke around for some fun routes. This cliff might be in Daniel Boone National Forest.

WEST COVE

Heading west on Hwy 52 out of Jamestown, look for a city picnic area on the left before you drop down the mountain. It is easy to find, as it is actually underneath a large sandstone rock shelter. There are a couple of picnic tables, and some trash cans there. Park here, and cross Hwy 52 heading north. You will gain a small creek bed, then turn left/west again, and eventually cross the creek. You will see a small bluff line. Follow it climbers left to start gaining the climbs. There are a few houses above, so be discreet, and try not to make too much noise or linger at the top outs. This crag has a good selection of short cracks, top ropes, and a few steep overhangs. It is also evidently a local beer drinking, trash chunking, artifact digging hangout, so don't expect normal park quality here. A few of the obvious cracks, and some of the faces have been climbed. This is probably one of the easiest approaches near the Fork. A good lazy day option. The rock continues around the cove for quite a ways, so a little exploring could be worthwhile. There are also some decent looking boulders here and there.

MISSION POINT

Heading west on Hwy 52 out of Jamestown, drive past the parking area for West Cove, and start down the mountain. You will pass a picnic area on your right, but continue down until you can see another pull off area on your right. As you drop off the mountain, you will be able to see the rock up on your left, above the road. Park at the pullout, then cross the road, and follow a steep creek bed up to the cliff. This area is below a church camp, so please be discreet, avoid staying on top, and please keep the noise down. This crag has seen a bit of development. The first known climb was 20+ years ago by Jeff Noffsinger and Patrick Turner - a nice corner under a very large roof, way down to climbers left. Look for a giant rock shelter, follow the obvious crack, you can sling a thread through near the top of the crack and retreat. There is also a large free standing pillar as you hike up to the cliff. There is a crack on the road side that goes to the top, reported to be 10+? A few of the other obvious line have been done as well. There are also a handful of bolted routes, FA unknown, climbers left after you hike in. This is a good sized crag, with a lot of options. Watch out for some trash, and lots of broken glass below the sport route area. That is pretty much the only trashy spot, which ironically is right below the church overlook. The rest of the crag is scenic, and clean.

WHITE OAK CREEK

This north facing cliff has some great cracks, a relatively short approach and is a great summertime crag. To get there, cross O&W Bridge and look for a road to the right after a few hundred yards that leads down to the river and a couple of campsites. Park here. Walk up hill, staying right of wash, passing two sets of boulders. Fifty yards further is the bluff. All climbs are to the right.

T ***Ham Jammin 9+**
Balance your way into a narrowing crack, passing a bush. Rap from tree on right. *FA: Wayne Roy and Mayling Toy*

T ***** Crescent Crack 10**
Start 10' right of Ham Jammin. Climb the obvious right-facing chimney/dihedral and hand crack to ledge. Rap from tree to left. *FA: Nathan Brown & Wayne Roy, 2005*

T *** Lightning Bolt Crack 11a

Climb up to the obvious beautiful splitter crack that splits the headwall. Use directional to avoid sharp edge. Short but fantastic! Rap from tree to left. *FA: Nathan Brown and Wayne Roy*

T ***Crack of Noon 9+

Climb the ramp/crack to a ledge below an awesome left-facing wide crack. Climb wide lie back crack to the top. Take several large pieces up to # 5 Camalot. Rap from large tree to left using 2 ropes (140'). *FA: Wayne Roy and Nathan Brown*

T Hell No! 9

Start 20' right of Crack Of Noon. Climb the obvious wide crack / flake for about 50' or so to a small ledge. Rap from a large scary flake on slings. *FA: Jeff Noffsinger and Patrick Turner*

T Huckleberry Jam 11c

Start 30 yards right and around the corner.
P1: Stay left of chimney and follow crack to horizontals and gain top of detached block 5.9
P2: Get some gear in and climb past 2 bolts to good ledge. Pull roof and rap from tree. *FA Nathan Brown and Wayne Roy, 2005*

T Moses Direct 11c

Start roughly 100 yards past Huckleberry Jam. Step off boulder and follow the crescent crack to the roof. Undercling left to bolt then continue left to top. *FA: Wayne Roy and Matt Ackley, 2005*

Blue Heron Overview

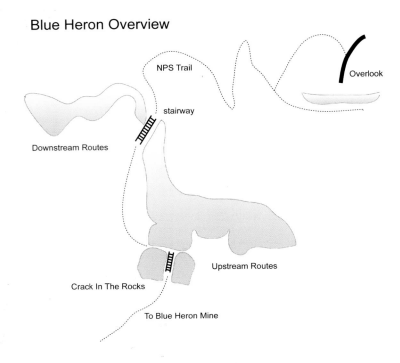

Wayne Roy , Lightning Bolt Crack, White Oak Creek.
Photo: Patrick Roy

Daniel Worley on Deliverance Corner, random cliff off some dirt road in the Fork. Photo: Katie Worley

BLUE HERON

Blue Heron is actually located just south of Whitley City, Kentucky, but it's included here because it's so close and lies within the Park. Stearns, Kentucky hosts a Big South Fork ranger station where you can pick up a BSF map. The Blue Heron climbing area is accessed from the Blue Heron Overlook. The routes are mostly slabby or vertical, with only a few that are steeply overhanging. Most of the climbing is sport, but there are numerous trad crack lines. Where protection is obvious from the ground, the routes have been developed as mixed. Mixed routes are noted in the description. There are a few projects that were still open at press time. Because the sandstone at Blue Heron is fairly soft, the bolts are generally ½" by 4", though some of the older routes still have 3/8" bolts. Inspect carefully before clipping!

Directions: Take US Highway 27 toward Whitley City. From the south, head approximately 4 miles into KY from the TN border. Take a left onto State Route 1651. Follow this for a few miles, paralleling the railroad tracks on the left. Watch for a fork in the road, immediately after passing over the tracks on a bridge. Take the left hand road at the fork, almost directly across from the Revelo, KY post office. This is State Route 742, and goes into the park. Once inside the BSF Park, take a left onto Gorge Overlook Road and go to its end. This is the Blue Heron Overlook.

From the north: Head west to Stearns on State Route 92. Go through Stearns toward the even smaller town of Revelo on Route 1651. Take State Route 741 to a junction with State Route 742. Head right on Route 742, and follow the above directions. Once on State Route 742, if you get to the Blue Heron Mine, you've missed Gorge Overlook Road.

Follow the paved trail toward the Blue Heron Overlook. Head right on a trail at a sign announcing the overlook. Take the trail downhill, and follow the sign to "Cracks in the Rock". You will eventually reach a long set of stairs. Facing out from the bottom of the stairs, the routes to your right are the "downstream" routes; those to the left are the "upstream" routes.

The following information appears courtesy of Paul Jakus and Ian McAlexander. Thanks guys!

ROUTES DOWNSTREAM FROM THE STAIRS

The Pantheon Ampitheater

S 1. Procrustes' Workbench 10b
Some loose rock. (6 bolts, shuts) 50'

S 2. ***Dead Souls 12b
Excellent. (7 bolts, anchors) 60'.

S 3. *Caesar's Stabbing 11a
5 bolts, anchors. 45'

S 4. **Et Tu, Brute? 10d
6 bolts, anchors. 50'

T 5. Bucket Boy 5
Follow huge flakes and discontinuous cracks. 60'

S 6. **Campobello Beauty 9
6 bolts, anchors. 50'

⑤ 7. *Carolina Club 10b
Look for the hidden hold. (7 bolts, anchors) 60'

⑤ 8. **Murphy To Manteo 10d
8 bolts, anchors. 60'

The following routes begin just downstream from the Carolina Slab.

🇹 9. Puddin' Jam 7
Ascend the crack/flake above the alcove. 60'

⑤ 10. ***Mirror Of Llunet 11b
Start just above a small "pond". Varied and interesting, especially if you do not touch the tree. (8 bolts, anchors) 75'

🇹 11. The Geothermal Jig 10a
Crack to chimney. 70'

⑤ 12. *Wit's End 10b
First bolt is high, at the top of a shallow left-facing dihedral. (7 bolts, anchors) 60'.

⑤ 13. *Route du Jour 10a
Start about 20' left of Wit's End. Start on an arete down low. (7 bolts, anchors) 55'

🇹 14. No One To Hear You Scream 8
"Crescent moon" shaped flake in a left-facing dihedral. Very old rap slings at top (established rope solo) 50'

🇹 15. Zack Be Nimble 8
The filthy right-facing corner, 20' left of No One To Hear You Scream. 50'

🇹 16. Crack The Keg 9
Stem the corner immediately left of the sharp arete.50'

⑤ 17. Beastie Boy (project)
A project on the face immediately right of Weenie Boy. (6 bolts, anchor) 50'

🇹 18. Weenie Boy 9+
Start: 50' left of Crack the Keg
The left-facing chimney has been toproped from the Beastie Boy anchors. 50'

🇹 19. Hello Nasty 9+
Start: A wide, mildly offwidth crack just left of Weenie Boy. Feed the crack a steady diet of big stuff, but bring a smaller piece (#3 Metolius TCU) for the exit. Rap from Ecliptic anchors.

⑤ 20. **Ecliptic 11c
Located immediately left of Hello Nasty. (8 bolts, anchors) 55'

⑤ 21. **Winter Solstice 10d
An excellent route that deserves more traffic. (6 bolts, shuts) 60'

Walk through a tunnel (called The Bauhaus) a bit further downstream from Winter Solstice, to a group of shady routes that are cool in the summer. This is the Springfield area, and includes two freestanding towers and the alley between the towers and the main wall. The towers are Springfield Elementary and Springfield Nuclear.

T **22. Sideshow Bob 10b**
Located left of the large left-facing dihedral directly behind Springfield Elementary. Begin in hand/finger crack that leads up to meet with the left-facing dihedral mentioned above. Undercling back left. Rap from anchors on Krusty. 70'

S **23. *Krusty The Clown 10b**
A fun arete just left of Sideshow Bob. (5 bolts, anchors) 70'

T **24. ***The Real Homer 10c**
Follow the discontinuous finger crack about 40' left of Krusty. Watch for the expanding flake at the top of the crack. Head right and top out. Rap from trees. 80'

Springfield Elementary

T **25. Principal Skinner 10b**
Mixed route with 3 bolts, anchors. Start at center of face, then work left to bolt. 75'

T **26. *Bart At The Blackboard 11c (mixed)**
Shares same start and anchors as Skinner, but climb up and right to a very high first bolt. Sling flakes along the way.
(5 bolts, anchors) 75'

Springfield Nuclear

S **27. ***Smithers Gets His Man 11c**
Megaclassic arete route. Watch for the loose flake on the right, near the end of the climb. (7 bolts, anchors) 65'

S **28. **Meltdown 11c**
Start just right of Smithers. (9 bolts, anchors) 65'

The Turret

Located on main wall between Springfield Nuclear and The Odyssey Block.

T **29. Access Fun 9+**
Obvious wide crack. Rap from trees, or face climb left to Fun anchors. 70'

S **30. ***Fun 11c (sport, almost)**
Classic. Bring one or two medium pieces for the start. Up the crack a bit, then follow bolts left. (6 bolts, anchors) 70'

The Odyssey Block

This is a third free-standing pillar.

S **31. ***Charybdis 10a**
Excellent, but sporting some runouts. An alert belay is recommended, as is the route. (7 bolts, anchors) 80'

S **32. **Scylla 10b**
Follow the left-facing dihedral, then right onto the face. (7 bolts, anchors) 70'

S **33. Song of the Sirens 10a**
Well-protected and fun. (7 bolts, anchors) 65'

T **34. Block Party 7**
A mixed route originally done without the bolt. Has some runout sections. Rap from Sirens anchors. 65'

T **35. A Gathering of Shades 11+**
Mixed route with 5 bolts. Face to crack. Belay at top, rap from Sirens anchors. 65'

ROUTES UPSTREAM FROM THE STAIRS

Cracks in the Rock Area

Numerous routes in this area are now off-limits under the management plan because they are within thirty feet of the USNPS maintained trail. The NPS has instituted the rule to keep hikers from getting accidentally bonked by rocks or gear. Out of respect for the plan, these routes are not reported in this guide. Please do not climb within thirty feet of the USNPS trail.

Magnanimous Block, The Greater

The maintained trail goes between two large blocks (the "Cracks in the Rocks"). Just before reaching the Cracks in the Rock Stairs, take an indistinct side trail to the right. This leads to Magnanimous Block, The Greater. The block has some excellent, sheltered bouldering.

T **36. *Slingblade 9+**
From base of giant oak tree, climb straight up through clean, white rock to highest point on the wall. Bring lots of slings. Descend by walking all the way back to the top of the stairway used on the approach. Please do not rap onto the maintained trail. 60'

T **37. Shell Shock 8**
Follow a broken crack right of the oak tree, to large black pockets. Ends at anchors. 50'

S **38. Sabre Dance 10d**
First bolt hanger missing. Big swing with possible deckage, if you fall early. (3 bolts, anchors) 35'

Magnanimous Block, The Lesser

Facing out from the rock as you exit the corridor from the "Cracks in the Rock", this block is to the left.

S **39. **Frosty The Lumberjack 11a**
Steep face 30' off the trail. (5 bolts, anchors) 40'

Walk further around the corner to a left-facing dihedral. All of the upstream routes past this point get a lot of sun. Warm in the winter, blazing in the summer.

T **40. Jonah's Pew 6**
Chimney in the corner. Three alternate exits. 50'

T **41. *Bandersnatch 9**
Follow the orange dihedral to the top. Rap from trees, or descend by walking back to the top of the stairs used on the approach. 75'

S **42. ***Morpheus 11c**
Begin 30' right of Bandersnatch. Classic. (9 bolts, anchors) 80'

T **43. *Insecurity Blanket 10d (mixed)**
Pro at the end of the steep section is difficult to find, but solid. Easy climbing above to natural rap anchor. (2 bolts) 80'

T **44. **Head Factor 12a**
A 2 bolt direct start to Insecurity Blanket.

T **45. **Colonel Forbin's Ascent 11a (mixed)**
Follow the gold, right-facing dihedral. Bring large gear for upper section. (1 bolt, anchors) 60'

T **46. The Garden Weasel 10a**
Follow the 40' crack to a face. 95'

S **47. **You Enjoy Myself 11c**
Excellent. Located on the left side of a huge, white flake detached from the main wall. (6 bolts, anchors) 60'

S **48. ***Drive Me To Firenze 11c**
Located to the right of YEM. Superb. (8 bolts, anchors) 60'

T **49. *Yaller Jambo 9**
Start just right of Drive Me To Firenze. Up the yellow, offwidth, handcrack and corner. Walk down to the right. 45'

T **50. Spit Spot 6**
Walk up behind the right side of YEM flake, then chimney for 20' to ledge. Get on the very top of the flake and step across to main wall. Continue to top. 40'

S **51. **Tweezer 11**
Located behind the right side of the YEM flake. Crimps to a right facing flake, then up. (7 bolts, anchors) 55'

T **52. **Holly And The Ivy 10b**
Toprope or lead the obvious wide crack.

T **53. Helping Friendly Book**
Project in a right-facing dihedral to overhang. Some bolts in place.

T **54. Unnamed**
Project in a left-facing dihedral above a swamp, to a face. Has one bolt in place.

T **55. *Nannerhead 10c (mixed)**
Starts about 200' right of Holly And The Ivy. Begin in shallow, right-facing dihedral. At an alcove where the crack heads right, step left and follow three bolts to the anchors. Watch for snakes on ledge near the second bolt. 80'

T **56. A Trad Looks At 40**
Project. Undercling left-leaning dihedral to vertical crack. Anchors in place.

Blue Heron Downstream

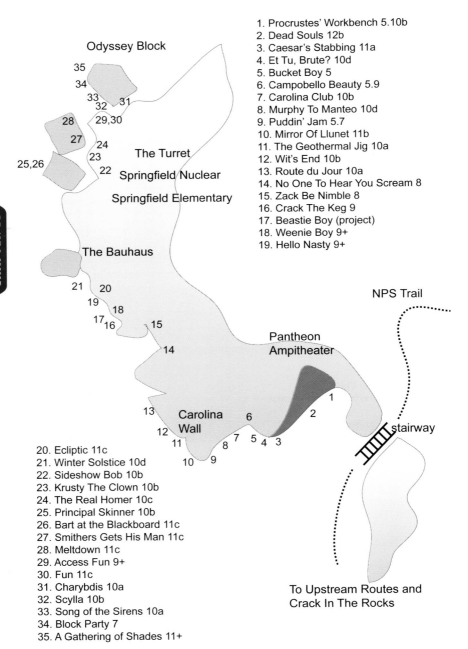

1. Procrustes' Workbench 5.10b
2. Dead Souls 12b
3. Caesar's Stabbing 11a
4. Et Tu, Brute? 10d
5. Bucket Boy 5
6. Campobello Beauty 5.9
7. Carolina Club 10b
8. Murphy To Manteo 10d
9. Puddin' Jam 5.7
10. Mirror Of Llunet 11b
11. The Geothermal Jig 10a
12. Wit's End 10b
13. Route du Jour 10a
14. No One To Hear You Scream 8
15. Zack Be Nimble 8
16. Crack The Keg 9
17. Beastie Boy (project)
18. Weenie Boy 9+
19. Hello Nasty 9+

20. Ecliptic 11c
21. Winter Solstice 10d
22. Sideshow Bob 10b
23. Krusty The Clown 10b
24. The Real Homer 10c
25. Principal Skinner 10b
26. Bart at the Blackboard 11c
27. Smithers Gets His Man 11c
28. Meltdown 11c
29. Access Fun 9+
30. Fun 11c
31. Charybdis 10a
32. Scylla 10b
33. Song of the Sirens 10a
34. Block Party 7
35. A Gathering of Shades 11+

Odyssey Block

The Turret

Springfield Nuclear

Springfield Elementary

The Bauhaus

NPS Trail

Pantheon
Ampitheater

Carolina
Wall

stairway

To Upstream Routes and
Crack In The Rocks

CHAPTER 11

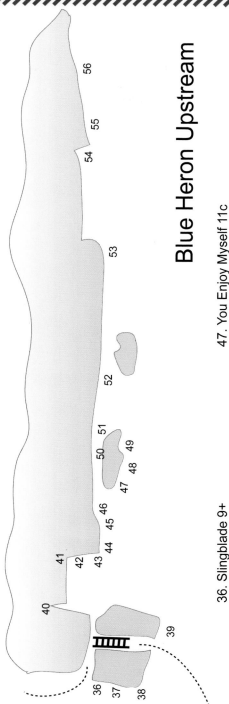

Blue Heron Upstream

36. Slingblade 9+
37. Shell Shock 8
38. Sabre Dance 10d
39. Frosty the Lumberjack 11a
40. Jonah's Pew 6
41. Bandersnatch 9
42. Morpheus 11c
43. Insecurity Blanket 10d.
44. Head Factor 12a
45. Colonel Forbin's Ascent 11a
46. The Garden Weasel 10a

47. You Enjoy Myself 11c
48. Drive Me To Firenze 11c
49. Yaller Jambo 9
50. Spit Spot 6
51. Tweezer 11
52. Holly and the Ivy 10b
53. Helping Friendly Book
54. Unnamed
55. Nannerhead 10c
56. A Trad Looks At 40

Marc Seitzman at the 2nd pitch belay on Tale Of The Scorpion, O&W
Photo: Jeff Noffsinger

A couple of pics of random cliffs in the Big South Fork...

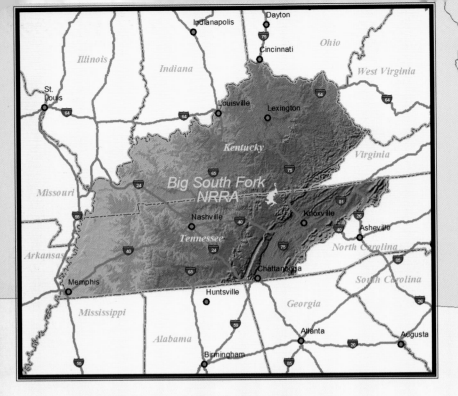

Big South Fork
National River
and Recreation Area

Big South Fork Landmarks

- ● Ford
- 🔲 Overlook
- ⊙ Park Attractions
- ≈ Rapids

Roads

- ——— State Road
- ▬▬▬ US Highway
- ┼┼┼ Scenic Rialroad

National Forest
State Forest
Deferred Acquisition Lands
⊙ County Seat
○ Town

Jamestown

Allardt

North

Miles

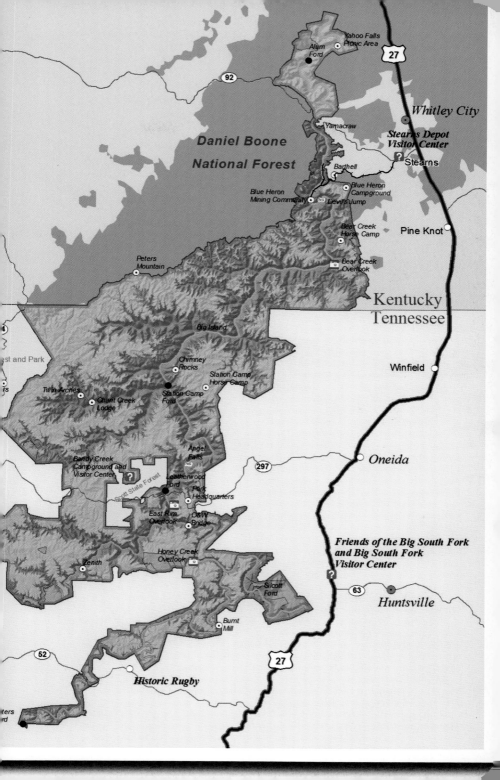

Yahoo Falls
Picnic Area

Alum
Ford

27

92

Whitley City

Daniel Boone

Yamacraw

*Stearns Depot
Visitor Center*

? Stearns

Barthell

Blue Heron
Campground

National Forest

Blue Heron
Mining Community

Devil's Jump

Pine Knot

Bear Creek
Horse Camp

Peters
Mountain

Bear Creek
Overlook

Kentucky
Tennessee

Big Island

Chimney
Rocks

Station Camp
Horse Camp

Winfield

Twin Arches

Charit Creek
Lodge

Station Camp
Ford

st and Park

4

Angel
Falls

Bandy Creek
Campground and
Visitor Center

?

297

Oneida

East Rim
Overlook

Leatherwood
Ford

Park
Headquarters

Scott State Forest

O&W
Bridge

Honey Creek
Overlook

*Friends of the Big South Fork
and Big South Fork
Visitor Center*

Zenith

?

Silcott
Ford

63

Huntsville

Burnt
Mill

52

27

Historic Rugby

ters
d

Bryan Murphey, Lucky Strikes
Photo: Jonathan Hollada

STARR MOUNTAIN 12
chapter

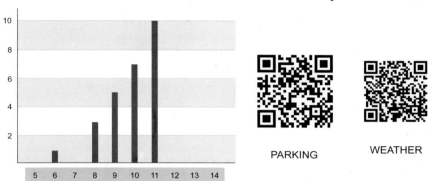

PARKING   WEATHER

For what it's worth, of all the areas in this guide, Starr Mountain is one of my favorites. This has little to do with the quality, or quantity of the climbing - in fact, it is a small cliff, with nowhere near the number of routes as other areas. Nestled in a secluded cove above the Hiwassee River, with a gorgeous view and a moderately "aerobic" hike in, it offers a welcome respite from the crowded scene of the more popular crags in the region.

The rock quality at Starr is excellent, with most routes following corners and cracks. There are no sport routes here, so bring your rack. Toproping is possible, but be extremely careful scrambling up the access gullies and around the top.

History

The first climbing activity at Starr can be traced to Atlanta climber Bob Ordner, who was taken to the cliff in 1978. Over the next few months, Bob, along with Shannon Stegg, Curtis Glass, Tom Woodruff and Phil Fisher and others, climbed most of the prominent plum lines. Due to its established informal ethic against bolting, the crag has since seen only sporadic development in the past few years.

Parking Area Coordinates

35° 13' 31.12" N
84° 31' 53.51" W

Location and Directions

From Atlanta, follow I-75 North to Highway 411 East (exit #293). Continue on 411 through Chatsworth, Georgia, over the Ocoee River, and through Benton, Tennessee. A few miles past Benton, cross the Hiwassee River. Proceed approximately .4 miles and turn right on Spring Creek Road, following signs for the Hiwassee State Scenic River Area (Gee Creek Wilderness Area). Set your odometer here, and continue for 2.3 miles, passing the ranger station on the right. The road turns to gravel. Continue to an obvious pulloff on the left, near a large culvert pipe, next to the railroad tracks.

From Knoxville or Chattanooga, follow I-75 North toward Cleveland, Tennessee. Exit onto Highway 64 East, and follow it for roughly 15 miles to Highway 411 North. Take Highway

411 North through Benton and follow the same directions as above.
Note: The town of Benton is a notorious speed trap. In fact, it was featured on a national nightly news program, in relation to the sheer volume of tickets written (ie: revenue collected) given the small size of the town. The weekly pilgrimage of paddlers heading to the Hiwassee and Ocoee presents a situation that is evidently too tempting to resist for local law enforcement.

From the parking pulloff, look for boulder "steps" leading up onto the railroad bed. Climb the embankment up onto the tracks and look for a trail heading uphill on the other side. Follow this trail up beside a waterfall/stream bed. At the waterfall, bear right on a flat, rocky trail, past a campsite. Scramble directly uphill above the campsite, winding your way through a blocky rock outcropping. Continue right along the cliff base to the first routes.

Camping

Gee Creek Campground has showers and campsites for a nominal fee and there is free camping all along the Hiwassee River. Also, halfway up the access trail, you will find an excellent flat ledge with a fire ring and space for a few tents, in close proximity to the waterfall.

Luxuries

Benton offers gas stations and a few restaurants, while the small city of Cleveland is only 20 miles away.

Emergency Services

Tennessee State Forest Office	(423) 263-0050
Ocoee Ranger Station	(423) 338-5201
Polk County Sheriff's Office	(423) 338-4540
Benton Police Department	(423) 338-5733
Dial 911	

FYI

The Hiwassee River and the nearby Ocoee River offer excellent whitewater paddling opportunities, as well as great fly fishing! (Of course, a Tennessee State Fishing license is required). The nearby Ocoee River was the site of the 1996 Olympic Games paddling events, and there are many rafting companies in the vicinity. At the very least, the Hiwassee provides a refreshing dip at the end of a day of climbing.

Cliff Layout

The trail meets the cliff on its left end, and almost all of the climbing occurs on the upper tier. The routes are listed left to right from this point. Please refer to the diagrams provided. There is also a trail that heads right and along the lower tier, where there are lots of easy beginner routes. Because all of the established climbing occurs from a ledge system, children and dogs should be kept close at hand. At times, the ledge narrows dramatically and reaching the base of the routes at the far end requires stepping past three dangerous notches. I recommend putting children and novices in a harness and belaying them across these tenuous sections.

CHAPTER 12

Starr Mountain - South End

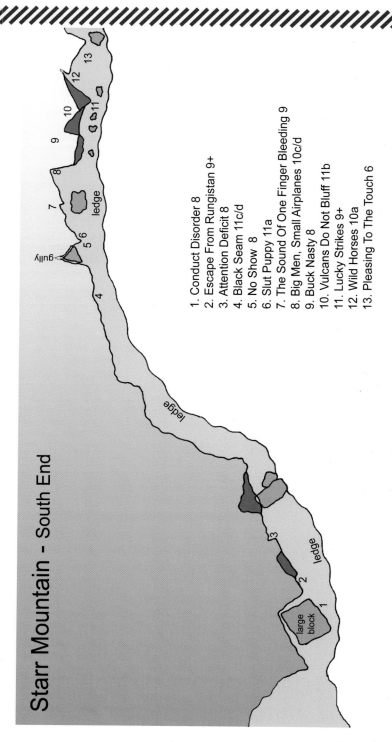

1. Conduct Disorder 8
2. Escape From Rungistan 9+
3. Attention Deficit 8
4. Black Seam 11c/d
5. No Show 8
6. Slut Puppy 11a
7. The Sound Of One Finger Bleeding 9
8. Big Men, Small Airplanes 10c/d
9. Buck Nasty 8
10. Vulcans Do Not Bluff 11b
11. Lucky Strikes 9+
12. Wild Horses 10a
13. Pleasing To The Touch 6

CHAPTER 12

1. Conduct Disorder 8
Start: On the outer face of the boulder. Climb the obvious short crack. *FA: John Fain and Greg Allen, 1980*

2. Escape From Rungistan 9+
Start: 30' right of Conduct Disorder. Climb a short finger crack and corner. The start is probably 5.10 but the corner is much easier. *FA: John Fain and Todd Anderson, 1980*

3. Attention Deficit 8
Start: 20' right of Escape From Rungistan. Climb a crack in a wide corner to a tree. *FA: Howie Cox and John Fain, 1979*

The trail continues right under a small fire blackened roof to an area with many overhangs. Proceed a short distance past a trailside roof crack to find....

4. **Black Seam 11c/d
Start: Just left of a vertical gully, 100' right of Attention Deficit. Teeter up a thin, black seam to a roof. Continue over the lip to the top. Note: Protection is small and very technical to place. Bring brass and small wires. *FA: Shannon Stegg and Stan Glass, 1983*

5. No Show 8
Start: 15' right of Black Seam. Follow a thin crack just left of a short arete. Pull a short roof and follow a right-facing corner, past ledges, to a slab finish. *FA: Scott Perkins, 1998*

6. *Slut Puppy 11a
Start: At a thin flake on the wall, 20' right of No Show. Pull over the flake and continue up the ramp to the top. *FA: Philip Fisher and Robyn Erbesfield, 1986*

7. The Sound Of One Finger Bleeding 9
Start: In a deep corner, just right of Slut Puppy. Climb an awkward, crispy, unpleasant left-facing corner to a pointed fin, then move right around a small roof. Proceed to a large roof; step left and up to the top. *FA: Howie Cox and Bob Ordner, 1979*

8. ***Big Men, Small Airplanes 10c/d
Start: Behind a boulder, by a cedar tree, 15' right of The Sound of One Finger Bleeding. Climb a shallow finger/hand crack in a left-facing corner, to a ledge. Continue over the roof, via a hand crack, to the top. *FA: Bob Ordner and Howie Cox, 1981*. Note: There is a two bolt anchor at the top of the corner. The corner, to the anchors, is 5.7 or 5.8.

9. Buck Nasty 8
Start: Past Big Men, Small Airplanes. Climb a right-facing corner to a roof. Scoot out left around the roof and follow easy but dirty ground to the top. *FA: Rich Janow and Alan Brock, 2012*

10. Vulcans Do Not Bluff 11b
Start: Near the left front of a shallow alcove, past Buck Nasty. Climb a corner to a crack splitting a white bulge. Continue over tiered roof to the top. *FA: Bob Ordner, Todd Anderson and Sean Cobourn, 1986. Upper roof FA: Robyn Erbesfield and Philip Fisher in 1986.*

11. ***Lucky Strikes 9+
A must do! One of the best routes at the cliff.
Start: 10' right of Vulcans Do Not Bluff. Climb a short arete. Pull a small roof and continue to the top. *FA: Howie Cox and Bob Ordner, 1981*

CHAPTER 12

Starr Mountain - Middle Section and North End

12
13
14
15
cable
step across
careful!
cleft
careful!
16
17
18
19
20
21
22
23
24
painted
symbols
25
26
27
23
24

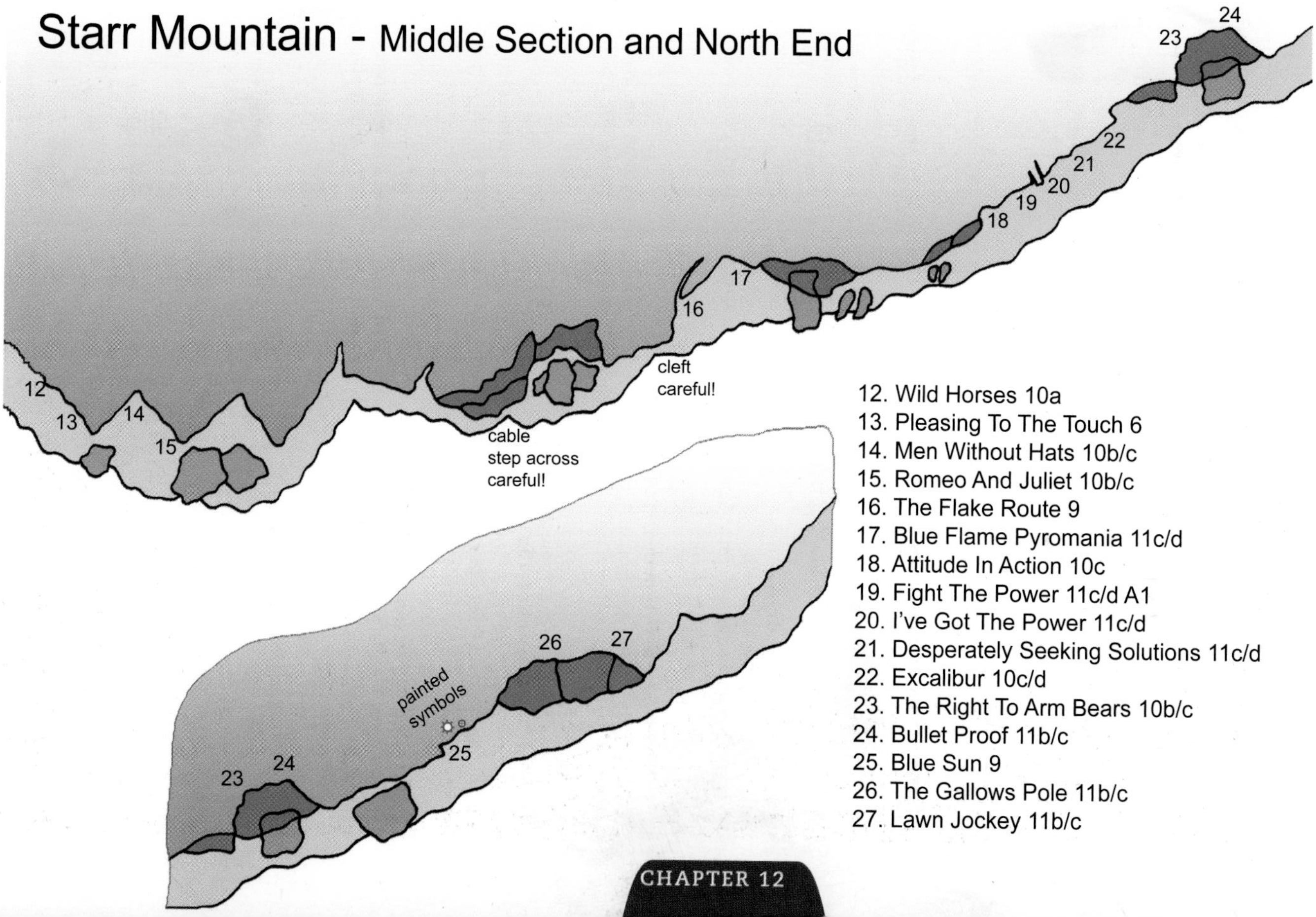

12. Wild Horses 10a
13. Pleasing To The Touch 6
14. Men Without Hats 10b/c
15. Romeo And Juliet 10b/c
16. The Flake Route 9
17. Blue Flame Pyromania 11c/d
18. Attitude In Action 10c
19. Fight The Power 11c/d A1
20. I've Got The Power 11c/d
21. Desperately Seeking Solutions 11c/d
22. Excalibur 10c/d
23. The Right To Arm Bears 10b/c
24. Bullet Proof 11b/c
25. Blue Sun 9
26. The Gallows Pole 11b/c
27. Lawn Jockey 11b/c

T 12. Wild Horses 10a
Start: 10' right of Lucky Strikes. Contrived. Meander up the face past a thin crack, avoiding any good holds, looking for difficulty, to the top. *FA: Tom and Darlene Woodruff, 1981*

T 13. **Pleasing To The Touch 6
Start: Same as for Wild Horses. Climb the obvious face and cracks with solid protection. *FA: Bob Ordner and Janet Dunn, 1988.*

T 14. **Men Without Hats 10b/c
Start: In a white corner, to the right of Pleasing To The Touch. Stem up the corner, skirt right around the roof. Note: There is a chain anchor below the roof. The corner is 5.8. *FA: Greg Allen and Shannon Stegg, 1989.*

T 15. **Romeo And Juliet 10b/c
Toprope the face and arete right of Men Without Hats, on small holds. *FA: John Vermont and Juliet Dickinson, 1992.*

Continue right between a large boulder and the wall. Step across a dangerous V-notch. Luckily, there is a cable bolted in for safety, so wear a harness and a runner/carabiner. Continue along a rubble-strewn ledge, past another tricky cleft and finally a third, narrow cleft that is very dangerous. There is no cable and it is slick and pebbly. Roping up is advised!

T 16. *The Flake Route 9
Start: Just right of the last cleft.
Climb an obvious flake/wide crack. Continue to the top. *FA: Mike Dunn and John Fain, 1987.*

T 17. **Blue Flame Pyromania 11c/d
Start: 20' right of The Flake Route, at a crack splitting an orange face. Climb the obvious finger crack to the bulge. Trend up and left on minimal protection, to the top. *FA: Philip Fisher, 1986.*

T 18. **Attitude In Action 10c
Start: 15' right of Blue Flame Pyromania. Cruise up a shallow seam in the white face (minimal pro), then step left beneath a large roof to a ledge. Continue to the top. *FA: Shannon Stegg and Curtis Glass, 1986.*

T 19. *Fight The Power 11c/d, A1
Start: 15' right of Attitude In Action. Climb a thin crack/seam to a huge pillar/flake pasted against the wall below a roof. Step right to a thin seam in the roof. Pull the roof and follow a short, shallow corner to the top. *FA: Bob Ordner and Howie Cox, 1980.*

T 20. **I've Got The Power 11c/d
Start: 5' right of Fight The Power. Start in a wide crack and then up a right-facing corner formed by a vertical, trapped pedestal. Go to the roof, then move right and up a short, right facing corner block to the top. *FA: Shannon Stegg and Curtis Glass, 1985.*

T 21. Desperately Seeking Solutions 11c/d
Start: 10' right of I've Got The Power. Toprope the middle of a steep white wall.

T 22. ***Excalibur 10c/d
A fantastic route with great pro and classic moves.
Start: 15' right of Desperately Seeking Solutions. Climb a shallow, right-facing corner, then move left around a small roof and up a left-facing corner. Pull a small roof and follow a wide left-facing corner to the top. *FA: Bob Ordner and Howie Cox, 1986.*

16

18

9

20

22

🎦 23. The Right To Arm Bears 10b/c
Start: 15' right of Excalibur, in a recessed alcove with a boulder in it. Two obvious crack systems are in the back of the alcove. Climb the right hand crack and steep face to the top. *FA: Mike Dunn and Bob Ordner in 1986.*

🎦 24. Bullet Proof 11b/c
Start: Just right of The Right To Arm Bears, from atop the boulder. Climb the orange face and roof. *FA: Philip Fisher and Robyn Erbesfield, 1986.*

Squeeze through the passage and continue right, scrambling over a boulder pile and down, to find two faint blue symbols painted on the rock.

🎦 25. Blue Sun 9
Start: In a shallow right-facing corner. Climb the corner, pull a short roof and follow a hand crack to the top. Variation: Climb the right hand crack at 5.10.

🎦 26. The Gallows Pole 11b/c
Start: About 20' right of Blue Sun, look for two roof cracks in a short face just above a wide, sandy ledge. Pull the roof via the left hand crack/weakness. Continue up the steep face to the top. Note: A small tree grows close to this route, perhaps making it an unpleasant endeavor. *FA: Greg Allen and Shannon Stegg, 1983.*

🎦 27. Lawn Jockey 11b/c
Led way before the advent of large cams - Yikes! Start: Right of The Gallows Pole. Start in a shallow incipient groove, then layback up to, and over, a wide roof crack to the top. Note: One or two large (#5.6) cams recommended. *FA: Shannon Stegg and Dave Caldwell, 1985.*

As you approach the beginning of the cliff, a trail cuts downhill sharply to the right and along the base of the lower tier. There are a few easy routes scattered across this section. The first two are very easy beginner sport routes, both have 2 or 3 bolts and anchors.

Lower Tier Sport Routes

Waterfall at Starr Mountain Photo: Chris Watford

Greg Kottkamp, Nagual
Photo: Andrew Kornylak

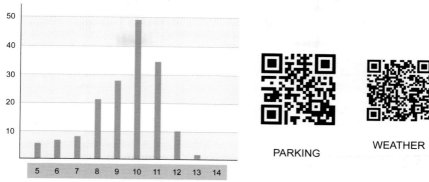

PARKING

WEATHER

King's Bluff stands as a testament to the hard work and dedication of a motivated group of climbers, who worked tirelessly to negotiate the acquisition of the land for the Southeastern Climbers Coalition. Hard work, donations and continued fundraising efforts will assure that King's Bluff stays open for all climbers to enjoy.

The rock at King's Bluff is limestone, with crisp, sharp holds guaranteed to shred the fingers. Often described as being like stacked boulder problems, most routes range in height from 30 to 50 feet with a few up to 70'. Problem solving and gymnastic moves are typical. The "Bluff" lies on the north side of the Cumberland River, facing south, which causes the cliff line to be ten degrees warmer at the base than at the top and mostly sheltered from wind. The summers can be extremely hot and humid, with the best climbing occurring in the early morning hours. Due to the extensive overgrowth, there is always shade along most of the trail and cliff line. During winter, the leaves fall allowing more sunlight to strike the cliff, keeping the area warmer and allowing for climbing even on the coolest days. Most locals will agree that fall is the best time to climb since it frequently rains in the spring.

A Few Notes

Though most of the routes are sport routes, there are also quite a few mixed routes, many of which can be done without gear. You may often see many of the locals climbing the so-called mixed routes and just running them out. Usually the bolts will protect the more difficult sections of the climb with gear designated for the easier part. Bringing a full set of nuts/stoppers and tri-cams will adequately protect any climb at the bluff. Cams should be carefully placed since the limestone can often fracture and break in some places. Most climbing can be done at the bluff with a dozen quick draws and a single 50m rope, as it is mostly a sport climbing area. The only way to set a toprope is by first climbing the route. At all anchors please use quick draws or slings to extend the anchors for top roping. This reduces wear on the anchors and extends their life. Due to the high humidity in the area, anchors, chains, cables, and slings are constantly being replaced. Even at press time, routes are being developed and old routes modified. Old bolts and anchors are being replaced, trails improved and new lines put in

History

Extensive route development began in the early 1990's as locals looked for an alternative

CHAPTER 13

to the long drives to Eastern Tennessee or Kentucky for climbing. Walt Wilkinson, aided by his wife Suzy Wilkinson and friend Terry Parker, spearheaded the initial development. As many of the original developers moved on, Joey Redman and Doyle Parsons took up the mantle of developing more lines. As the next millennium begins, Joey Redman continues as the primary developer of the area by leading efforts on trail development, route development, and the all important effort of turning the area over to the Southeastern Climbers Coalition for oversight. Many locals in the area continue to assist him in the efforts. They can often be seen sacrificing their time toiling on the trails, clearing brush, and replacing old bolts instead of climbing. Great appreciation should be given to these few who work so hard to make the "Bluff" a better place to climb.

Location and Directions

From Nashville, take I-24 North toward Clarksville. At exit 11, turn left and head into Clarksville on Highway 76. Continue for about 3.2 miles to a stoplight (junction with Highway 41A). Pass through the stoplight with a super Wal-Mart on the left. Continue on another 3 miles. After climbing a hill, look for an Amoco station on the right. To the left is Max Court Road. Turn on Max Court and continue 100 yards. You will see a big sign that says "King and Queen's Bluff". Park in the Woodsmen of the World parking lot during the week, or in front of the communications businesses during the weekends only. Do not park in front of the gate so as not to impede emergency vehicles.

From Fort Campbell, Kentucky, follow 41A south past Fort Campbell and through Clarksville. After crossing the Lewis Memorial Bridge, turn right onto Riverside Drive (41A South By-pass). At Gary Matthews Jeep dealership (2.3 miles from the bridge), fork left staying on the main by-pass. Continue for another 2.7 miles. You will see a Texaco on the right as you start to crest a hill. Turn right just after the gas station onto Max Court. The rest is the same as above.

The foot approach is very short. From the parking lot, pass through the gate. Continue to the top of the hill and cul-de-sac. To the left of the bulletin board is the trail that heads downhill. Follow the trail down to the head-wall cliff and then turn left. Continue following the trail as it descends along the cliff edge. Climb down the stairs to the trail below. At the base of the stairs, facing the cliff, King's Bluff West lies to the left, while King's Bluff East lies to the right.

Camping/Luxuries

There is no camping at King's Bluff as of now. The area is currently inside the city limits of Clarksville so accommodations are going to be hotels or crashing at a generous local's house. There are loads of restaurants and eateries in Clarksville. The New York Bagel Cafe on Madison Street has good early morning bagels and gourmet "yuppie" coffee. The best pizza in town can be had at the Black Horse Brew Pub located on Franklin Street.

Emergency Assistance

Call 911 for local EMS and police services. The local rescue services have done emergency rescues down at the "Bluff" before, but be prepared to assist in case someone needs evacuating.

Regulations

The Southeastern Climbing Coalition (SCC) owns a major part of the area. Access is open to anyone. In order to prevent vandalism and dumping, a chain-link fence with a secured gate has been put up. Specific information for access, including the combination to the gate's lock, can be obtained by contacting a local climber or through the SCC for the latest information. In general, the gate is always open on weekends and holidays. Access during the week can easily be arranged. The SCC website is http://www.seclimbers.org. Click on the King's Bluff tab.

FYI

This climbing area is owned and/or managed by the Southeastern Climbers' Coalition. If you're going to climb in this area or other Coalition areas regularly, please become a member of the SCC. Membership in the SCC defrays the maintenance costs and also helps promote increased access for climbers through alliances with landowners and further climbing area aquisitions. By becoming a member of the SCC, you become a part-owner of this and other climbing areas owned by the Coalition. To become a member of the SCC, please visit http://www.seclimbers.org.

Acknowledgements

All of the information for this chapter was graciously handed to me, complete and print-ready by Scott Griggs and Hank Smith. This is basically an exact reprint of their guidebook, with new access and route info. Additionally, the Smith/Griggs guidebook lists other small crags in the area that may be worth visiting. The information presented here should prove more than adequate.

Cliff Layout

King's Bluff is most easily described as having two broad divisions: The stretch of cliffline to the left of the access stairs and the cliffline to the right of the stairs. The routes left of the stairs are described going right to left and the routes to the right of the stairs are described from left to right. Information on bolt count and anchor type is subject to change. Topo-pics of routes, listed with route numbers, correspond to the text. Note: In the last several years, small name/grade plaques have been installed at the bottom of the routes. Some may be missing but most should still be present.

CHAPTER 13

SOUTHEASTERN CLIMBERS COALITION

www.seclimbers.org

Navigator Wall

Horror Wall

Politicians Wall

The Beach

High Water Wall

The Orchard

Dynamic Wall

Cake Walk Wall

Walt's Wall

Max Court

King's Bluff East

trail and stairs

King's Bluff West

Cumberland River

Not To Scale

Lonesome Wall

The Alley

King's Bluff Overview

The Quiet Zone

KINGS BLUFF WEST

Note: There is a cave at the top of the cliff, just right of the stairs. It contains a V2 boulder problem done by Hank Smith. Begin with a sit start underneath where the cable handrail ends. Traverse right to just past the cave center. Be careful not to fall and roll down the cliff.

S L1. Tarheel Flake 9+
Follow a face to the right side of a flake. Trend left to finish. (3 bolts, anchors) *FA: Terry Parker*

S L2. Leviathan 11b
Climb a short flake to upper face. (2 bolts, Tarheel anchor) *FA: Terry Parker*

S L3. Helping Hands 12a
Face climb. (3 bolts, anchors) *FA: Walt Wilkinson*

S L4. Journey Above 11d
2nd pitch to Helping Hands. Continue through the upper roof. Gear. *FA: Mark Ilgner*

S L5. The Saga Continues 9-
3 bolts, cable anchors on ledge, common w/ New Drill). *FA: Walt Wilkinson*

S L6. *New Drill In Town 11a
3 bolts, cable anchors on column/ledge. Same as Saga. *FA: Walt Wilkinson*

S L7. *Keystone 5
3 bolts, Saga/New Drill anchors. *FA: Walt Wilkinson*

S L8. **The Second Pitch 6 (5.9 over the bolt/roof)
Extension starts from the Saga/New Drill/ Keystone anchors. 3 bolts, no permanent anchors. Sling some natural features at top. *FA: Walt Wilkinson*

S L9. Whirlwind 10c
3 bolts, cable anchors. *FA: Walt Wilkinson*

S L10. Clifford The Big Red Dog 8
3 bolts, ring anchors. *FA: Hank Smith / Joey Redman / Doyle Parsons / Scott Griggs*

S L11. After Lunch 9+
Starts right under the power lines. (2 bolts, ring anchors) *FA: Walt Wilkinson*

Lonesome Wall

Lonesome Wall has some of the hardest climbing at King's Bluff. The routes are fairly short, but are technical and crimpy.

S L12. A Fine New Edition 8
3 bolts, chain anchors. *FA: Joey Redman, Hank Smith, Scott Griggs, Doyle Parsons*

S L13. Mister Green Jeans 8
3 bolts, chain anchors. *FA: Joey Redman*

S L14. Captain Kangaroo 10a
Short face and over a small roof. 3 bolts, chains. *FA: Jeff Noffsinger*

S L15.***Baby Kangaroo 8
3 bolts, anchors. Goes over a classic overhang. *FA: Joey Redman*

S L16. Anchors Away 7
3 bolts, chain anchors. *FA: Joey Redman*

S L17. Short And Sporty 10c
Climb just right of the obvious flake. 2 bolts, ring anchors. *FA: Joey Redman*

S L18. Sportin' Doylies 4
Climb the right-facing flake. 4 bolts, ring anchors. *FA: Doyle Parsons*

S L19. Shorty Doylies 8
Face climb left of the flake. 3 bolts, ring anchors. *FA: Terry Parker*

S L20. Beginner's Luck 5
4 bolts, shares anchors with Shorty' Doylies. *FA: Joey Redman*

S L21. Community Effort 8
3 bolts, chain anchors. *FA: Joey Redman*

S L22.*Prelude To Harvest 11d/12a
Thin face leads past a bulge. Finish at ledge below high roof. 5 bolts, chain anchors. *FA: Terry Parker*

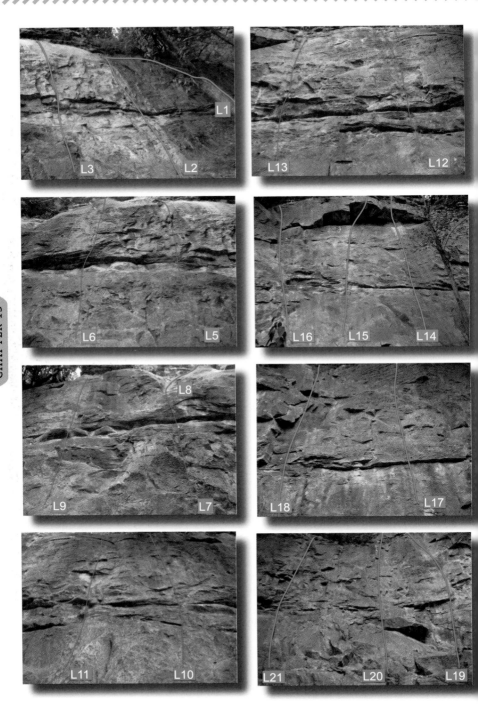

CHAPTER 13

CHAPTER 13

S L23. Mortal Wound 13
Thin face. Finish on the last part of Prelude. Mixed, requires gear. *FA: Mark Ilgner*

S L24. Three Wishes13b
Thin overhanging face. (3 bolts, anchors) *FA: Arno Ilgner*

S L25. Ground Zero 12c
Steep face just right of the obvious corner. 4 bolts, shares anchors with Three Wishes. *FA: Joey Redman*

S L26.***Ritz Bits 10c
Short face past a short overlap and a dihedral. Finish on a crimpy headwall. 5 bolts, chain anchors. Varied climbing. *FA: Terry Parker and Suzy Wilkinson*

S L27.**The Straight And Narrow 11a
Climb just left of the dihedral. (4 bolts, chain anchors) *FA: Walt Wilkinson*

S L28.*My Little Secret 11a
5 bolts, chain anchors. *FA: Terry Parker*

S L29. Too Heavy To Fly 11d
3 bolts, chain anchors. *FA: Walt Wilkinson*

S L30.**Northern Invader 12a
Starts in front of bolt on rock platform. 5 bolts (Last bolt and chain anchors common w/ Baby) *FA: Rick Harwick*

S L31. Baby, I'm Ten Inches Long 11d
5 bolts, chain anchors. *FA: Walt Wilkinson*

S L32. Mustang Sally 11a
4 bolts, chain anchors. *FA: Terry Parker*

S L33. The Process 10a
Follows a short, shallow dihedral to upper face. 4 bolts, chain anchors. *FA: Joey Redman*

S L34. Happy Hour 9
2 bolts, chain anchors. *FA: Joey Redman*

S L35. Born On The 4th Of July 9
2 bolts, chain anchors. *FA: Joey Redman*

The Alley

Over the years, The Alley has expanded so much that it now comes close to The Quiet Zone. The first route, Learning to Crawl is only a short distance to the right of The Quiet Zone's last route, Pocket Pool. This area is rich in moderate short climbs and provides a good place for novice leaders to cut their teeth.

M L36. Cataract 11a
Jog up a bit, past a short overlap. Trend left to chains. 3 bolts, chain anchors. *FA: Walt Wilkinson and Terry Parker*

M L37.*Static Cling 11b
Goes just left of a small right-facing corner. 4 bolts, chain anchors. *FA: Walt Wilkinson, Doyle Parsons and Suzy Wilkinson*

S L38.*Cricket Serenade 9
Starts at right end of railroad tie. Climb the right side of a dihedral, step right past a small overlap, then up. 4 bolts, ring anchors. *FA: Walt Wilkinson and Terry Parker*

M L39. Grin N' Bare It 10c
Starts at left end of railroad tie. Climb the thin seam in the back of the dihedral. Step left onto the steep face then up past a small roof. 4 bolts, anchors. *FA: Walt Wilkinson and Terry Parker*

S L40.**Scarface 10d
Climbs up and through a large patch of lighter colored rock. 4 bolts, chain anchors. *FA: Joey Redman*

S L41.*Luther's Fury 9
Face to a short left-facing flake. 5 bolts, chain anchors. *FA: Paul Mitchell*

S L42. Engineering A Goat Rope 7
Climb a shallow dihedral and step right to ledge. Follow a left-facing dihedral. 3 bolts, eyebolt anchors. *FA: Walt Wilkinson*

S L43.**The Bearded One 8
Pull the overhang on the huge jug. 4 bolts, ring anchors. *FA: Paul Mitchell*

Mark Ilgner, Ritz Bits
Photo: Andrew Kornylak

L44. Beam Me Up Scotty 8
Starts where trail begins to narrow. 4 Bolts, ring anchors shared with The Bearded One.

L45. Blanket Party 8
Climb to the right side of the ledge. Top may be somewhat overgrown in summer. 2 bolts, eyebolt anchors. *FA: Walt Wilkinson*

L46. Captain Hook 7
Starts near a set of old stone steps. Vertical jug haul. 4 bolts, chain anchors. *FA: Terry Parker*

L47. Seismic Activity 4
Short and blocky. 3 bolts, rings. *FA: Joey Redman*

L48. Demolition Zone 5
Blocky face just right of a short dihedral. 2 bolts, ring anchors. *FA: Joey Redman*

L49. Independence Day 7
3 bolts, ring anchors. *FA: Joey Redman*

L50. Bob The Builder 7
3 bolts, ring anchors. *FA: Joey Redman*

L51. Thomas The Train 6
3 bolts, ring anchors. *FA: Joey Redman*

L52. Dip In The River 5
3 bolts, ring anchors. *FA: Joey Redman*

L53.**Hammer Time 8
Start on top of rock shelf, in front of tree. 4 bolts, ring anchors. *FA: Hank Smith*

L54. Learning To Walk 8
Start on top of a 2' high rock shelf. 4 bolts, chains. *FA: Joey Redman*

L55. Learning To Crawl 4
Go up right side of 15' high bulge with stump on top. 4 bolts, cable anchors in tree. *FA: Joey Redman*

L56. Pocket Pool 9
Climb a face to a right-facing dihedral/bulge. 2 bolts, eyebolt anchors. *FA: Walt Wilkinson*

L57. Nine To Five 9
3 bolts, eyebolt anchors. *FA: Walt Wilkinson*

L58. Old Fart 8
4 bolts, chain anchors. *FA: Paul Mitchell*

L59. Chimney Sweep 5
Route stays right of blocky corner. 3 bolts, ring anchors. *FA: Walt Wilkinson*

The Quiet Zone

This area is the farthest west from the stairs where climbing is permitted. Please do not go further west to the Forbidden Zone. Further access to the Forbidden Zone is being negotiated. Also, as the name implies, keep noise levels low in this area so as not to disturb the landowners above.

L60. Stone Dagger 9
This is the first route to the left of the big blocky corner. Starts above a "hole" in base of wall. 5 bolts, cable anchors in tree. *FA: Jeff Noffsinger*

L61. *Name In The Guidebook 11a
Pulls a roof. 4 bolts, chains. Consider stick-clipping the 1st bolt. *FA: Walt Wilkinson*

L62. Brickyard 10a
Climb the right side of a 15' flake that starts 15' off the ground, then over a 3' roof. 1 bolt, chain anchors. *FA: Walt Wilkinson*

L63. Tight Squeeze 10b
Climb the face just right of the dihedral. 4 bolts, chains. *FA: Doyle Parsons*

L64.**To Good To Be True 10b
Goes over an obvious 3' overhang. 3 bolts, chain anchors. *FA: Walt Wilkinson*

L65. Murphy's Law 11a
Climb just left of an arête past a short roof and steep face. 4 bolts, chain anchors. *FA: Walt Wilkinson*

L66. Competitive Edge 10a
Starts on top of two stacked boulders. Skirts the left side of roof. 4 bolts, chain anchors. *FA: Walt Wilkinson*

L67.*Integrity 10c
Starts 5' left of two stacked boulders. 5 bolts, chain anchors. *FA: Walt Wilkinson*

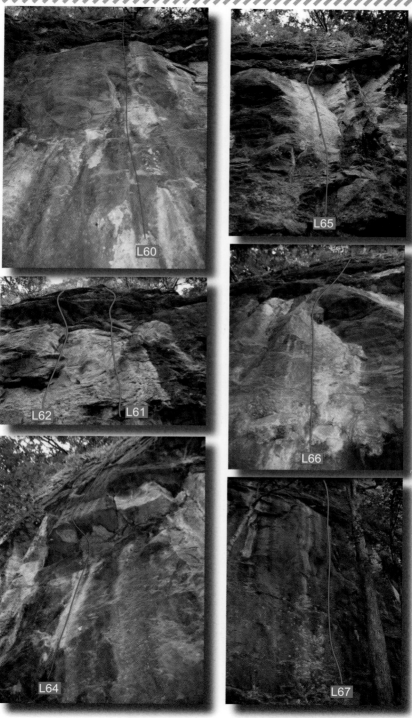

S L68.*Thin And Crispy 10b
Starts in front of trees. 5 bolts, chain anchors. *FA: Terry Parker*

M L69.*A Break From The Heat 9
Climb the obvious right-facing crack/flake. 3 bolts, chain anchors. *FA: Walt Wilkinson*

T L70. Snoop'n And Poop'n 8
Has chain anchors. Wide, shallow dihedral right of rotten flakes. *FA: Walt Wilkinson and Harold Schoecklmann*

S L71.*Easy For Now 9
Follows a shallow dihedral. 3 bolts, chain anchors. *FA: Walt Wilkinson*

S L72.*Elevator Shoes 10a**
Classic King's Bluff climbing. A must do! 3 bolts, chain anchors. *FA: Walt Wilkinson*

S L73. Forged Identity 12b
5 bolts, chain anchor. *FA: Mark Ilgner*

S L74. White Line Fever 11c
Route goes up wide white streak. 5 bolts, chain anchors. *FA: Doyle Parsons*

M L75. Under The Eye Of The Vulture 11c
This is the last route at this end of the cliff. 4 bolts, chain anchors. *FA: Walt Wilkinson*

KING'S BLUFF EAST (Right Side)

This area lies just to the right of the stairs. The routes are fairly short but worth doing.

S R1. Just A Pinch 10b
Short face to triangular roof. 2 bolts, anchors above cave. *FA: Walt Wilkinson*

S R2. A New Slant 10b
Follows a left-leaning corner. 2 bolts, shares anchor with Just A Pinch. *FA: Mark Ilgner*

S R3. No Prescription Needed 12a**
Stick clip recommended. 4 bolts, ring anchors. *FA: Terry Parker*

S R4. For Girly Girls Only 12b
4 bolts, eye-bolt anchors. *FA: Suzy Wilkinson*

S R5. Green 9
2 bolts, cable anchors in tree. Consider stick clipping the first bolt. *FA: Joey Redman*

S R6. Shave And A Haircut 9
Climb a short dihedral past a small overlap. Stick clip first bolt. 2 bolts, chain anchors. *FA: Walt Wilkinson*

Walt's Wall

Walt's Wall begins as you descend down the steep trail and has some excellent longer routes.

M R7. Caged Bowling Ball 10c
Face to a short corner to top. 8 bolts, anchors. *FA: Walt Wilkinson*

S R8. After The Ball Was Over 9
Blocky face. 6 bolts, anchors. *FA: Walt Wilkinson*

M R9.*Just Gimme Three Steps 9**
Go left at 3rd bolt and do a 10a direct finish to anchors. *FA: Walt Wilkinson*

M R10. Joint Venture 10c
6 bolts, anchor. *FA: Terry Parker, Walt Wilkinson and Fred Vail*

S R11. Striking Out On Your Own 10d
Start on Joint Venture, then go right to the corner/crack (under roof) then straight up. *FA: Walt Wilkinson*

S R12.*You Only Get Two Tries 10a**
Climb to the left side of a small roof. 5 bolts, anchor. *FA: Walt Wilkinson*

M R13. Born To Be Freed 10a
Face to blocky roof. 1 bolt , chain anchors. *FA: Walt Wilkinson*

T R14. Process Molasses 10c
Climb thin crack up left side of flake. At the cave continue to anchors on tree above. *FA: Hank Smith*

T R15. The Natural 7**
Short fun crack to a chain anchor. Chain anchors in cave. *FA: Terry Parker*

S R16.**Pulsator 11d
Climbs an often wet tufa. 5 bolts, chain anchor. Powerful route. *FA: Terry Parker*

S R17. Delores 11c
Climb a stalactite-looking feature 10' right of Pulsator. 3 bolts, rings. *FA: Arno and Mark Ilgner*

S R18. Hit Sequel 9+
Crimpy vertical face. 3 bolts, cable anchor. *FA: Terry Parker*

S R19. Eliminator 10c
4 bolts, cable anchor. *FA: Terry Parker*

Cake Walk Wall

This popular area has many moderate and easy routes. This area is the 2nd busiest after The Alley.

S R20. In The Rocking Chair 10a
Begins just after the drainage. Crimpy, short face. 3 bolts, cable anchors in tree. *FA: Walt Wilkinson*

S R21.*New Purchase 7
4 bolts, eye-bolt anchors. *FA: Walt Wilkinson*

S R22. Hat Pin With A Sledge Hammer 8
Vertical face past high bulges. 4 bolts, anchors. *FA: Walt Wilkinson*

M R23. Little Buttons 6
4 bolts, anchors. *FA: Walt Wilkinson / Suzy Wilkinson*

S R24. Jurassic Raccoon 7
Slab to corner. 4 bolts, eye-bolt anchors. *FA: Walt Wilkinson*

S R25. Little Fox 6
4 bolts, chain anchors. Interesting start. *FA: Paul Mitchell*

T R26.*Leaping Ladder 6
Route goes up a crack in the left side of big flake. Chain anchors. *FA: Terry Parker*

T R27.*Skin And Bones 10b
Shallow left-facing corner to roof. Undercling roof to top. Popular toprope. Chain anchors. *FA: Ted Burke*

T R28.**Whadyathink? 8
Right side of flake. Excellent route. Cable anchors. *FA: Terry Parker*

S R29. Rambo Strikes Back 8
Climb the dihedral. 3 bolts, anchors. *FA: Hank Smith*

S R30. The Sharper Image 10c
Crimpy face. 4 bolts, cable anchors. *FA: Terry Parker*

S R31. Here And Now 12a
Face and short roof 15' right of Sharper Image. 3 bolts, rings. *FA: Arno and Mark Ilgner*

S R32. Birthday Boy 10a
Left-facing flake past roof. 4 bolts, chain anchors. *FA: Joey Redman*

S R33. Cedar Tree Massacre 12a
Starts from cedar stump. Crimpy face. 4 bolts, chain anchors. *FA: Emmanuel Lacoste*

The Dynamic Wall

This area starts as the trail begins to descend again. Here are some of the more longer and technical routes at the bluff. This area requires some small gear.

M R34. Between Stress And Success 10c
Face to roofs. 6 bolts, anchors. *FA: Terry Parker*

M R35. Between Chance And Choice 10b
6 bolts, last bolt and anchors shared with Stress and Success. *FA: Terry Parker*

M R36. Put The Pain Aside 11c
Face past two short roofs. 8 bolts, eye-bolt anchors. *FA: Walt Wilkinson*

T R37.***Wired For Sound 9
Cable anchors in tree. Goes left over a small overhang. Fun climbing. *FA: Walt Wilkinson*

M R38.**Another Hard Decision 10d
Climb up through the right side of the overhang. 2 bolts, anchors. *FA: Walt Wilkinson*

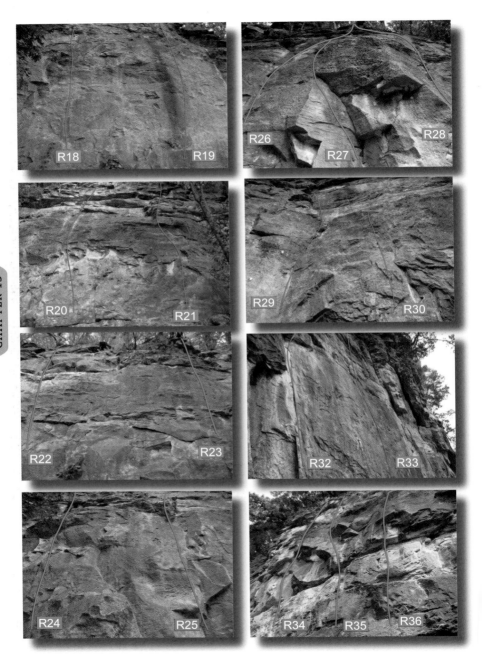

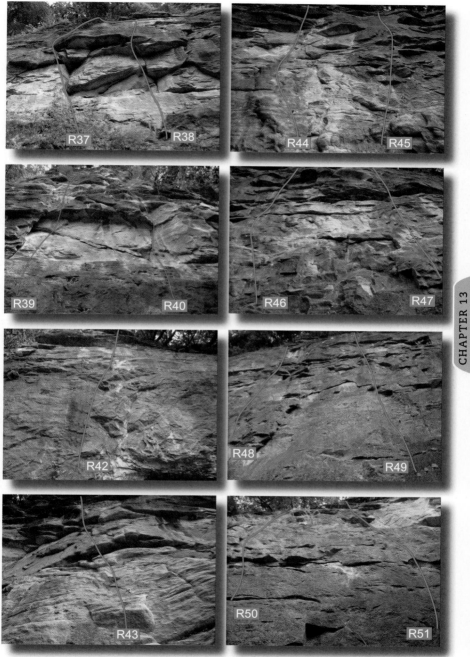

M R39. Traveling Through Time 10b
Right-facing flake past roof. 6 bolts, anchors. *FA: Walt Wilkinson*

S R40.***When Old Friends Meet 10b
Face to ledge, then up a a series of corners and roofs. This is the longest and best route on Dynamic Wall. 6 bolts, anchors. *FA: Walt Wilkinson*

S R41. The Final Frontier 10b
6 bolts, anchor. *FA: Sean Steward*

The Orchard

The Orchard probably has the best concentration of moderate climbs at King's Bluff. It is also on private property, so please be respectful and keep noise and commotion to a minimum.

S R42.*The Renewal 10b
Starts before the trail descends. Face to roof. 4 bolts, chain anchors. Stick clip the 1st bolt. *FA: Scott Griggs*

S R43. **Tennessee Chainsaw Massacre 10b
Climb a right-facing flake and on past several roofs. 3 bolts, chain anchors. *FA: Doyle Parsons*

S R44.*Don't Stop To Smell The Roses 10c
Featured face to a big roof with tufa column. Bring a runner to sling the column and go for the top. 6 bolts, sling a column, chain anchor. *FA: Walt Wilkinson*

S R45.*Open Book Of Wisdom 9
Starts on top of stump. Climb the left wall of a left-facing corner. 5 bolts, chain anchors.

S R46.*No Expectations 9
5 bolts, chain anchors. *FA: Doyle Parsons*

S R47.*The Dagon Meets A Dancer 8+
Blocky holds lead to a left-facing flake. 5 bolts, chain anchors. *FA: Walt Wilkinson*

S R48. Plum Tuckered Out 10d
4 bolts, eye-bolt anchors. *FA: Walt Wilkinson*

S R49. Wonders Never Cease 8+
Block flake to a large flake. 4 bolts, anchors. *FA: Walt Wilkinson*

S R50. Perch Of The Monster 8+
Starts just left of a right-facing corner. 5 bolts, chain anchor. *FA: Walt Wilkinson*

S R51.**Maybe A Little Ether 10b
Face, dihedral, roof. 4 bolts, eye-bolt anchors. *FA: Walt Wilkinson*

S R52.*Daddy's Bolt Ladder 11a
9 bolts, chain anchors. Originally an aid route. *FA: Paul Mitchell*

S R53.**Stack 'Em Three Deep 10c
5 bolts, chain anchors. Trust the rock on the finishing moves. *FA: Walt Wilkinson*

S R54 The Doyle Parsons Project 11b
5 bolts, anchor. Climbs the face directly under Stack Em Three Deep. Pulls a small roof at the top. *FA: Mark Ilgner and Scott Griggs*

S R55. Stands To Reason 10b
4 bolts, anchor. *FA: Terry Parker*

S R56. Hard To Quit 10b
Arete to corner. 5 bolts, anchor. *FA: Terry Parker*

S R57. Barb's Grimace 10d
5 bolts, anchor. *FA: Emmanuel Lacoste*

S R58.***Standing Room Only 10d
3 bolts, chain anchors. A bit run-out near the top. *FA: Terry Parker*

S R59.***The First Plum 10b
4 bolts, chain anchors. Consistently excellent moves. *FA: Walt Wilkinson*

S R60.*Just An Ol' Hole 10c
4 bolts, chain anchors. *FA: Scott Griggs*

S R61.***L.A.G. 9
Go up to flake, then right and around or straight over the top. A must do! 5 bolts, chain anchors. *FA: Emmanuel Lacoste*

S R62. Reachy 8
Slabby face. 3 bolts, anchor. *FA: Suzy Wilkinson*

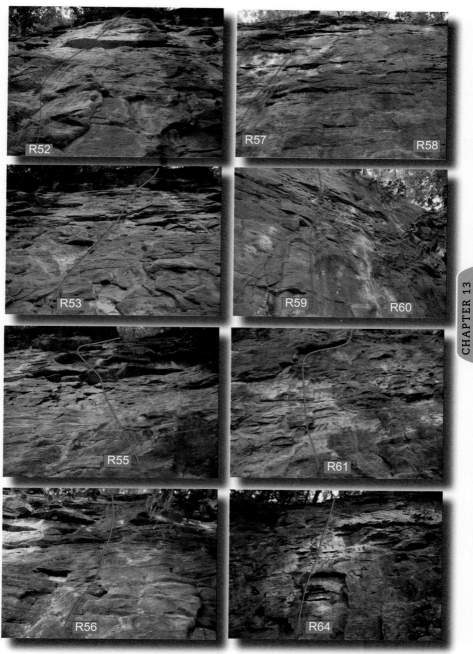

R52 R57 R58 R53 R59 R60 R55 R61 R56 R64

ⓢ R63. Slippery When Wet 7
Slab. 4 bolts, anchor. *FA: Suzy Wilkinson*

ⓢ R64. Ian's Playground 4
4 bolts, anchor. *FA: Joey Redman*

ⓢ R65. Steel Headed Woodpecker 7
Slab. 4 bolts, anchor. *FA: Suzy Wilkinson*

ⓢ R66. Charlotte's Web 7
Slab. 7 bolts, anchor. *FA: Suzy Wilkinson*

ⓢ R67.*Pop Off 6
Good warm up for the area. 4 bolts, chain anchors. *FA: Paul Mitchell*

ⓢ R68.*Poison Ivy 8
5 bolts, anchors. *FA: Paul Mitchell*

ⓢ R69. Slip Sliding Away 8
Starts just before trail heads right and down. 4 bolts, anchor.

High Water Wall

This area has a few outstanding longer routes.

M R70. Knee Knocker 11b
Overhanging corner past roof to ledge. Anchors on ledge. *FA: Walt Wilkinson and Suzy Wilkinson.*

ⓢ R71. Undeterminable Monster 11c
Short arête to steep face. 4 bolts, chain anchors. *FA: Walt Wilkinson*

ⓢ R72. Yellow Streak 11b
Overhanging face. 5 bolts, anchor. *FA: Mark Ilgner and Scott Griggs*

ⓢ R73.**Drainpipe 11a
6 bolts, cable anchors. *FA: Walt Wilkinson*

ⓢ R74. Heartache 10a
Starts at a cave at ground level. 4 bolts, chain anchors. *FA: Suzy Wilkinson / Walt Wilkinson*

M R75. Army Ants 10b
Climb a face t the right margin of a roof. 5 bolts, chain anchors. *FA: Walt Wilkinson*

ⓢ R76. Bloody Knuckles 9
3 bolts, chains. *FA: Emmanuel Lacoste*

ⓢ R77. Lions And Tigers And Bears Oh My! 9
3 bolts, chain anchors. *FA: Suzy Wilkinson*

The Beach

This area lies where the rock reaches the river. During winter, this is a popular area since it receives plenty of sunshine and stays warm. During summer, you can take a quick dip in the river to cool off. You will attract boating crowds from the Cumberland River if you climb here in the summer.

ⓢ R78. Stahlschmidt Warm Up 5
Climbs a face just left of a crack. 2 bolts, anchor. *FA: John Stahlschmidt*

T R79. Singing In The Rain 6 (trad)
Follows an often dirty and overgrown handcrack. *FA: Emmanuel Lacoste*

T R80. Pretty On Video 510b
A thin finger crack that ends at eye bolt anchors. *FA: Walt Wilkinson*

ⓢ R81.**Almost As Mean As Suzy 10b
Steep and fun. 5 bolts, eye-bolt anchors. Stick clip. *FA: Walt Wilkinson*

M R82. Civic Action 11a
4 bolts, cable anchors in tree. *FA: Walt Wilkinson*

ⓢ R83. Big Guns Of Navarone 11c
Vertical face. 8 bolts, anchor. *FA: Walt and Suzy Wilkinson*

ⓢ R84.**The Nagual 12b
A must do route with guaranteed air time. 6 bolts, chain anchors. *FA: Doyle Parsons*

ⓢ R85. Home Improvement 11b
6 bolts, eye-bolt anchors. *FA: Walt Wilkinson*

Politicians Wall

Politicians Wall starts just as the trail heads up from the beach and back into the trees. If The Beach is too hot to climb, this area provides a more shaded and less traveled area.

CHAPTER 13

R81 R82 R83 R84 R85

R86 R87

R88 R89

S R86. As The Crow Flies 11b
6 bolts, anchors. Stick clip. *FA: Walt Wilkinson and Doyle Parsons*

S R87. Magnetic Feet 11d
4 bolts, chain anchors. *FA: Walt Wilkinson*

S R88.*Cheese Eater 11a
3 bolts, chain anchors. *FA: Walt Wilkinson and Doyle Parsons*

S R89. Position Of Power 11a
3 bolts, chain anchors. Route is often overgrown on top during the summer. *FA: Walt Wilkinson and Doyle Parsons*

Horror Wall

Horror Wall is about fifty meters from Politicians Wall, along a thin and often overgrown trail, however the short hike is worth it. The climbs are not only good but rarely see any traffic on even the busiest day.

S R90. Paranoia 11a**
5 bolts, eye-bolt anchors. *FA: Walt Wilkinson / Doyle Parsons*

S R91. Four Winds 11b**
4 bolts, chain anchors. *FA: Walt Wilkinson / Doyle Parsons*

M R92. Necrophobia 11b
4 bolts, cable anchors. *FA: Walt Wilkinson / Doyle Parsons*

Navigator Wall

Navigator Wall lies about 500 yards further along the river. When the river is low, it is easier to walk along the rock bank to the area. To get there, follow the river to the big green sign. At the sign, continue for another 30-50 yards until a faint trail cuts up to the cliff. There is also an old cable that runs down to the river's edge that can be used as a guide. If you want superb and secluded climbing on some of the longest routes at King's Bluff, then Navigator Wall is the best place to go.

M R93. Shoot The Rapids 10b R
3 bolts, chain anchors. *FA: Walt Wilkinson*

S R94. Any Port In A Storm 11b
6 bolts, chain anchors. *FA: Walt Wilkinson*

S R95. Rudder A' Midship 5.11a
4 bolts, chain anchors. *FA: Walt Wilkinson / /Suzy Wilkinson*

M R96. Man Overboard 9+**
1 or 2 bolts, chain anchors. *FA: Walt Wilkinson / Suzy Wilkinson*

M R97. Walk The Plank 10d
3 bolts, shared anchors. *FA: Walt Wilkinson / Terry Parker*

M R98.*Cracked By A Bludgeon 9
2 bolts, eye-bolt anchors. *FA: Walt Wilkinson*

S R99. Crow's Nest 9+
4 bolts, cable anchors. *FA: Walt Wilkinson*

M R100. Keel Hauled 11b
4 bolts, cable anchors. *FA: Walt Wilkinson / Suzy Wilkinson*

M R101.*Cast Adrift 9
4 bolts, cable anchors. *FA: Walt Wilkinson*

S R102. Backstabber 9+
5 bolts, chain anchors. *FA: Walt Wilkinson*

View from Black Mountain
Photo: Paul Mashburn

BLACK MOUNTAIN 14
chapter

PARKING

WEATHER

Black Mountain is a cluster of rock formations sprinkled along a ridgeline, similar to Sandrock or Rocktown. Compared to other areas in the guide, it is a minor one, but as is often the case, it offers a different and enjoyable diversion for the adventuresome climber.

The routes are fairly short, usually 25' to 80', and the rock is varied: pockets, cobblestones, slots, and slopers are the general rule. Black Mountain was developed in the late 1980's by a small group of Knoxville climbers, including Glenn Ritter and Tony Robinson. Now it is almost exclusively a toproping area, though there is some talk of restoring and replacing some of the bolts and anchors that were removed in the early 90's, pending the implementation of a new climbing management plan.

As an aside, I have found it a little odd that Black Mountain has not become a major bouldering destination, as it has much in common with other boulderfields in the region such as Stone Fort and Horsepens 40.

Location and Directions

Black Mountain lies west of Knoxville, off of I-40, near the towns of Crossville and Rockwood. From I-40, get off at the Crab Orchard exit, turn south onto Bat Town Road and follow it for 1.5 miles to a three-way intersection. Turn left onto Owl Roost Road and continue to a split. Stay straight onto Black Mountain Road and follow it up Black Mountain. Park at a pulloff a few hundred yards before the radio tower if you wish to climb at the Front Area. For the Back Area, park at the base of the tower.

Camping

Camping at Black Mountain is not permitted.

Luxuries

Crossville is a sizeable little town and should have everything you need.

Emergency Services

Simply dial 911

Regulations

At one time, Black Mountain was owned by the United Methodist Church, which graciously allowed the area to remain open to the general public. It was recently purchased by the Tennessee Parks and Greenways association, so climbing and other recreation opportunities are assured. The TPGA is in the process of formulating a climbing management plan, which may include a provision for the use of fixed anchors on a limited scale. For now, take some long pieces of webbing or sections of rope for setting up topropes. Black Mountain also lies along Section 5 of the Cumberland Trail, so there are many options for hiking and loop trails that meander around some of the historical sites in the area.

FYI

Black Mountain is a very pretty area, and a botanist's dream come true, with many different species of lush ferns, pitcher plants and other flora.

Cliff Layout

Black Mountain is essentially several clusters of boulders and rock formations. Just take a rack, a rope, some long slings (a crashpad?) and explore. Climb whatever looks appealing.

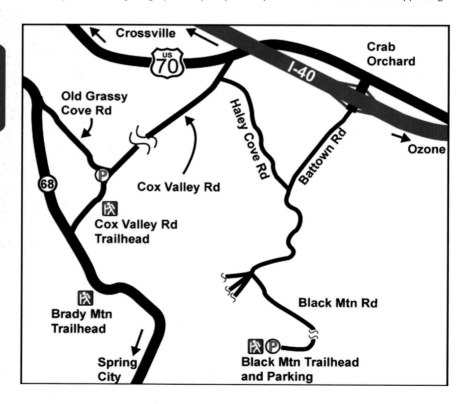

CLIMBING GYM LIST

Rainy days are bound to happen. Here's a list of gyms in the three major cities of the region - Chattanooga, Knoxville and Nashville.

CHATTANOOGA

DIRECTIONS

TBA Gym
3804 St. Elmo Avenue Suite 102
Chattanooga, TN 37409
(423) 822-6800 www.tbagym.com

Urban Rocks Gym
1007 Appling Street Chattanooga, TN 37406
(423) 475-6578 www.urbanrocksgym.com

High Point Climbing and Fitness
215 Broad Street Chattanooga, TN 37402
www.highpointclimbing.com

NASHVILLE

Climb Nashville
3630 Redmon St #1 Nashville, TN 37209
(615) 463-7625 www. climbnashville.com

The Crag at Cool Springs
121 Seaboard Ln Franklin, TN 37067
(615) 661-9444 www.iloverockclimbing.com

The Ascent
831 Park Ave Murfreesboro, TN 37129
(615) 796-6545 www.climbyourrock.com

KNOXVILLE

The Climbing Center at River Sports Outfitters
2918 Sutherland Ave Knoxville, TN 37919
(865) 523-0066
www.riversportsoutfitters.com/climbing-center

Fall Creek Falls
Photo: Lori Walden

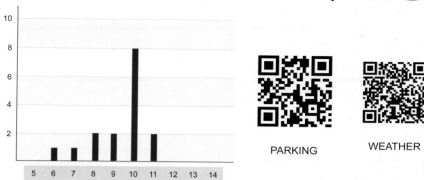

PARKING   WEATHER

Fall Creek Falls State Resort Park, which lies between Pikeville and Spencer, Tennessee, is a fully developed park, complete with swimming pools, campgrounds, nature trails, bike paths and a golf course. It also happens to be situated in one of the most scenic and spectacular areas of the Cumberland Plateau, and is home to 256' high Fall Creek Falls, the tallest waterfall in the eastern United States.

History

There's not a great deal of documented climbing information on Fall Creek, though it seems that it has been used for years by local camps, schools and church groups, primarily for rappelling and toprope climbing.

Location and Directions

There are two entrances to Fall Creek Falls State Park: the North Entrance and the South Entrance.
The North Entrance: From Pikeville, Tennessee, take TN 30 northwest to the park entrance on the left. From Spencer, take TN 30 southeast to the park entrance on the right.
The South Entrance: From Spencer, Tennessee, take TN 111 south, to the park entrance on the left. From Dunlap, take US 127 north to TN 8. TN 8 turns into TN 111, and the entranceios on your right.

Camping

There are over 200 campsites at Fall Creek, spread over three campgrounds. All of the sites have tables, grills, water and electrical hookups, as well as central shower facilities. Campers must register at the check-in station. There are no primitive campsites, except those along the Upper or Lower Cane Creek Overnight Loop Trails. Phone the park headquarters at (423) 881-3297 or 1-800-250-8611.

Luxuries

Fall Creek has an inn, restaurants and lodges, which sleep groups of twenty. Work on your golf game on the award-winning 18 hole, 72 par (whatever that means...) golf course. Phone for reservations at 1-800-250-8610. The golf pro shop number is (423) 881-5706.

Regulations

Climbers must fill out a registration and release at the park headquarters. The release also details where climbing is allowed within the park. There are bluffs, overlooks and cliffline all over the park, but in essence, no climbing is allowed at, or within 300 yards of Fall Creek Falls, Piney Falls, or Cane Creek Falls. Most areas can be accessed with written permission from the park office, however. The Ranger in the area is Ray Cutcher, who is also a climber. Look him up when you get there for the lowdown. The following is a list of rules and regs for climbing in the Park.

1. No rappelling or climbing at Fall Creek Falls, Piney Falls, Cane Creek Falls, or within three hundred yards either side of the waterfalls. These falls areas may be climbed or rappelled with special written permission the park manager or his designate.
2. Climbing and rappelling may be done anywhere in the park with the exception of areas where danger might exist to other park visitors. This however does not mean that climbing is prohibited if the area chosen by the climber might be visited by other park visitors. This simply means that areas that are regularly visited with attractions other than climbing are to be avoided.
3. Protection devices, such as pitons, bolts, cables, or any other device that causes permanent damage is not to be used. Exceptions will be made in certain cases, but must be permitted first by park officials. Failure to comply with this rule can result in permission for future climbs to be denied. No exceptions will be made for rappelling.
4. It is the policy of the park to require that individuals planning to participate in climbing or rappelling activities check in at Park Headquarters before and after the activity.
5. All climbers and rappellers must be off the rocks one hour before sunset. No overnight camping allowed except at designated areas.
6. Any incidents resulting in personal injury or damage to property must be reported to the superintendent or other park official.
7. The permit must be carried on the individual at all times during the activity.

FYI

A popular climbing spot is Millikan's Overlook, named for noted ornithologist Dr. Glen Millikan, who fell to his death while collecting bird egg specimens. If anyone has any additional info on climbing at Fall Creek Falls, please forward it to me at the address on the inside cover.

THE TENNESSEE PALISADES

The Tennessee Palisades are located at the mouth of the Cane Creek Gorge, across from Buzzard's Roost. To get there from I-40, take highway 111 south from Cookeville, Tennessee. Pass through Sparta, then turn left (east) on highway 284. Turn left on highway 30 approximately 5 miles to the park road sign.

It's best to park just outside the park boundary and walk the fire road that is on the west side of the road just inside the park boundary. Walk about 10 minutes to the field. Walk across the field past the shooting range, staying to the left of the range, and continue in pretty much in the same direction. As the terrain drops off on either side, try to stay on the ridge. Continue down a short hill, staying on the ridge, looking for the drop-off to the left. The rappel spot is a small rock platform with the perfect rap tree sticking out at a 45 degree angle over the void. This rap route follows Rock-a-Billy King. There are several watershed gullies that can be used to approach the cliff but rapping in is easier. Approximate approach time from vehicle to rap is 15 to 20 minutes along mostly level terrain.

Be sure to bring two 50 meter ropes, minimum, because it's about a 160' rap. It may

CHAPTER 15

be difficult to locate the rap tree the first time, but if you go too far you will come to the waterfall. From here you can either go back up a bit and look for the tree, or rappel from the left side of the falls. The easiest way out is to climb Rock-a-Billy King and follow the same route as the approach. If you wish to hike out, follow the cliff past Double D and ascend the watershed to join the ridge mentioned earlier.

Introduction

From Jeff Dopp, who graciously provided this information:
"Sometime in the fall of 1996 my friend Frank and I were on our way to Buzzards Roost on the loop road at Fall Creek Falls. Frank was looking across the gorge at some big cliffs and told me to pull over. We stood at an overlook and just gawked for a while. A passing Ranger told us those cliffs were called the "Palisades", and, noticing our gear, informed us that we needed to register at the Main Office before climbing in the park. He also said that we needed an overnight pass to go to the Palisades.

In the months that passed after this day we studied road maps and topos for the location and best approach to these cliffs . We discovered a fire road in the back of an abandoned campground just outside the park boundary that accessed a park road that led to a watershed that appeared to lead to where we thought the cliff may be. Our first attempt was a bit of a bushwhack, but as we followed the stream down consecutively steeper terrain we finally emerged on a large rock platform at the brink of a 100' waterfall.

To either side there was beautiful rock - we had found Mecca ! We rapped in and pretty much rubbernecked all afternoon. Realizing the late hour, we looked for the most obvious line out, a prominent dihedral that led to the top. Leading, I reached a ledge about 40' from the top with a tree, and spotted to my dismay, an ancient piece of webbing about two feet up the tree and strangling it. This was probably the oldest bit of sling I'd ever seen! Oh well, so much for the first ascent. Since that day, we have yet to find any trace of previous visitors, and we've tried to leave none. As far as we know, all of these routes are first ascents. Some follow cracks or corners and it's quite possible that someone has climbed them. Palisades is a wonderful place to climb, especially for those looking for a bit of adventure. Treat the area with respect and leave no trace."

Palisades Main Wall

T 1. Woody 8
Follow obvious crack to a tree ledge. *FA: Jeff Dopp and Frank Jackson, 1997*

T 2. Atomic Fireball 11a
Climb ledges to gain a crack to a small right-facing dihedral. Follow crack to tree ledge. *FA: Jeff Dopp and Frank Jackson, 1997*

T 3. Red Road 10 R
Climb the center of a large aroowhead shaped formation. Follow gorgeous red rock to the tree ledge. *FA: Jeff Dopp and Frank Jackson, 1997*

T 4. Pappy's Corner 7
Climb the obvious left-facing dihedral to ledge/top.

T 5. Granny's Biscuits 10
Climb small corners and face just right of Pappy's. *FA: Jeff Dopp and Frank Jackson, 1997*

T 6. Butter Beans 10
Climb the face 10' right of Granny's Biscuits. *FA: Jeff Dopp and Frank Jackson, 1997*

7. Jackwood 10+
Start at the base of an obvious off-width chimney. Step right and face climb to a small gold corner then straight up to the rim. *FA: Jeff Dopp and Frank Jackson, 1997*

8. M.O.'s 10+
Follow a shallow, indistinct, left-leaning corner to its end, then follow the face to the rim. *FA: Jeff Dopp and Frank Jackson, 1997*

9. Family Man 10
Start: 20' left of Gordita and climb straight to the rim. *FA: Jeff Dopp and Frank Jackson, 1997*

10. ***Gordita 9
Climb the beautiful crack straight up for 135'! *FA: Jeff Dopp and Frank Jackson, 1997*

11. The Flake Route 11
Locate a chimney just left of Cookie. Face climb just left of the chimney, step over a bulge and climb to the right-arching flake above. Climb the flake, pull past a thin crack and face climb to a tree ledge. *FA: Jeff Dopp and Frank Jackson, 1997*

12. **The Cookie 10c
This is the 30' tall "cookie shaped" boulder with a crack in the center. Climb the crack and continue up the headwall, past a horizontal, and on to a tree ledge. *FA: Jeff Dopp and Frank Jackson, 1997*

13. Sorry Rocky 10
Previously inhabited by an unhappy flying squirrel.
Start from a ledge on the left side of the waterfall. Climb the corner to a huge roof. Traverse left to a ledge, then step up and right to a crack. Fly to the top. *FA: Jeff Dopp and Frank Jackson, 1997*

Right Side of Waterfall

14. ***Rock A Billy King 9
Locate a cave just to the right of the waterfall. Walk about 100' right of the cave. Climb cracks and face to a right-facing gold dihedral. Climb the corner for 15' to a horizontal crack leading across the left face. Step left around the corner and climb to a large hanging flake. Step onto the flake and follow the arete to the top and the main rap station. *FA: Jeff Dopp and Frank Jackson, 1997*

15. Double D 8
Start at the extreme right edge of the Big Bowl, just before the walk out. Climb flakes to a crack and follow the crack to a ledge at the base of the large dihedral with a big hueco on the left wall. Climb the dihedral to a ledge and rap off or exit right. *FA: Jeff Dopp and Frank Jackson, 1997*

16. Moist Gift 6
Turning the corner to the descent gully, look to the left. Face climb to a ledge, then follow a left-arching off-width to the same ledge as Double D. *FA: Jeff Dopp and Frank Jackson, 1997*

Continue walking right to an area named Genesis. There are no route descriptions but a topo has been included.

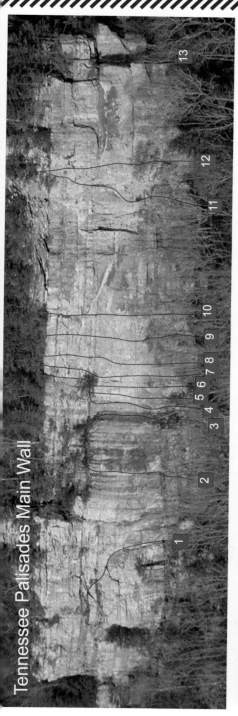

Tennessee Palisades Main Wall

Tennessee Palisades - Genesis Wall

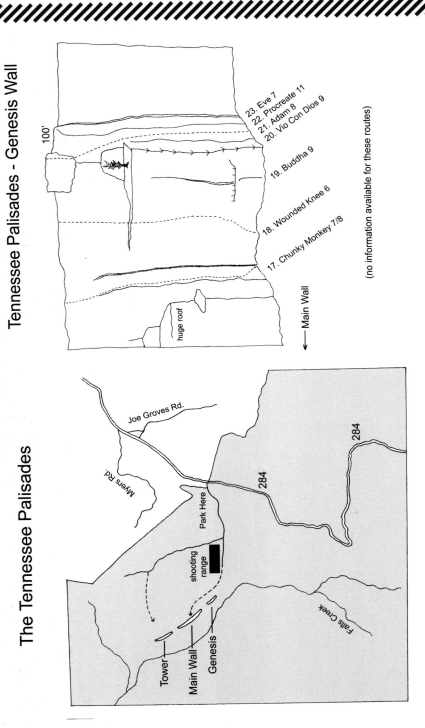

100'

23. Eve 7
22. Procreate 11
21. Adam 8
20. Vio Con Dios 9

19. Buddha 9

18. Wounded Knee 6

17. Chunky Monkey 7/8

(no information available for these routes)

huge roof

← Main Wall

The Tennessee Palisades

Joe Groves Rd.

Myers Rd.

Park Here

shooting range

284

284

Falls Creek

Tower

Main Wall

Genesis

The Tennessee Palisades as seen from Buzzard's Roost

Photo: Jeff Dopp

Cane Creek Falls, Savage Gulf
Photo: Lori Walden

SAVAGE GULF

STONE DOOR

PARKING

WEATHER

Savage Gulf State Natural Area lies just south of Fall Creek Falls, and is another fairly undocumented area for the adventurous explorer to visit. Originally acquired in 1973 to protect and preserve one of the last stands of virgin timber in the United States, the park now encompasses over 12,000 acres, and contains 55 miles of trails and ten primitive campgrounds. It is an excellent place to take novice climbers to learn the rudiments of toprope setups.

History

The main climbing at Savage Gulf has occurred at the Great Stone Door, a prominent cleft in the bluff used by Indians to access the top from the valley floor. When you visit Savage Gulf, you will see miles of cliffline, but bear in mind that much of the rock is of poor quality, so choose wisely. In some ways, the choice is made for you, since climbing is restricted to certain areas.

Vanderbilt University has used the Stone Door as part of its outdoor education program for many years, as a place to teach beginning climbing and rappelling. There are many undocumented established routes, usually following obvious lines, but a large portion of the rock is loose and blocky.

Location and Directions

There are two entrances to Savage Gulf, and each has a ranger station.
The Savage Gulf Entrance- From Dunlap, follow TN 8/111 to a left turn onto TN 399. The entrance will be a few miles down on the right.
The Stone Door Entrance- From McMinnville, follow TN 56 to Beersheba Springs. Turn left on a side road marked with a state park sign and follow it to a fork. Bear right to the entrance/ranger station.

To get to the base of the routes, scramble down through the Door to the bottom. The topo (reprinted here courtesy of Chris Hall) begins here.

Camping

Savage Falls Camp, Stage Road Camp, Sawmill Camp, and Stone Door Camp all offer nice campsites. Stop at the ranger station for information.

Luxuries

McMinnville is probably the closest town of any size.

Emergency Assistance

The Savage Gulf Ranger Station	(931) 779-3532
The Stone Door Ranger Station	(931) 692-3887

Regulations

All climbers and hikers should be out by sundown. Camping is allowed only in established campgrounds. Check at the ranger stations for updated information.

Cliff Layout

Please refer to the map and topo.

T 1. His Majesty 5
Climb ledges and bulges to a tree. 60'

T 2. Vanderbilt Wall Area 5.5 to 5.8
Toprope any one of several obvious lines to the rim. 65'

T 3. Overhang Direct 7
Follow a crack through an obvious overhang. 65'

T 4. Rude Awakenings 11
Climb a thin finger crack in the left wall of a prominent dihedral, to a tree ledge. 50' *FA: Roger Fleming FFA: Arno Ilgner and Mark Ilgner*

T 5. Monster Movie 9
Start: Just right of Rude Awakenings. Follow a wide crack. As it curves to join Black Widow, continue up a thin crack and overhangs to the ledge. 50' *FA: Steve Anderson and Arno Ilgner*

T 6. Black Widow 8
Follow a corner/crack to the top. 50'

T 7. Cornflake Crack 5
Climb a crack in the right wall of the dihedral to the tree ledge. 50'

T 8. Chimney 5
Start: Behind a large block. Climb the obvious chimney to the top. 120'

T 9. Campsite Dihedral 10
Climb the left-hand corner and crack to a ledge. Continue on steeper ground to the top. 145' *FA: Arno Ilgner and Steve Anderson*

T 10. The Last Pin 9
Start: Just right of Campsite Dihedral. Climb to join Campsite Dihedral, then continue to the ledge. 45'

T **11. Horny Toad 6**
Follow the outside edge of the Campsite Dihedral to the ledge. 35'

T **12. Hard Up 10**
Start: On the ledge above Campsite Dihedral. Continue straight up the face to the top. 60'
FA: Arno Ilgner and Steve Anderson

There is an easy scramble just right of Hard Up that provides access to the top of the cliff.

T **13. High and Dry 9**
Start: 45' right of Campsite Dihedral
P1: Climb to a large ledge with a bolt belay. 30' (5.9)
P2: Move right and up through a rotten overhang. Continue up and slightly right, step left to a ledge beneath a large block. Traverse right past a horn, step left to a belay. 60' (5.6)
P3: Wander to the top. 30' (5.6) *FA: Bernie Ilgner and Kenny Parker*

T **14. Directissima 5**
Start: 25' right of High and Dry
P1: Climb a corner to the large ledge. 25' (5.5)
P2: Follow a bushy chimney to a ledge. 50'
P3: Continue up a slightly overhanging dihedral to the top. 40' *FA: Arno Ilgner and Bernie Ilgner* Note: Can be done in one long pitch.

T **15. The Nose 5**
This is the popular route of the area.
P1: Climb the first pitch of Directissima
P2: Step right and up to a sloping ramp. Climb past the overhang, then left past a small tree. Continue to the rim. *FA: Kenny Parker and Arno Ilgner*

1. Foster Falls
2. Savage Gulf / Stone Door

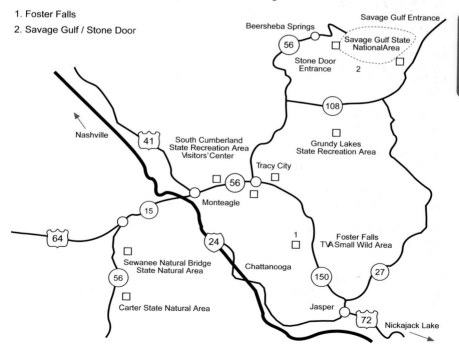

CHAPTER 16

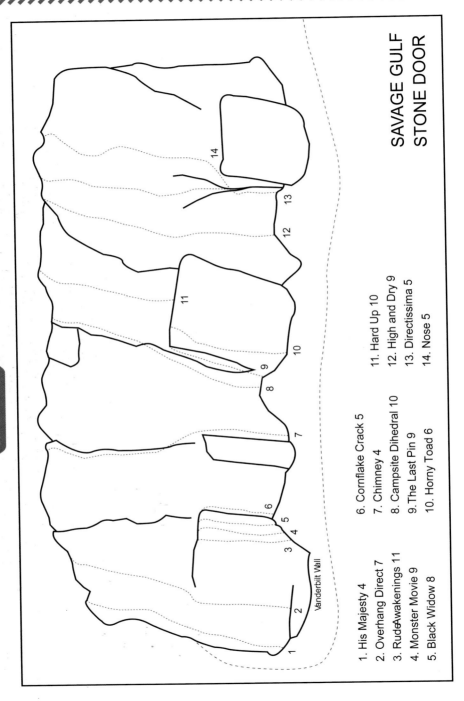

SAVAGE GULF
STONE DOOR

1. His Majesty 4
2. Overhang Direct 7
3. RudeAwakenings 11
4. Monster Movie 9
5. Black Widow 8

6. Cornflake Crack 5
7. Chimney 4
8. Campsite Dihedral 10
9. The Last Pin 9
10. Horny Toad 6

11. Hard Up 10
12. High and Dry 9
13. Directissima 5
14. Nose 5

Vanderbilt Wall

SCC

SOUTHEASTERN CLIMBERS COALITION

www.seclimbers.org

I hope that you have enjoyed this book, and that it inspires you to get out and explore the great climbing opportunities that we have in the Deep South. In addition, hopefully it will inspire you to GET INVOLVED. The Dixie Cragger's Atlas is a avid supporter of both the Southeastern Climber's Coalition and The Access Fund. Both organizations are working daily for YOU - influencing legislation on a state, local and national level, buying climbing areas, sponsoring trail days, maintaining fixed anchors

's Race Track
o: Charles Sutherland

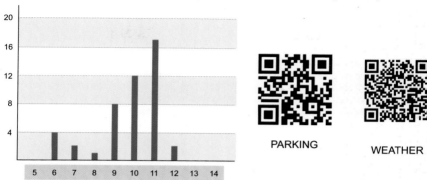

PARKING

WEATHER

Devil's Racetrack is an obvious series of rock fins on the east side of I-75, between Jelico and Knoxville, Tennessee, near Cove Lake State Park and the town of Jacksboro. The area has a variety of traditional gear routes and sport climbs in all grades, making it an excellent outing for climbers of all skill levels. Vaguely reminiscent of West Virginia's Seneca Rocks, the rock is solid for the most part, and the bolts and rap anchors seem to be well placed. The routes that go to the top end at an airy, knife edge ridge with excellent views (of the interstate). Is it a destination crag? No, but worthy of a visit or two.

History

History is somewhat spotty, but it seems that Knoxville locals Bob Cormany, Craig Stannard and Stan Wallace climbed a bit here in the 1970's. In later years, it is likely that prolific first ascensionists Glenn Ritter, Kenny Campbell and Tony Robinson left their mark as well. It seems that with the discovery of the nearby Obed and Clear Creek, activity at Devil's Racetrack slowed down for a number of years, but there has been some recent new activity.

Location And Directions

Take the Caryville exit off of I-75 (exit #134). Take Veteran's Memorial Highway for .5 miles, following signs for Cove Lake State Park. Take the first left turn into the visitor's center. The park visitor's center has facilities and local information. The camping is just off the main Park Loop road.
From the camping area, take a right onto Loop Road. Continue past Ward, Jackson, and Bruce Gap roads. Bruce Gap has a 4 way stop and is also known as Butter and Eggs Road. Go .3 miles past Butter and Eggs Road, and make a left on a dirt road. The road is just past 319 Loop Road, and is between a run down house with turkeys and chickens in the yard and a fairly nice newer house with a red tin roof. Go .2 miles on the gravel road to the parking area. The parking area is at a bend in the road, where a dirt road is blocked off by large boulders to prevent vehicle access. There are two dirt roads after the boulders. The right one ends at a creek and the bushwhack bak up is miserable. Better to take the left road, which parallels the creek for about half a mile. Look for a creek crossing at a place where the creek is wider, with large boulders in it, then head uphill via a steep, eroded trail, to the base of the cliffs. Follow the cliff face a couple hundred yards to the left (north) to get to the prominent rock fins that you can see from the highway.

Camping

The nearest camping area is Cove Lake State Park. It is mostly an RV park, so it isn't very scenic, but it has great facilities, with hookups and picnic tables at every site, showers, swimming pool, tennis courts, etc. There is no camping allowed at the cliff or parking area.

Luxuries

The nearest town is Jacksboro, which has a pretty fair selection of food and supplies. Just head northeast a couple of miles on US2 Cove Lake visitors can enjoy badminton, shuffleboard, horseshoes, field games, volleyball, playgrounds, ping-pong, tennis, and many other activities including a paved walking and bicycling trail. Recreation equipment is available on a free checkout system at the boat dock in the summer months or in the park office during the winter months.

Emergency Assistance

Dial 911
Cove Lake State Park   (423) 566- 9701
Note: Devil's Racetrack is not a part of Cove Lake State Park. Rescue or emergency assistance is likely to be carried out by local Caryville or Jacksboro fire services.

Regulations

None at this time. Devil's Racetrack lies along the Cumberland Trail, so hikers, daytrippers and birdwatchers also use the area. Act accordingly. Cove Lake State Park has no jurisdiction over the private land used to access the cliffs.

FYI

Parking and access leaves a bit to be desired. There have been quite a few instances of vandalism and break-ins, so don't leave anything of value in your car. It seems that bored locals will vandalize a car simply out of spite, regardless of any valuables that might be contained within.

The Cumberland Trail trailhead hiking directions are provided at the Cove Lake State Park visitor's center, but the trail actually leads several strenuous miles away from the start of the climbs. The trail ends up at the top of the climbs and then it is necessary to scramble down a gully to the base. It is easier to come in at the bottom as described.

Route Information

This route guide was provided by Kenny Campbell and Rusty Deal, from an old Knox Rocks newsletter. Additional information was provided by John Nowell and Andy Weltner.

CHAPTER 17

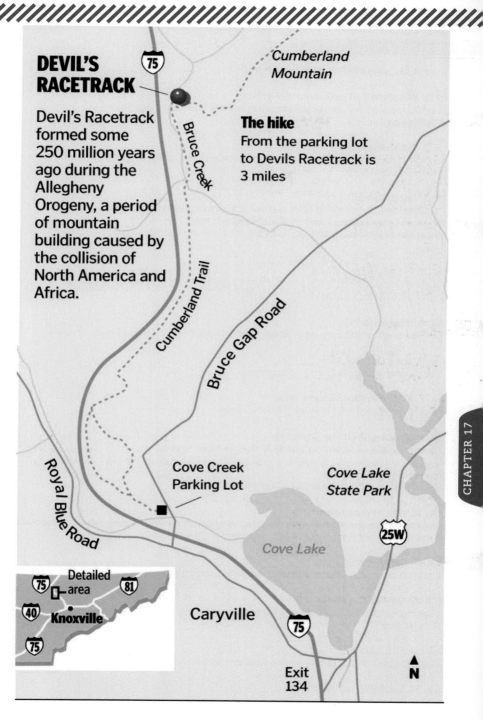

DEVIL'S RACETRACK

75

Devil's Racetrack formed some 250 million years ago during the Allegheny Orogeny, a period of mountain building caused by the collision of North America and Africa.

Cumberland Mountain

The hike
From the parking lot to Devils Racetrack is 3 miles

Bruce Creek

Cumberland Trail

Bruce Gap Road

Royal Blue Road

Cove Creek Parking Lot

Cove Lake State Park

25W

Cove Lake

Detailed area

75 · 81

40 · Knoxville

75

Caryville

75

Exit 134

N

Routes are listed right to left (West to East)

🔲 1. Welcome To The Jungle 11d (mixed)
The first route on the obvious overhanging nose of the main spire. Shares the 2nd pitch with Russian One-Step.

🔲 2. Green Eggs & Ham 8
Just left of the Jungle, work through some loose rock to a notch behind a flake and continue to belay on One Step.

🔲 3. Sonic Temple 8
P1: Climb face to a large lie-back and belay from fixed anchors on ledge.
P2: Move left at big crack and continue straight to top.
Variation: Frayed Knot 10 R/X. From the right end of the belay ledge, climb up a thin flake.

🅢 4. ***Lucy In The Sky 9
Follow the obvious bolt line for 150' of fun! Finish at chains or continue to top and rap off eye bolts. (9 bolts, chains)

🅢 5. *Gargoyle 11d
Thin finger crack and long stem. Shares anchor with Trick-or-Treat. (5 bolts, chains)

🅢 6. Trick Or Treat 10b
Slightly overhanging crack. (5 bolts, chains)

🅢 7. Malice In Wonderland 10b/c
Face route left of Trick Or Treat. (4 bolts, shuts)

🅢 8. Dancing With The Devil 11b
Thin steep face. Shares anchor with Malice. (4 bolts, shuts)

🅢 9. Flesh Gordon 11c
Starts 100' uphill from Dancing Chains. (4 bolts, anchor)

🅢 10. **Rumpleforeskin 11c
Starts on ledge above Flesh Gordon, on a steep detached face. Runout on easy ground to the first bolt. Cool position! (6 bolts, chains)

🔲 11. Fat Man's Squeeze 6
Starts on the inside flake of Rumpleforeskin. Classic chimney moves.

🅢 12. Day At The Races 9
Start: 30' uphill of Rumpleforeskin. Scramble up ledge to first bolt. Negotiate way to top. (7 bolts, chains)

🅢 13. ***Little Wing 10b
Start 60' uphill of Day At The Races. Slab to a lie-back. A Must Do! (8 bolts, chains)

🅢 14. Look Ma, No Head! 11b
Follow bolts up an overhanging face, then up easy ground to chains. (5 bolts, chains)
Note: Bring some runners for slinging horns.

🅢 15. Wet Willie 10a
Just left of Look Ma. (5 bolts, chains)

🅢 16. Tree Rash 11c
Thin, hard start. (5 bolts, chains)

South Face (The Alley)

Listed from left to right (West to East)

🆃 17. Psycho Lizards 10a
Start: 30' uphill from the Jungle. Climb face to small roof. Pull roof and continue to top, skirting the edge of the flake.

🅢 18. Zombie Stomp 11c
Pulls through the same roof system as Psycho Lizards. (6 bolts, ends at chains above roof)

🆃 19. Vapor Trail 11a
Climb straight up through the off-width roof crack between Zombie Stomp and Santa Claws.

🆃 20. Santa Claws 10c
Climb short face to a roof with horizontal cracks. Pull roof and head for the tree 70' up.

🆃 21.**Russian One Step 7
P1: Start on obvious ramp-like ledge. Traverse left for 70' to a belay ledge.
P2: Pull bulge and climb nose to top.

🅢 22. Palm Tree 8
Starts at base of the large tree. Clip 5 bolts and rap or lower off tree.

🅢 23. Bounty Hunter 9
Start just right of Palm Tree. Follow short diagonal crack. Move left and belay at a suspicious, dead tree. (5 bolts, dead tree). Note: Back up the belay with some gear.

🆃 24. Great Balls of Fire 7
Follow large diagonal crack. Belay on ledge.

🆃 25. Little Ol' Lady 6
Climb up crack system and belay under a large, overhanging nose. (not pictured)

Moon Rock (No topo)

🆃 26. Moon Doggies 6
Climb up the nose of Moon Rock, clip 2 old pins and belay from chains at top.

🆃 27. Vertical Imbalance 9
Start: Just right of Welcome To The Jungle. Pull through 2 small roofs protected by bolts, then follow the small crack to chains on top.

🆃 28. Kix Tracee 9
Start: 25' left of Vertical Imbalance. Climb up suspect rock and skirt large roof to right. Continue to top.

🆃 29. Natural Lite 7
Start: On the back side of Moon Rock. Climb jugs and sling big horns. Belay from chains.

On the lower wall there are four trad routes:

T **Egocentric 8**
It starts almost in the middle of the wall and pulls a small roof. There are rap anchors on
top.

T **Unnamed 9+**
Starts just right of Egocentric

T **Unnamed 8**
Starts left of Egocentric.

Cracked 8
The huge crack visible from Moon Rock.

There are also two sport routes on the lower slab, put up by Steven Dryer. The left route
is a 9 with a long run-out at the roof at the top. To the right is a 5.8 retrobolt of an old gear
route, beginning in a left-facing dihedral.

Devil's Racetrack - North Face

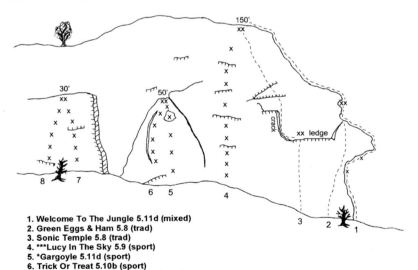

1. **Welcome To The Jungle 5.11d (mixed)**
2. **Green Eggs & Ham 5.8 (trad)**
3. **Sonic Temple 5.8 (trad)**
4. *****Lucy In The Sky 5.9 (sport)**
5. ***Gargoyle 5.11d (sport)**
6. **Trick Or Treat 5.10b (sport)**
7. **Malice In Wonderland 5.10b/c (sport)**
8. **Dancing With The Devil 5.11b (sport)**

Devil's Racetrack - North Face cont'd.

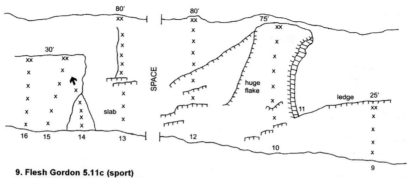

9. Flesh Gordon 5.11c (sport)
10. **Rumpleforeskin 5.11c (sport)
11. Fat Man's Squeeze 5.6 (trad)
12. Day At The Races 5.9 (sport)
13. ***Little Wing 5.10b (sport)
14. Look Ma, No Head! 5.11b (sport)
15. Wet Willie 5.10a (sport)
16. Tree Rash 5.11c (sport)

* Re-printed from a previous edition of the Dixie Cragger's Atlas

Devil's Racetrack - South Face (The Alley)

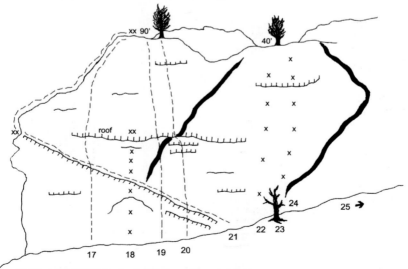

17. Psycho Lizards 5.10a (trad)
18. Zombie Stomp 5.11c (sport)
19. Vapor Trail 5.11a (trad)

20. Santa Claws 5.10c (trad)
21. **Russian One Step 5.7 (trad)
22. Palm Tree 5.8 (sport)

23. Bounty Hunter 5.9 (sport)
24. Great Balls of Fire 5.7 (trad)
25. Little Ol' Lady 5.6 (trad)

Kelly Brown caught between Blue Sky, Green Water (North Clear Creek

OBED/CLEAR CREEK 18
LILLY BLUFF chapter

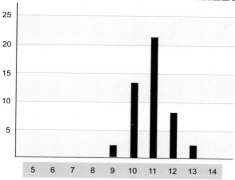

LILLY BRIDGE
PARKING

WEATHER

Many years ago when I was putting together the first Dixie Cragger's Atlas, I made it a priority to include information on the then up-and-coming Obed and Clear Creek. Development was occurring at a feverish pace, the area was huge, the number of routes staggering. I had no idea where to begin. Glenn Ritter provided me with many notes, maps and topos - a great starting point to be sure. The remote nature of the cliffs there, and the fact that I live in Atlanta (four hours away) made the task even more daunting. I was not a local and was worried about the route developers giving up any info for inclusion. Well, my fears were quickly allayed by Kelly Brown, prolific route developer and "Keeper Of All Knowledge" with regards to the Obed. Kelly spent countless hours taking me around, reviewing notes, providing me with updates and new route info. Without his help, along with Greg Houston, Mark Dew, James Gose and others, I'm not sure what I would have done. I am forever grateful.

Fast forward almost fifteen years, and now Kelly has authored his own guidebook to the area titled **The Obed - A Climber's Guide To The Wild And Scenic**, published by Greener Grass Publishing. It is an excellent guidebook, current and complete, with lots of great action photos and route pics. I encourage anyone visiting the Obed to grab a copy.

For this reason, I have included a brief chapter with pertinent details and a section covering Lilly Bluff. This has been done with the first time, occasional or travelling climber in mind. Should you want to visit the other areas, grab a copy of Kelly's book or hike on down and ask around. The locals are friendly and will point you in the right direction.

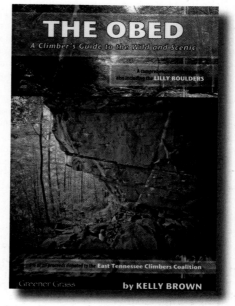

CHAPTER 18

The Obed Wild and Scenic River National Park is nestled in the rugged contours of the Cumberland Plateau, west of Knoxville, Tennessee. It is here that the Obed River and the Clear Creek merge together, tumbling down through deep gorges lined with capstone, forming one of the largest and most recently-developed climbing areas in the Southeast. Typical of the river-carved sandstone of the region, the rock is steep and overhanging. The routes are difficult, pumpy and usually involve a bit of roof climbing, so fitness is a virtue. The majority of routes in the Obed/Clear Creek are sport routes, typically ending at a double bolt or cold shut anchor below the canyon rim, so toprope opportunities are virtually non-existent. There are also quite a few excellent gear routes, mostly in North Clear Creek.

History

Known for its excellent whitewater, the area has drawn hardcore paddling enthusiasts from all over the country for years. It is likely that a few of these paddlers were also climbers and may have done some exploration of the sandstone cliffs above the rivers.

In 1973, Knoxville climber Bob Cormany visited the area on a tip from a University Of Tennessee Entomology professor, who was involved in a spider study on the Obed River. Bob, along with Craig Stannard, Clint Lothrop, and David Maxwell, led or toproped many of the obvious, protectable lines at Clear Creek and Lilly Buttress. At Lilly Buttress, Stan Wallace led the route Rocking Chair. This enthusiastic group routinely camped at the Lilly Boulders pulloff and probably did many of the classic boulder problems that are still enjoyed today, including the classic Welcome to Clear Creek, a stellar handcrack at the far end of Lilly Boulders. This group disbanded in the late 70's, embarking on careers and families and nearly all of them moved away from the Knoxville area.

The cliffs lay dormant throughout most of the 1980's. In 1990, prolific route developers Glenn Ritter and Tony Robinson, both from Knoxville, began exploring the steep sandstone band above the Obed. Not afraid of steep, airy terrain, this pair systematically picked the plum lines, including the classic Tierrany and many others. Offering a wealth of impressive routes on impeccable, white sandstone, the Obed side is well worth the 25 minute hike-in.

It was only a matter of time before an ever-growing crew of motivated climbers descended on the neighboring Clear Creek. The Clear Creek side began development as a mixed crag and most routes at North Clear required natural gear in addition to the bolts. This has changed somewhat in recent years, with new routes being primarily fully bolted. Not surprisingly, the first ascensionists of many of the original lines have returned to fully equip them. These days, a rack of quicks is all you need for a fine day of cragging, nevertheless, there are several worthy traditional crack and corner routes.

The most recent development on the Clear Creek side has been at South Clear, downstream and around the corner from where the creek makes a sharp bend to the left. Outstanding areas such as Blue Crystal, the Image Wall and the Stephen King Library are testimony to the efforts of Kelly Brown, Greg Houston, Rob Turan, James Gose, Bruce Henderson, Glenn Ritter and a handful of other dedicated climbers. There are several "satellite" crags in the Obed/Clear Creek drainage, including the bluff above Lilly Bridge (Lilly Buttress), the Y12 Crag, the Inner Circle and the Lilly Boulders. Oddly enough, Lilly Buttress, the most easily accessible cliff in the park, was not developed until the mid 1990's.

Location and Directions

From Atlanta or Chattanooga, take I-75 North to I-40 West. Exit onto US 27 at Harriman, Tennessee.
From Knoxville, take I-40 West to Harriman.

From Nashville, take I-40 East and exit onto 298 North at Crossville, Tennessee. Follow 298 until it dead-end into 62 and turn right. Go about two miles and turn right on Ridge Road. Follow the directions below for the rest.

From Harriman, follow US 27 North to Wartburg, Tennessee. From Wartburg, take Highway 62 to Lancing. From Lancing, proceed for three miles to Ridge Road on the left, at an obvious sign. Turn left on Ridge Road and follow it into the Park. Specific directions for each climbing area are given from this point, and can be found at the beginning of each section, as well as below.

CLEAR CREEK

After turning onto Ridge Road, follow it for approximately 2.5 miles, to Doc Howard Road, on the left. Follow Doc Howard a few hundred yards to a parking area on the right, in a grassy field. Note: This parking area is provided by the adjacent landowner, as a convenience to climbers. There is a wooden collection box at the entrance, so throw a few bucks in when you park. The trail to the Clear Creek begins at the end of this parking area. For North Clear and the Inner Circle, follow the first obvious descent trail on the right, to the cliff base, following a gully/ramp system. To access South Clear Creek and areas farther downstream, continue along the rim trail, which leads to the prominent point that delineates North Clear and South Clear. Follow the trail to the left and look for a well-worn descent trail on the right after a few hundred yards. This trail comes down next to Shroom and Colorado Boy. Clear Creek access is best figured out using the accompanying maps and diagrams.

Clear Creek is divided into two distinct areas: North Clear and South Clear. As the accompanying map illustrates, the Clear Creek makes a sharp bend to the left midway down the canyon. The cliffline comes to an obvious, prominent point. North Clear is the cliffline upstream from the Point Buttress, while South Clear runs from the point downstream. North Clear and South Clear are further subdivided into small sections, each with its own name and usually containing a high concentration of routes.

NORTH CLEAR CREEK

From the parking area off Doc Howard Road, take the obvious trail into the woods and left along the canyon rim. After a short distance, look for a trail on the right, which is the access trail for North Clear. (For South Clear, stay on the rim trail.) Upon reaching the cliff base, walk right (upstream) to Inner Circle, or left (downstream) for the rest of North Clear.

THE INNER CIRCLE

To reach Inner Circle, take the first descent gully to the right, after leaving the Clear Creek parking area. Upon reaching the cliff base, turn right and walk upstream. The Inner Circle is a compact, steep amphitheater that stays dry in the rain. A 60-meter rope is recommended. The routes are listed right to left.

LITTLE CLEAR CREEK

Park at Lilly Bridge, near the toilets. Follow a rocky trail upstream from the toilets for approximately 100 yards or so. Look for a stream crossing marked by orange tape in a tree. Cross the creek and angle uphill and right, following more tape (?) to intersect the cliff after a few hundred yards.

LILLY BOULDERS

Continue up the hill for a few hundred yards, and look for a hidden pulloff on the right, blocked by several boulders. This is the old pulloff for Lilly Boulders, but parking and camping are no longer allowed. There is a new trail from the Lilly Bluff Overlook parking lot at the top of the hill, to Lilly Boulders.

OBED AND Y12

Proceed from Lilly Bridge to the top of the hill. Just after the crest, there is a parking area/ pulloff on the left to access the overlook balconies atop Lilly Buttress. Drive to the back cul-de-sac and park. Follow the obvious trail toward the overlook for about 200 yards and look for a newly-marked trail to the right. This trail skirts east along the hillside toward the Obed. After about 2/3 mile, look for a piece of orange survey tape on the left, marking a faint footpath on the left. To reach Y12, take this trail down a few ledgy downclimbs and scrambles to the right. You will soon come to a narrow ledge, high above the ground, with a fixed safety rope strung across it. (?) Be very careful here! Note: Dogs should have no problem with this access.
Continue right along the cliff base, passing the first identifiable route. Soon you will come to a wet corner with a waterfall. There are three routes on a ledge to the left, but for the rest of the cliff, cut downhill, away from the cliff base and around the corner.

For the Obed, continue on the main trail, crossing a creek, to reconnect with the old logging road near Arch Rock, out on the ridge/peninsula. For West Obed, turn right and follow the logging road for about ten minutes. An obvious trail skirts down and left along a creekbed to the cliff base. For the Tierrany Wall, turn left and follow the road down almost to the end of the point. Look for a well-worn trail down and right. Scramble down this "dog-friendly" gully to the cliff base and walk right.

LILLY BLUFF

Follow the same directions as above, but do not turn onto Doc Howard Road. Instead, follow Ridge Road down a steep grade, and park at Lilly Bridge, where there are conveniently located toilets. The trail goes up the hillside on the opposite side of the bridge, to the cliff base.

Camping

Camping is not allowed at established overlooks or the Lilly Boulders. The closest camping is at the Nemo Bridge/Norris Campground, which is $7.00 per night and has a great swimming hole. Frozen Head State Park is about 10 minutes west of Wartburg on Highway 62. The campsites are $10.00 per day, and there are clean, hot showers. The most convenient camping is at The Lilly Pad, operated by Del and Marte Scruggs, very gracious local residents. Del has a great setup, with picnic tables and several campsites. There is a fee per night. Pay it 'cause it's worth it. Del's is located along Ridge Road, on the right before heading downhill toward Lilly Bridge.

Luxuries

There are toilets conveniently located at Lilly Bridge and at the Lilly Overlook parking area, just up the hill. Nearby Wartburg features the World's Scariest Hotel (think Norman Bates, but worse...) as well as several good restaurants. Both Harriman and Crossville have a wide selection of hotels, restaurants, laundromats, a hospital and a movie theater.

Emergency Assistance

Dial 911
Morgan County Sheriff's Department   (423) 346-6262
Roane Medical Center (in Harriman)   (423) 882-4141
Obed River Park Headquarters   (423) 346-6294

Regulations

Since the area is a National Park, standard rules and regulations apply: No alcohol is permitted on Park property. Firewood cutting is prohibited. There are fire restrictions during dry periods. The park staff have been proactive in developing and enforcing a "climber friendly" management plan that is currently in place. New route development is done by permit only. In recent years, locals have been replacing non-stainless bolts and anchors. For information, contact the Park Headquarters at 208 North Maiden Street P.O.Box 429 Wartburg, TN 37877. The phone number is (423) 346-6294.

When visiting the Obed-Clear Creek, keep in mind that the park property is nestled in and among private land and homes. The following is an excerpt from a 1994 "Rock and Ice" article by Rob Turan and Glenn Ritter:

"Most of the trails accessing the climbing areas are on private land, which the owners have graciously allowed people to cross. They may not understand climbers, but they do accept them. A word is in order here about Southern etiquette. Don't screw up a good thing by not waving back to local residents (landowners or not) when they wave at you. Better yet, wave first. The people in Wartburg and Morgan County are friendly and generous. Take the time to talk to them. Your friendly attitude can go a long way in preventing animosity toward future climbers."

This is sound advice for visiting all of the climbing areas in this book. Unfortunately, folks from other parts of the country still cling to images of white sheets, burning crosses, moonshiners, inbreeding and scenes from "Deliverance". Fortunately, these cliches have all but vanished and fine Southern hospitality is the rule rather than the exception.

FYI

The Obed, Clear Creek, Daddy's Creek and the Emory River offer some of the finest whitewater boating in the United States, with rapids ranging from Class II to Class V, depending on the water level. There are 18 different paddling trips, covering over 140 miles of water. Highlights include the hairball run of Daddy's Creek as well as the 20-mile wilderness trip on the upper Clear Creek. The Catoosa wildlife management area, adjacent to the park property, offers excellent mountain biking opportunities.
Also of interest is nearby Oak Ridge, home to the American Museum of Science and Energy. During World War II, the federal research facilities at Oak Ridge played a crucial role in the Manhattan Project, producing the high grade enriched uranium for the first A Bomb. In later years, the research focus has expanded to include studies in physics, medicine, quantum mechanics and energy production. Some of the world's brightest minds (and thickest glasses) can no doubt be found at Oak Ridge. Oh yeah, almost forgot...there are one or two pretty good bars in Oak Ridge as well, should you crave a little nightlife action.

CHAPTER 18

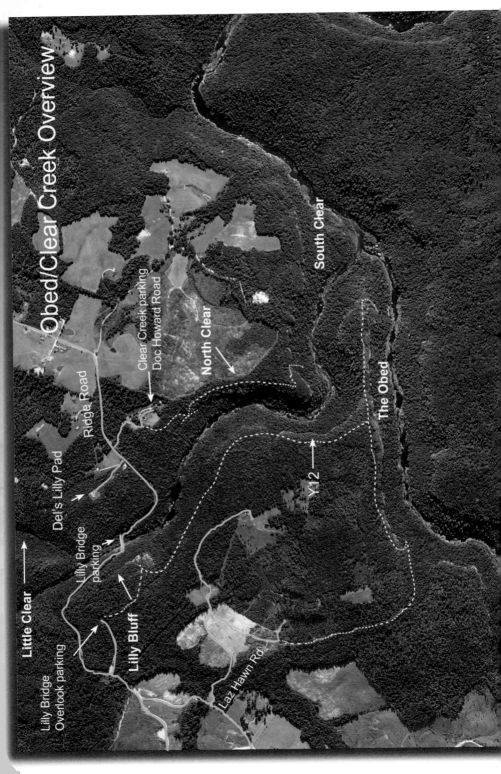

Obed/Clear Creek Overview

Little Clear

Del's Lilly Pad

Ridge Road

Clear Creek parking
Doc Howard Road

North Clear

South Clear

The Obed

Y-12

Lilly Bridge Overlook parking

Lilly Bridge parking

Lilly Bluff

Laz Hawn Rd.

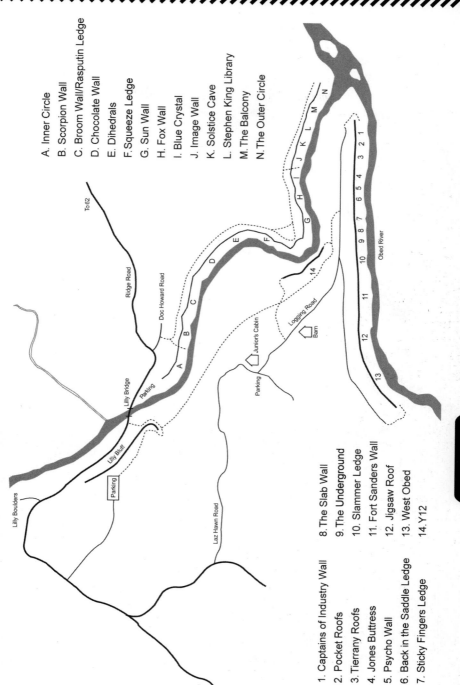

A. Inner Circle
B. Scorpion Wall
C. Broom Wall/Rasputin Ledge
D. Chocolate Wall
E. Dihedrals
F. Squeeze Ledge
G. Sun Wall
H. Fox Wall
I. Blue Crystal
J. Image Wall
K. Solstice Cave
L. Stephen King Library
M. The Balcony
N. The Outer Circle

1. Captains of Industry Wall
2. Pocket Roofs
3. Tierrany Roofs
4. Jones Buttress
5. Psycho Wall
6. Back in the Saddle Ledge
7. Sticky Fingers Ledge
8. The Slab Wall
9. The Underground
10. Slammer Ledge
11. Fort Sanders Wall
12. Jigsaw Roof
13. West Obed
14. Y12

CHAPTER 18

1. Lilly Boulders
2. Lilly Bluff
3. North Clear Creek
4. South Clear Creek
5. Y12
6. Obed River
7. Little Clear Creek

To Frozen Head

Wartburg

To Crossville

62

27

Lancing

62

Ridge Road

Doc Howard Road (gravel)

Clear Creek 3

Lilly Bridge

7

2

1

Genesis Road

To Crossville

Laz Hawn Road (gravel)

5

4

6

Obed River

CHAPTER 18

Cliff Layout

The layout is probably best explained using the photos, topos and maps included. Note: This guide describes most of the obvious and popular routes in the drainage, but some obscure routes may have been left out.

LILLY BLUFF

From the parking area at Lilly Bridge, near the public bathrooms, walk across the bridge and follow an obvious trail up the hill. This trail intersects the cliff base at a tall, prominent wall. This wall is directly below the tourist overlook deck and railing, so climbing is not permitted. Walk right about 200 feet, to an impressive, left-facing corner with a stellar finger crack leading to a roof. The routes are listed left to right.

T 1. **Neanderthal 11d**
Start: In a pretty, left-facing dihedral.
P1: Follow the overhanging finger crack to anchors. (10)
P2: Continue right out blocky roofs on surprisingly good protection, to the top. (11d)

Continue around the corner to the first sport route.

S 2. **Borderline 11d**
Start: 20' right of the corner. Stick clip. Follows a roof flake up high. (7 bolts, shuts)
FA: Mike McKee

S 3. *Alien 10d
Start: Just left of a blocky corner, 15' right of Borderline. High stick clip. (8 bolts, shuts)
FA: Mike McKee

S 4. ***Tarantella 10a**
Start: Just right of Alien, on the adjacent wall. Scamper up the ugly corner for a few moves. Climb just left of the arete. The start is often wet. Unclip the first bolt to prevent rope drag. (9 bolts, shuts) *FA: Lisa McKee*

S 5. **Electric Sky 12a**
Start: Just right of Tarantella. Stick clip. Follow right side of the arete to finish out blocky roofs. (9 bolts, shuts) *FA: Mike McKee*

S 6. *Whippersnapper 11a
Start: Just left of a small cave, on a low angle slab. (9 bolts, shuts) *FA: James Gose*

S 7. **Lounge Lizard 11b**
Start: 30' right of Whipper Snapper, on a slab. Start on a slab. Continue up the left side of an arete and out a roof slot. (10 bolts, shuts) *FA: Bruce Henderson*

S 8. *Rocking Chair 9
Start: 20' right of Lounge Lizard. Climb just right of an ugly right-facing corner to an anchor below the roof. (6 bolts, shuts) Stays dry in rain. The extension out the roof crack above is 11. *FA: Craig Stannard, Bob Cormany*

S 9. Electric Chair 10b/c
Starts just to the right of Dead Baby Ducks. Follow 5 bolts over a small roof to an anchor.

CHAPTER 18

🅢 10. Boogie Man 12d
Start: Just right of a wide chimney/crack, from a ledge. Goes up to and out a flat roof with a fixed quickdraw. (8 bolts, chains at lip) *FA: Kelly Brown*

🅢 11. Clyde The Mega Dude 11b/c
Start: 15' right of Boogie Man. Stays dry in rain. (6 bolts, chain anchor) *FA: Kelly Brown*

🅢 12. *Blasphemy 13b
Starts just right of Clyde. Steep face to a roof with a jagged crack. (7 bolts, anchor) *FA: Kelly Brown*

🅢 13. ***Heresy 11c
Start: Just left of a wide crack, 30' right of Clyde. Stick clip. Stay left of the crack, then out the big roof with fixed draws. (8 bolts, chains) Ironically, the crux is on the lower face. The roof is 10c. Stays dry in rain. *FA: Kelly Brown*

🅣 14. Dead Baby Ducks 11
Starts in the wide chimney just right of Heresy. Continues out the wide roof crack. *FA: Craig Stannard and Bob Cormany, 1970's*

🅢 15. *Wheatward Bound 12b
Start: 15' right of the wide crack. Stick clip. Tackle the big roof, via fixed draws. (7 bolts, chains at lip) Stays dry in rain. *FA: Kelly Brown*

🅢 16. Baccer Spit 11b
Start: Just right of Wheatward Bound. Stick clip. A bouldery start gives way to better holds. (4 bolts, shuts under roof) Stays dry in rain.

🅢 17. Junior's Big Brown Beaver 11d
Start: Just right of Baccer Spit. (4 bolts, anchors) *FA: Kenny Campbell and Junior Campbell.*

🅢 18. Thrifty Mule 11a
Start: 10' right of Junior's. (4 bolts, anchors) Shares anchor with Junior's.

🅢 19. First Laugh 10c
Start: 10' right of Unnamed. (5 bolts, anchors) *FA: Mike McKee*

🅢 20. Last Laugh 10c
Start: Next to First Laugh. (5 bolts, shuts) Shares anchor with First Laugh. *FA: Mike McKee*

🅢 21. Standing Ovation 11c
Start: 10' right of Last Laugh. Starts in some left-facing flake features. (4 bolts, shuts)

Continue walking right for about 100 yards, past a void with no routes, to an arete.

🅢 22. Aneurism 11c
Start: On the left side of the arete. Roughly follow the arete. (8 bolts, shuts) *FA: James Gose*

🅣 23. Mixed Nuts 10a (mixed)
Start: On the face of a right-facing dihedral, just around from Aneurism. Climb past two bolts to a crack. Continue to shuts at a bushy ledge. *FA: Bruce Henderson*

24. Dirty Deeds 10a
Start: 25' right of the dihedral. Climb a steep, smooth brown wall. (4 bolts, shuts)
FA: James Gose

25. Done Dirt Cheap 10a
Start: Just right of Dirty Deeds. (5 bolts, shuts) Shares anchors with Dirty Deeds.
FA: James Gose

26. Drive By 11c
Start: 50' right of Dirt Cheap. Climb a smooth, brown wall. (5 bolts, anchors)
FA: Kenny Campbell

27. **Organized Crime 11d
Start: 12' right of Drive By, next to a single bolt from an abandoned project. Stick clip. A
bouldery, funky start. (5 bolts, shuts) *FA: Mike McKee*

28. *La Familia 12b/c
Start: 10' right of Organized Crime. Stick clip. Another funky start. (6 bolts, anchor)
FA: Kenny Campbell

29. **Yakuza 12b
Start: 6' right of La Familia. (6 bolts, anchor) Shares anchor with La Familia.
FA: Kenny Campbell

30. *Gangsta 12a
Start: 10' right of Yazuka. Angles up and right. (5 bolts, shuts) *FA: Kenny Campbell*

31. **Temporary Insanity 12b/c
Start: Just left of the huge boulder. (4 bolts, anchor) Shares anchor with Gangsta.
FA: Sam Krieg

Continue right around the prominent, huge boulder…

32. *Ode To The Quitter 12b/c
Bouldery down low. (6 bolts, anchors) *FA: Sam Krieg*

33. **Body Hammer 12a
Start: 15' right of the boulder. Stick clip. Bouldery start. (6 bolts, shuts) *FA: Kenny Campbell*

34. **Egyptian 11d
Start: Just right of Body Hammer. High stick clip. (6 bolts, shuts) *FA: Mike McKee*

35. *Osiris 11c
Start: Just right of Egyptian. Scramble up left-facing blocks to start. (6 bolts, anchor)
FA: John Nowell

36. *Paraphernalia 10b/c
Start: 10' right of John's Route. (6 bolts, shuts) *FA: James Gose*

37. Ticks Are For Kids 10a
Start: Just right of Paraphernalia. (7 bolts, shuts) Shares first bolt with Paraphernalia.
FA: James Gose.

38. Ivy League 11b
Start: 10' right of Ticks. Scramble up to the first bolt. (7 bolts, shuts) The fourth bolt is upside down in roof. *FA: James Gose*

39. Evil Weed 11a
Start: Just right of Ivy League. (7 bolts, shuts) Shares anchor with Poison Ivy. *FA: Kenny Campbell*

40. Poison Ivy 11a
Start: 6' right of Evil Weed. Starts on sculpted, pocketed rock. Very pretty. (7 bolts, 2 biner anchor) *FA: James Gose*

41. Crack 11c/d
100' right of Ivy League. A bolted crack - My Heavens! Follows a thin finger crack in a steep wall past 7 bolts to an anchor.

42. **Blade Loafer 10c
Start in a handcrack. Finish in a dihedral/crack. (5 bolts, shuts) *FA: Originally a Stan Wallace trad route done in 1979.*

43. Heiroglyphics 11c
Start: 12' right of Blade Loafer. (6 bolts, shuts) *FA: Mike McKee*

44. *Dinosaur Jr. 10c
Start: 10' right of Heiroglyphics. Stick clip. Layaway in a vertical slot, then finish up a handcrack to a ledge. (5 bolts, shuts) *FA: Stan Wallace and Bob Cormany, 1979*

45. Trickin' The Weasel 11d
Start: 10' right of Dinosaur Jr. (6 bolts, no anchor)

46. Motion Sickness 10b
Start: 10' right of Trickin' The Weasel, near the end of the cliff. Begin in a vertical hand slot. (6 bolts, shuts) *FA: James Gose*

At this point, the cliff is very close to the road. For accessing these last routes, it is easiest to park at the bridge, walk up the road, and scramble up to the cliff base via a short trail. Do not park along the road.

LILLY BOULDERS

This unlikely little bouldering area is tucked neatly out of view on the south hillside above Clear Creek. Essentially a long low cliff band with scattered boulders and formations nearby, the area has become extremely popular with the bouldering set. Problems of all levels of difficulty can be found, but most tend to be on the upper end of the scale, due to the steep, cave-like nature of the boulders.

To get there, drive uphill from Lilly Bluff and Lilly Bridge. Just before the crest of the hill, look for an old pulloff on the right with space for two or three cars. The pulloff is blocked by several large boulders. If there is no room to park, continue up the hill and park at the Lilly Overlook. There is a trail downhill that crosses the road to the boulder field. Camping is not allowed. From the pulloff, cross the creek and follow the trail along the hillside to the boulders. A spot pad is recommended. The entire area is outlined in detail in Kelly Brown's excellent book *Obed - A Climber's Guide To The Wild and Scenic.*

Lilly Bluff - Left End

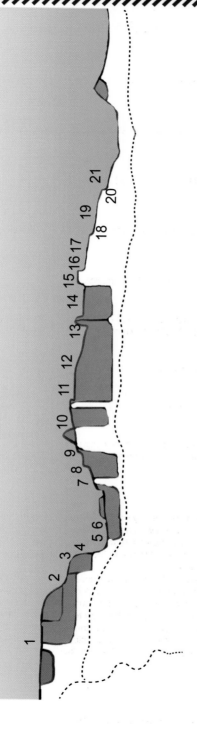

1. Neanderthal 11d
2. Borderline 11d
3. Alien 10d
4. Tarantella 10a
5. Electric Sky 12a
6. Whippersnapper 11a
7. Lounge Lizard 11b

8. Rocking Chair 9
9. Electric Chair 10b/c
10. Boogie Man 12d
11. Clyde the Mega Dude 11b/c
12. Blasphemy 13b
13. Heresy 11c
14. Dead Baby Ducks 11

15. Wheatward Bound 12b
16. 'Baccer Spit 11b
17. Junior's Big Brown Beaver 11d
18. Thrifty Mule 11a
19. First Laugh 10c
20. Last Laugh 10c
21. Standing Ovation 11c

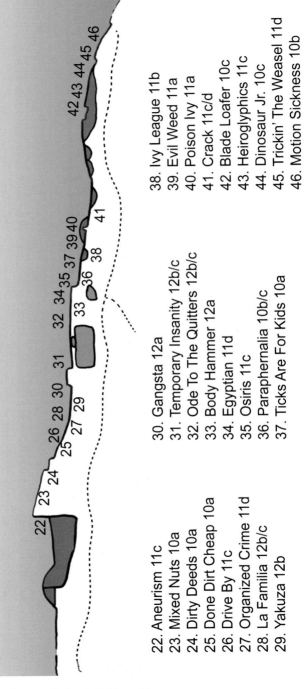

Lilly Bluff – Right End

22. Aneurism 11c
23. Mixed Nuts 10a
24. Dirty Deeds 10a
25. Done Dirt Cheap 10a
26. Drive By 11c
27. Organized Crime 11d
28. La Familia 12b/c
29. Yakuza 12b

30. Gangsta 12a
31. Temporary Insanity 12b/c
32. Ode To The Quitters 12b/c
33. Body Hammer 12a
34. Egyptian 11d
35. Osiris 11c
36. Paraphernalia 10b/c
37. Ticks Are For Kids 10a

38. Ivy League 11b
39. Evil Weed 11a
40. Poison Ivy 11a
41. Crack 11c/d
42. Blade Loafer 10c
43. Heiroglyphics 11c
44. Dinosaur Jr. 10c
45. Trickin' The Weasel 11d
46. Motion Sickness 10b

EAST TENNESSEE CLIMBERS COALITION

ETCC

 STAY IN TOUCH
Visit Us On Facebook

OBEDCLIMBERS@GMAIL.COM

Wes Powell Photo

OTHER PLACES

This guidebook covers the most popular publicly accessible climbing areas in Tennessee. It does not by any means cover **all** of the climbing areas in Tennessee. Not by a long shot. The "Gods of Geology" have smiled upon the Volunteer State and there are miles upon miles of cliffline tucked into the coves and ridges from Chattanooga northeast up the Cumberland Plateau and Walden's Ridge toward Knoxville and the Great Smoky Mountains. Unfortunately, most of it is on private land - owned by individual landowners, timber companies, mining companies or land trusts. It would be disingenuous of me to say that these vast expanses of rock have not been touched by a climber's hand, or that they are currently not being explored, however, in most cases it is done "under the radar" (ie: trespassing). Not condoning it, but it's simply the case.

There are also many areas where climbing is allowed but landowner preference or community consensus precludes them from being publicized. In years past, one could count the number of explorers on two hands; even still, it's surprising how much cliffline has been explored. It's not uncommon to climb a route at a remote cliff, only to find an old fixed piton or rap sling at the top. These days, the climber population has skyrocketed (in Chattanooga in particular), and as expected, more of them are out looking than ever before. Is there another Tennessee Wall lurking out there? No, but there are still enough off-the-beaten-path areas for the anti-social crowd avoiders to explore.

In some cases, areas that are off limits have gotten shut down due to trespassers. Not a good thing, since it ruins any chance of ever having productive negotiations regarding future access. In other cases, advocacy groups like the Southeastern Climbers Coalition have purchased land or negotiated easements to allow climbing. Deep Creek, one of the largest "new" climbing areas in Tennessee, is the result of negotiations between the State Forestry Commission and the SCC - still an ongoing process. Details are still being ironed out and it's a work in progress.

Who knows what the future holds? One thing is for certain: Climbers are drawn to new rock like bees to honey. It's up to us how these cliffs get developed, how land managers and owners view the climbing community, and how we act together to ensure continued access.

Listing By Grade

Name	Grade	Type	Page
Escape From Rungistan	8	SM	180
Flim Flam	8	FF	101
Green Eggs And Ham	8	DR	236
Hammer Time	8	KB	199
Hat Pin With A Sledge Hammer	8	KB	205
Have A Vol Tonight	8	BP	38
High Road	8	CR	63
Ice House	8	BSF	158
Jacob's Ladder	8	FF	112
Knoxville Boys	8	LF	46
Long Slab	8	FF	97
Man With The Blue Guitar	8	LF	50
Megasaurus	8	BP	35
Mister Green Jeans	8	KB	193
Nine To Five	8	KB	199
No One To Hear You Scream	8	BSF	166
No Show	8	SM	180
On The Side	8	FF	109
Palm Tree	8	DR	237
Poison Ivy	8	KB	211
Rambo Strikes Back	8	KB	205
Reachy	8	KB	208
Reception	8	BP	36
RJ Cam	8	FF	120
Ruff And Nasty, The	8	FF	121
Shell Shock	8	BSF	168
Shorty Doylies	8	KB	193
Slip Sliding Away	8	KB	211
Snake Charmer	8	BSF	151
Sonic Temple	8	DR	236
Suicide Blonde	8	BSF	153
Sweet Surrender	8	FF	113
Under The Eye Of The Vulture	8	KB	203
Unnamed	8	DR	238
Visions Of Jesus Freaks	8	LF	47
Vols And Chains	8	BP	38
Vols To The Wall	8	BP	38
Whadyathink?	8	KB	205
Woody	8	FCF	221
Zach Be Nimble	8	BSF	166
Suicide Direct	8 C2	BSF	153
Bear Mountain Picnic	8+	FF	99
Bearded One, The	8+	KB	196
Dogon Meet A Dancer, The	8+	KB	2
I Should Have Stolen A Cadillac	8+	BP	
Jesus Does The Rambo Hang	8+	BP	
Perch Of The Monster	8+	KB	2
Wonders Never Cease	8+	KB	2
The Saga Continues	9-	KB	1
He Said, She Said	9-/10c	FF	1
Bushmaster	9 A3	BSF	1
Aerobic Arete	9	CR	
After The Ball Was Over	9	KB	2
Americus	9	BP	
Ankles Away	9	FF	
Another Year Gone	9	CR	
Bandersnatch	9	BSF	1
Bloody Knuckles	9	KB	2
Blue Sun	9	SM	1
Born On The 4th Of July	9	KB	1
Bounty Hunter	9	DR	23
Campobello Beauty	9	BSF	1
Cast Adrift	9	KB	2
Chimney Sweep	9	KB	19
Choss Corner	9	BSF	1
Crack The Keg	9	BSF	1
Cracked By A Bludgeon	9	KB	2
Cricket Serenade	9	KB	1
Crybaby Crack	9	BSF	15
Day At The Races	9	DR	23
Dihedral	9	FF	9
Dubstep Polka	9	LF	5
Easy Enough	9	CR	7
Elephant Ears	9	FF	11
Escalade Escapade	9	CR	6
Flake Route, The	9	SM	18
Gordita	9	FCF	22
Grand Arch	9	BP	3
Green	9	KB	20
Grey Matter	9	FF	10
Happy Hour	9	KB	19
Harrison's Crack	9	BSF	15
Harrison's Ford	9	BP	3
Hell No!	9	BSF	16
High And Dry	9	SG	22
Holy War	9	FF	1

Name	Grade	Code	Page
Corners	10	CR	61
Crack Head	10	BSF	157
Cresent Crack	10	BSF	161
Espresso Route	10	BSF	150
Family Man	10	FCF	222
Flake Right	10	CR	76
Granny's Biscuits	10	FCF	221
Guillotine	10	BSF	158
Hard Up	10	SG	229
Hemophiliac	10	BSF	159
Hidden Jewel	10	BSF	158
Honey Corner	10	CR	76
Medicine Man	10	BSF	147
Panty Raid	10	FF	117
Quickie	10	BSF	145
Sorry Rocky	10	FCF	222
South Face	10	BSF	157
Trad Corner	10	CR	62
Tree Route	10	BSF	160
Vertigo	10 A2	BSF	156
Salsa Del Diablo	10 A3	BSF	150
Red Road	10 R	FCF	221
Brown Streak	10+	CR	64
Climbing With Uncle Pervy	10+	BSF	147
First Responder	10+	BSF	150
Jackwood	10+	FCF	222
Just Another Corner	10+	BSF	147
M.O.'s	10+	FCF	222
Smith & Wesson Oil	10+	BSF	157
Tricky Offwidth	10+	BSF	145
Rhino Load	10+ A2	BSF	141
Runaway Train	10+ A2	BSF	142
Tomb With A View	10+ A2	BSF	151
Abe's Lincoln	10a	BP	35
Birthday Boy	10a	KB	205
Born To Be Freed	10a	KB	203
Captain Kangaroo	10a	KB	193
Charybdis	10a	BSF	167
Crawdaddy	10a	FF	85
Dirty Deeds	10a	OLB	251
Done Dirt Cheap	10a	OLB	251
Easy For Now	10a	KB	203
Garden Weasel, The	10a	BSF	169
Geothermal Jig, The	10a	BSF	
Heartache	10a	KB	
Hidden in Plain Sight	10a	FF	
Horseshoe	10a	FF	
In The Rocking Chair	10a	KB	
Lay Lady Lay	10a	FF	
Lovingood Route	10a	CR	
Mammplitude	10a	FF	
Murphy's Law	10a	KB	
Name In The Guidebook	10a	KB	
Nine Hundred Foot Jesus	10a	BP	
Nomadosaurus	10a	BP	
Orange Peel	10a	CR	
Psycho Lizards	10a	DR	
Rainbow Inn	10a	BP	
Rehab	10a	FF	
Route du Jour	10a	BSF	
Song Of The Sirens	10a	BSF	
Special	10a	FF	
Tallboy	10a	CR	
Tarantella	10a	OLB	
Tea And Strumpets	10a	FF	
The Process	10a	KB	
Throb	10a	BP	
Ticks Are For Kids	10a	OLB	
Tiers Of My Years	10a	BP	
Unnamed	10a	BSF	
Wet Willie	10a	DR	
Wild Horses	10a	SM	
You Only Get Two Tries	10a	KB	
Mixed Nuts	10a	OLB	
Under The Big Top	10a A0	BSF	
Steal The Air	10a/b	BP	
Almost As Mean As Suzy	10b	KB	
Army Ants	10b	KB	
Between Chance And Choice	10b	KB	
Brickyard	10b	KB	
Carolina Club	10b	BSF	
Dutch Maiden	10b	FF	
Earflaps	10b	FF	
Final Frontier	10b	KB	
First Plum, The	10b	KB	
Fish Eyed Fool	10b	FF	

Route	Grade	Type	Page
Excalibur	10c/d	SM	184
Good vs Evil	10c/d	FF	116
Heaven's Gate	10c/d	BSF	160
Mitch's Bitch	10c/d	FF	116
Ride The Comet	10c/d	BSF	159
Saved By Zeroes	10c/d	FF	101
Spider Tropic	10c/d	BP	36
Tit For Tat	10c/d	FF	115
After The Fire	10d	BP	28
Alien	10d	OLB	249
Another Hard Decision	10d	KB	205
Antigone	10d	BP	28
Barb's Grimace	10d	KB	208
Beefaroni	10d	BP	38
Conan The Vegetarian	10d	BP	38
Cracksmith's Delight	10d	BP	24
Et Tu, Brute?	10d	BSF	165
Finding The Trust	10d	FF	122
Foster Child	10d	FF	99
Fox's Earth	10d	BP	38
Fragile Holdings	10d	CR	76
Gentry Route	10d	CR	75
Jack The Stripper	10d	BP	38
Machete Mayhem	10d	CR	77
Murphy To Manteo	10d	BSF	166
Plum Tuckered Out	10d	KB	208
Pond Scum	10d	FF	85
Pump Me 'Til I'm Goofy	10d	FF	124
Quark Variation	10d	BP	29
Royal Flesh	10d	BP	38
Sabre Dance	10d	BSF	168
Scandalous Intentions	10d	BP	37
Scarface	10d	KB	196
Seepasaurus	10d	BP	34
Something's Always Wrong	10d	FF	95
Standing Room Only	10d	KB	208
Striking Out On Your Own	10d	KB	203
Sweet Feet	10d	FF	112
Walk The Plank	10d	KB	213
Who Shot Bambi?	10d	BP	25
Winter Solstice	10d	BSF	166
Insecurity Blanket	10d	BSF	169
Republican Give-Away-Program	10d/11a	FF	120
Carpet Bagger	11-	BSF	14
Dog And Pony Show	11-	BSF	1
Happy Ending	11-	BSF	14
Cave Man	11	FF	12
Dead Baby Ducks	11	OLB	25
Dickel's For Drinking	11	CR	
Five Fun	11	BSF	14
Flake Route, The	11	FCF	22
Green Elbow	11	BSF	14
Powerline Crack	11	CR	7
Rude Awakenings	11	SG	22
Tweezer	11	BSF	16
Vine Line, The	11	BSF	14
Cyclops	11 A2+/3	BSF	14
Box Car Willies	11 A3	BSF	14
Lifto	11 A3	BSF	14
Wayne's World	11 A3	BSF	15
Captain Hook	11 A3+	BSF	14
Cave Route	11+	BSF	14
Gathering Of Shades, A	11+	BSF	16
Ambition Ammunition	11a	BP	2
Atomic Fireball	11a	FCF	22
Bird In Hand	11a	BP	3
Caesar's Stabbing	11a	BSF	16
Cataract	11a	KB	19
Cheese Eater	11a	KB	21
Civic Action	11a	KB	21
Confederate, The	11a	FF	10
Crankasaurus	11a	BP	3
Daddy's Bolt Ladder	11a	KB	20
Dance Of The Vampires	11a	BP	3
Dead Parent's Society	11a	BP	2
Drainpipe	11a	KB	21
Evil Weed	11a	OLB	25
Finger Puppets	11a	FF	10
Frosty The Lumberjack	11a	BSF	16
Gold Finger	11a	FF	12
Half Beast	11a	FF	12
Humane Bomb	11a	FF	11
Junkyard	11a	FF	10
King Jesus	11a	BP	
King Of Dreams	11a	BP	2
Left Hook	11a	FF	11

Name	Grade	Type	No.	Name	Grade	Type	No.
Clyde The Mega Dude	11b/c	OLB	250	Sharon The Ho	11c	BP	
Gallows Pole, The	11b/c	SM	186	Smithers Gets His Man	11c	BSF	
Honeycomb	11b/c	BSF	142	Standing Ovation	11c	OLB	
Joker's Wild	11b/c	BP	27	Tree Rash	11c	DR	
Lawn Jockey	11b/c	SM	186	Undeterminable Monster	11c	KB	
Live And Let Dihedral	11b/c	LF	49	White Line Fever	11c	KB	
Lynn's Route	11b/c	FF	93	Wristlets	11c	FF	
Shock and Awe	11b/c	FF	115	You Enjoy Myself	11c	BSF	
Three Gs, The	11b/c	FF	118	Zombie Stomp	11c	DR	
Vulgarian Crack	11b/c	BSF	158	Bart At The Blackboard	11c	BSF	
Aneurism	11c	OLB	250	Solar System	11c A2+	BSF	
Beefeater, The	11c	BP	24	Bent	11c/d	CR	
Big One, The	11c	FF	104	Birthday Route	11c/d	BSF	
Big uns Of Navarone	11c	KB	211	Black Seam	11c/d	SM	
Carpet Bagger	11c	FF	101	Blue Flame Pyromania	11c/d	SM	
Classical Crack	11c	LF	45	Crack	11c/d	OLB	
Defpotec	11c	BP	38	Desperately Seeking Solutions	11c/d	SM	
Delores 11c	11c	KB	205	Dumkopf	11c/d	FF	
Drive By	11c	OLB	251	Ground Strike	11c/d	FF	
Drive Me To Firenze	11c	BSF	169	Hammerhead	11c/d	FF	
Ecliptic	11c	BSF	166	Handcuffed	11c/d	FF	
Eleven Long Haired Friends Of Jesus	11c	BP	27	I've Got The Power	11c/d	SM	
Evil Times	11c	CR	72	Life's Rich Pageant	11c/d	BP	
Flesh Gordon	11c	DR	236	Love It Or Leave It	11c/d	BP	
Forged Identity	11c	KB	203	Fight The Power	11c/d A1	SM	
Fun	11c	BSF	167	Baby, I'm Ten Inches Long	11d	KB	
Gnash and Grab	11c	CR	77	Borderline	11d	OLB	
Heiroglyphics	11c	OLB	252	Egyptian	11d	OLB	
Heresy	11c	OLB	250	Fit Makes The Fashion	11d	BP	
Hips Don't Lie	11c	FF	114	Gargoyle	11d	DR	
Hoosier, The	11c	FF	89	Greed	11d	FF	
Huckleberry Jam	11c	BSF	162	Hard To Fathom	11d	BP	
Jesus And The Prom Queen	11c	BP	27	If I Had A Shotgun	11d	FF	
Meltdown	11c	BSF	167	Journey Above	11d	KB	
Moral Dilemma	11c	BSF	145	Junior's Big Brown Beaver	11d	OLB	
Morpheus	11c	BSF	168	Magnetic Feet	11d	KB	
Moses Direct	11c	BSF	162	Neanderthal	11d	OLB	
Osiris	11c	OLB	251	Organized Crime	11d	OLB	
Pocket Pool	11c	BSF	143	Pulsator	11d	KB	
Power Tropic	11c	LF	51	Right Hook	11d	FF	
Put The Pain Aside	11c	KB	205	Street Crime	11d	FF	
Rumpleforeskin	11c	DR	236	Tall Cool One, The	11d	BP	
Rust Bucket	11c	CR	68	Trickin' The Weasel	11d	OLB	

Name	Grade	Type	Page
Filthy Pig	12b/c	FF	87
Gun Bunny	12b/c	FF	86
La Familia	12b/c	OLB	251
Launch Pad	12b/c	FF	105
Leap Of Faith	12b/c	LF	47
Ode To The Quitter	12b/c	OLB	251
Sweat This	12b/c	BP	37
Temporary Insanity	12b/c	OLB	251
Big Bopper, The	12c	FF	86
Cave Route	12c	LF	52
Drill Sergeant, The	12c	BP	37
Escalade Crusade	12c	CR	73
Evolution Number Nine	12c	LF	47
Grifters (Deuces' Wild)	12c	CR	69
Ground Zero	12c	KB	196
Humpty Pumpty	12c	BP	29
Liars	12c	FF	89
Meridians Of Light	12c	BP	28
Pocket Wilderness	12c	BP	23
Predator	12c	CR	66
Proposition #One	12c	FF	111
Sly Man	12c	BP	33
Annie Sprinkle's Christmas	12c/d	LF	47
Arms Control	12c/d	LF	48
Bottle Rocket	12c/d	BP	28
Meeks Route	12c/d	BP	31
Next To The Last Boy Scout, The	12c/d	LF	48
Prison Of The Mind	12c/d	FF	122
Shake, Rattle and Hum	12c/d	BP	32
Boogie Man	12d	OLB	250
Butt Trumpet	12d	FF	109
Cock The Hammer	12d	FF	97
Darkie The Bum Beast	12d	FF	97
Eclipse	12d	FF	97
Escapism	12d	CR	66
Kids With Guns	12d	FF	98
Radline (Redline)	12d	CR	65
Saab Story	12d	FF	85
Scarlet Begonias	12d	CR	66
Sponge	12d	FF	98
Tom And Jerry	12d	FF	86
Tweekasaurus	12d	BP	34
Crimp Knob	12d/13a	FF	98

Name	Grade	Type
Copperhead	13	CR
Mortal Wound	13	KB
Under Water Ninja Moves	13+?	FF
Abacus	13a	FF
Big Timers	13a	BP
Cyclop's Belly	13a	LF
Gas Chamber	13a	FF
Oh Man	13a	BP
Psychospasm	13a	CR
Soul Sounds	13a	BP
Squeeze The Trigga	13a	FF
Talking Flakes	13a	BP
After Dark	13a/b	FF
Crackerjack Kid	13a/b	LF
Crunch Junkie	13a/b	FF
Guest Appearance	13a/b	FF
Autocratic For The People	13b	FF
Big Empty, The	13b	FF
Blasphemy	13b	OLB
Snatch	13b	FF
Three Wishes	13b	KB
Viper	13b	BP
Au Naturale	13b/c	BP
Coolio	13b/c	LF
Kill Or Be Killed	13c	FF
La Bamba	13c	CR
Creature Feature	13c/d	CR
Praise Ye Jah!	13c/d	BP
Conflict, The	13d	FF
Apes On Acid	13d/14a	CR
Paradigm Shift	14?	FF
Fire In The Hole	14a	FF
Pieta	14a	BP
Explorer Route	A1	BSF
Wide Corner	A1	BSF
High Plains Drifter	A3	BP

Alphabetical Listing

Name	Grade	Type
A Break From The Heat	8	KB
A Fine New Edition	8	KB
Abacus	13a	FF
Abe's Lincoln	10a	BP
Access Fun	9+	BSF
Acquittal, The	11b/c	FF

Name	Grade	Crag	Page		Name	Grade	Crag	Page
Aerobic Arete	9	CR	70		Bart At The Blackboard	11c	BSF	167
After Dark	13a/b	FF	97		Battery Warmup	11a/b	FF	124
After Lunch	9+	KB	193		Beam Me Up Scotty	8	KB	199
After The Ball Was Over	9	KB	203		Bear Mountain Picnic	8+	FF	99
After The Fire	10d	BP	28		Bearded One, The	8+	KB	196
Afterburner	5	FF	105		Beefaroni	10d	BP	38
AIDS Crack	7	BP	24		Beefeater, The	11c	BP	24
Ain't No Skin Off My Back	9+	BSF	160		Beginner's Luck	5	KB	193
Alien	10d	OLB	249		Bent	11c/d	CR	77
All The Way To Heaven	11a/b	FF	113		Between Chance And Choice	10b	KB	205
Almost As Mean As Suzy	10b	KB	211		Between Stress And Success	10c	KB	205
Ambition Ammunition	11a	BP	24		Big Bopper, The	12c	FF	86
Americus	9	BP	35		Big Empty, The	13b	FF	97
Anchors Away	7	KB	193		Big Men, Small Airplanes	10c/d	SM	180
Aneurism	11c	OLB	250		Big One, The	11c	FF	104
Ankles Away	9	FF	98		Big Timers	13a	BP	31
Annie Sprinkle's Christmas	12c/d	LF	47		Big uns Of Navarone	11c	KB	211
Another Hard Decision	10d	KB	205		Bird In Hand	11a	BP	33
Another Year Gone	9	CR	63		Birthday Boy	10a	KB	205
Anthony's Face	10	BSF	159		Birthday Route	11c/d	BSF	143
Antigone	10d	BP	28		Black Seam	11c/d	SM	180
Any Port In A Storm	11b	KB	213		Black Widow	8	SG	228
Apes On Acid	13d/14a	CR	73		Blade Loafer	10c	OLB	252
Arete Butler	9+	FF	101		Blade Runner	10	BSF	158
Arms Control	12c/d	LF	48		Blanket Party	7	KB	199
Army Ants	10b	KB	211		Blasphemy	13b	OLB	250
As The Crow Flies	11b	KB	213		Block Party	10	BSF	148
Attila The Nun	11a/b	BP	38		Block Party	7	BSF	168
Atomic Fireball	11a	FCF	221		Bloody Knuckles	9	KB	211
Atrophy	11b/c	FF	98		Blue Flame Pyromania	11c/d	SM	184
Attention Deficit	8	SM	180		Blue Sun	9	SM	186
Attic Toys	12a	LF	48		Bob The Builder	6	KB	199
Attitude In Action	10c	SM	184		Body Hammer	12a	OLB	251
Au Naturale	13b/c	BP	36		Boogie Man	12d	OLB	250
Autocratic For The People	13b	FF	111		Borderline	11d	OLB	249
Baby Kangaroo	8	KB	193		Born On The 4th Of July	9	KB	196
Baby, I'm Ten Inches Long	11d	KB	196		Born To Be Freed	10a	KB	203
Baccer Spit	11b	OLB	250		Bottle Rocket	12c/d	BP	28
Backstabber	9+	KB	213		Bottled Up Warrior	12b/c	FF	95
Bad Moon Rising	11a R	BSF	159		Bottom Feeder	12a/b	FF	85
Basilisk	5	BP	27		Bounty Hunter	9	DR	237
Bandersnatch	9	BSF	168		Box Car Willies	11 A3	BSF	142
Barb's Grimace	10d	KB	208		Boys Of Argon	8	BP	35

Name	Grade	Col	Page	Name	Grade	Col	Page
Brickyard	10b	KB	199	Classic Corner	8	BSF	143
Brokeback Mountain	11b/c	FF	117	Classical Crack	11c	LF	45
Brown Book	12a	LF	49	Claw, The	12	CR	74
Brown Streak	10+	CR	64	Clifford The Big Red Dog	8	KB	193
Buck Nasty	8	SM	180	Climbing With Uncle Pervy	10+	BSF	147
Bucket Boy	5	BSF	165	Clyde The Mega Dude	11b/c	OLB	250
Bullet Proof	11b/c	SM	186	Cock The Hammer	12d	FF	97
Bushmaster	9 A3	BSF	156	Cold Shoulder	10c	FF	109
Butt Trumpet	12d	FF	109	Colonel Forbin's Ascent	11a	BSF	169
Butter Beans	10	FCF	221	Community Effort	8	KB	193
Caesar's Stabbing	11a	BSF	165	Competitive Edge	10c	KB	199
Caged Bowling Ball	10c	KB	203	Conan The Vegetarian	10d	BP	38
Campfire Crack	10c	BSF	159	Conduct Disorder	8	SM	180
Campobello Beauty	9	BSF	165	Confederate,The	11a	FF	108
Campsite Dihedral	10	SG	228	Conflict, The	13d	FF	93
Captain Hook	11 A3+	BSF	141	Cookie, The	10c	FCF	222
Captain Hook	4	KB	199	Coolio	13b/c	LF	49
Captain Kangaroo	10a	KB	193	Copperhead	13	CR	66
Carolina Club	10b	BSF	166	Coral Methane	10c/d	BP	36
Carpet Bagger	11c	FF	101	Cornered Market	8	FF	109
Carpet Bagger	11-	BSF	143	Corners	10	CR	61
Cast Adrift	9	KB	213	Cornflake Crack	5	SG	228
Castle Arete	9+/10	CR	61	Cottonmouth	12a/b	CR	65
Catapult	12+	CR	72	Crack	11c/d	OLB	252
Cataract	11a	KB	196	Crack Head	10	BSF	157
Cave Man	11	FF	121	Crack Of Dawn	11b	BP	23
Cave Route	12c	LF	52	Crack of Noon	9+	BSF	162
Cave Route	11+	BSF	141	Crack The Keg	9	BSF	166
Cedar Tree Massacre	12a	KB	205	Cracked	8	DR	238
Charlie Kable Solo Chimney	7	CR	65	Cracked By A Bludgeon	9	KB	213
Charlotte's Web	7	KB	211	Crackerjack Kid	13a/b	LF	45
Charybdis	10a	BSF	167	Cracksmith's Delight	10d	BP	24
Cheese Eater	11a	KB	213	Crankasaurus	11a	BP	34
Chesnutt Arete	12b	CR	70	Crash Into Me	11b	FF	114
Chesnutt Route	12a	CR	69	Crawdaddy	10a	FF	85
Chesnutt Sport	12b	CR	68	Creature Feature	13c/d	CR	73
Chesnutt's Route	12a/b	FF	124	Cresent Crack	10	BSF	161
Chimney	7	CR	63	Cricket Serenade	9	KB	196
Chimney	5	SG	228	Crimp Knob	12d/13a	FF	98
Chimney Sweep	9	KB	199	Crow's Nest	9+	KB	213
Choss Corner	9	BSF	148	Crunch Junkie	13a/b	FF	104
Cinderella	12a	BP	25	Crybaby Crack	9	BSF	158
Civic Action	11a	KB	211	Cuyahoga Falls	12b/c	BP	24

Five Fun	11	BSF	145	Greed	11d	FF	91
Flake Right	10	CR	76	Green	9	KB	203
Flake Route, The	9	SM	184	Green Eggs And Ham	8	DR	236
Flake Route, The	11	FCF	222	Green Elbow	11	BSF	148
Flesh Gordon	11c	DR	236	Grey Matter	9	FF	104
Flim Flam	8	FF	101	Grifters (Deuces' Wild)	12c	CR	69
For Girly Girls Only	12b	KB	203	Grin N' Bare It	10c	KB	196
Forged Identity	11c	KB	203	Ground Strike	11c/d	FF	87
Formula Rock	11b	BP	37	Ground Zero	12c	KB	196
Foster Child	10d	FF	99	Guest Appearance	13a/b	FF	111
Four Winds	11b	KB	213	Guillotine	10	BSF	158
Fox's Earth	10d	BP	38	Gun Bunny	12b/c	FF	86
Fragile Holdings	10d	CR	76	Gutbuster	12a/b	FF	104
Framed	12a	FF	91	Half Beast	11a	FF	121
Freddie's Mercury	9+	BP	35	Half Man	10c	FF	121
French Curl	6	BP	34	Half Moon	10c	BSF	160
Frosty The Lumberjack	11a	BSF	168	Ham Jammin	9+	BSF	161
Fun	11c	BSF	167	Hammer Time	8	KB	199
Gallows Pole, The	11b/c	SM	186	Hammerhead	11c/d	FF	87
Gangsta	12a	OLB	251	Handcuffed	11c/d	FF	86
Garden Weasel, The	10a	BSF	169	Happy Ending	11-	BSF	145
Gargantua	12a	BP	29	Happy Hour	9	KB	196
Gargoyle	11d	DR	236	Hard To Fathom	11d	BP	27
Gas Chamber	13a	FF	93	Hard To Quit	10b	KB	208
Gathering Of Shades, A	11+	BSF	168	Hard Up	10	SG	229
Geekis Khan	11b	BP	38	Harder	10b/c	LF	52
Gentry Route	10d	CR	75	Harrison's Crack	9	BSF	158
Geothermal Jig, The	10a	BSF	166	Harrison's Ford	9	BP	35
Gideon's Corner	10b/c	LF	49	Hat Pin With A Sledge Hammer	8	KB	205
Girly Man	11a/b	FF	120	Have A Vol Tonight	8	BP	38
Git R' Done	11b	BSF	145	He Said, She Said	9-/10c	FF	117
Glory	12a	FF	108	Head Factor	12a	BSF	169
Glue Sniffer	12	CR	60	Heart Of Gold	12a	FF	91
Gnash and Grab	11c	CR	77	Heartache	10a	KB	211
Gold Finger	11a	FF	122	Heaven's Gate	10c/d	BSF	160
Golden Girl	10c	FF	122	Heiroglyphics	11c	OLB	252
Good vs Evil	10c/d	FF	116	Hell No!	9	BSF	162
Gordita	9	FCF	222	Hello Nasty	9+	BSF	166
Grand Arch	9	BP	33	Helping Hands	12a	KB	193
Grand Larceny	12a	FF	87	Hemophiliac	10	BSF	159
Granny's Biscuits	10	FCF	221	Here And Now	12a	KB	205
Gravity Boots	7	FF	105	Heresy	11c	OLB	250
Great Balls Of Fire	7	DR	237	Hidden in Plain Sight	10a	FF	118

Route	Grade	Crag	Page	Route	Grade	Crag	Page
Left Hook	11a	FF	115	Men Without Hats	10b/c	SM	184
Legends In Their Own Minds	11a	BP	30	Meridians Of Light	12c	BP	28
Lemoine	11b	CR	61	Midnight Plowboy	10b	FF	117
Leviathan	11b	KB	193	MILF	9	FF	111
Liars	12c	FF	89	Mirror Of Llunet	11b	BSF	166
Life's Rich Pageant	11c/d	BP	28	Miss Prissy	9	FF	99
Lifto	11 A3	BSF	141	Miss Scarlet	9+	FF	101
Lightning Bolt Crack	11a	BSF	162	Mister Green Jeans	8	KB	193
Line Drive	7	LF	51	Mitch's Bitch	10c/d	FF	116
Lions And Tigers And Bears	9	KB	211	Mixed Arête	9	CR	68
Little Buttons	6	KB	205	Mixed Nuts	10a	OLB	250
Little Fox	6	KB	205	Moist Gift	6	FCF	222
Little Ol' Lady	6	DR	237	Monkey Boy	12a	LF	47
Little Wing	10b	DR	236	Monster Movie	9	SG	228
Live And Let Dihedral	11b/c	LF	49	Moon Dance	9	BSF	160
Lone Justice	12	CR	60	Moon Doggies	6	DR	237
Long Slab	8	FF	97	Moonscape	10b	FF	103
Look Ma, No Head!	11b	DR	236	Moral Dilemma	11c	BSF	145
Loonasaurus	11b	BP	35	Morpheus	11c	BSF	168
Looters	12a	FF	91	Mortal Wound	13	KB	196
Lost Horizons	11a	BP	26	Mosaic	11a	CR	70
Lounge Lizard	11b	OLB	249	Moses Direct	11c	BSF	162
Love It Or Leave It	11c/d	BP	26	Motion Sickness	10b	OLB	252
Lovingood Route	10a	CR	70	Moving Target	9	FF	89
Low Self Opinion	9+	LF	52	Mrs. Treated	11a	FF	111
Lucky Streak	9+	CR	63	Murphy To Manteo	10d	BSF	166
Lucky Strikes	9+	SM	180	Murphy's Law	10a	KB	199
Lucy In The Sky	9	DR	236	Mustang Sally	11a	KB	196
Luther's Fury	9	KB	196	My Little Secret	11a	KB	196
Lynn's Route	11b/c	FF	93	Nagual, The	12b	KB	211
M.O.'s	10+	FCF	222	Name In The Guidebook	10a	KB	199
Machete Mayhem	10d	CR	77	Nannerhead	10c	BSF	169
Magnetic Feet	11d	KB	213	Narcissism	10b	FF	98
Malice In Wonderland	10b/c	DR	236	Natty Light	11a	CR	63
Mammplitude	10a	FF	108	Natural Lite	7	DR	237
Mammy	9	FF	101	Natural, The	7	KB	203
Man Overboard	9+	KB	213	Neanderthal	11d	OLB	249
Man With The Blue Guitar	8	LF	50	Necrophobia	11b	KB	213
Maybe A Little Ether	10b	KB	208	New Drill In Town	11a	KB	193
Medicine Man	10	BSF	147	New Purchase	7	KB	205
Meeks Route	12c/d	BP	31	New Route	11d/12a	FF	97
Megasaurus	8	BP	35	New Slant, A	10b	KB	203
Meltdown	11c	BSF	167	Next Corner	9+	BSF	143

Route	Grade	Type	Page
Reach	12a/b	FF	89
Reachy	8	KB	208
Real Homer, The	10c	BSF	167
Reception	8	BP	36
Red Road	10 R	FCF	221
Refrigerator Crack	12a	BP	36
Rehab	10a	FF	106
Renewal, The	10b	KB	208
Reptile	12a	FF	108
Republican Conservationist	10c	FF	120
Republican Give-Away-Program	10d/11a	FF	120
Rhea County Gun Club	12b	BP	33
Rhino Load	10+ A2	BSF	141
Ricochet Rabbit	12+	CR	66
Ride The Comet	10c/d	BSF	159
Right Hook	11d	FF	115
Right To Arm Bears, The	10b/c	SM	186
Ritter's Arete	10c	LF	50
Ritz Bits	10c	KB	196
RJ Cam	8	FF	120
Rock A Billy King	9	FCF	222
Rocking Chair	9	OLB	249
Rocks Are For Climbing	9	CR	60
Rode Hard, Put Up Wet	10b	FF	106
Rolffed	9+	FF	106
Rollo	11a	FF	104
Romeo And Juliet	10b/c	SM	184
Route du Jour	10a	BSF	166
Royal Flesh	10d	BP	38
Rudder A' Midship	11a	KB	213
Rude Awakenings	11	SG	228
Ruff And Nasty, The	8	FF	121
Rumpleforeskin	11c	DR	236
Runaway Train	10+ A2	BSF	142
Russian One Step	7	DR	237
Rust Bucket	11c	CR	68
Saab Story	12d	FF	85
Sabre Dance	10d	BSF	168
Salsa Del Diablo	10 A3	BSF	150
Sampson's Gym	11a/b	BP	35
Sand Dollars	9	BP	38
Santa Claws	10c	DR	237
Satisfaction	12a/b	FF	86
Saved By Zeroes	10c/d	FF	101
Scandalous Intentions	10d	BP	37
Scarface	10d	KB	196
Scarlet Begonias	12d	CR	66
Scary Jerry	12	BSF	145
Scylla	10b	BSF	167
Second Pitch, The	6	KB	193
Secret Passage	12a	FF	120
See the Egress	7	FF	118
Seepasaurus	10d	BP	34
Seismic Activity	5	KB	199
Shake, Rattle and Hum	12c/d	BP	32
Shallow Water	12b	LF	49
Sharon The Ho	11c	BP	29
Sharper Image, The	10c	KB	205
Shart In Your Armor	9	CR	72
Shave And A Haircut	9	KB	203
Shell Shock	8	BSF	168
Shirley's Temple	9	BP	38
Shock and Awe	11b/c	FF	115
Shoot The Rapids	10b R	KB	213
Short And Sporty	10c	KB	193
Shorty Doylies	8	KB	193
Sibling Rivalry	7+/9	FF	117
Sideshow Bob	10b	BSF	167
Singing In The Rain	6	KB	21
Size Matters	10b	FF	11
Skin And Bones	10b	KB	20
Skipper	9	FF	8
Sleepless Nights	9+	CR	6
Slim Pickins	11a	BP	3
Sling Blade	10c	BSF	14
Slingblade	12b	CR	6
Slingblade	9+	BSF	16
Slip Sliding Away	8	KB	21
Slippery When Wet	7	KB	21
Sloppy When Wet	5	FF	12
Slut Puppy	11a	SM	18
Sly Man	12c	BP	3
Smear, Queer and Fear	11b	FF	1
Smith & Wesson Oil	10+	BSF	1
Smithers Gets His Man	11c	BSF	1
Smokestack Crack	7	CR	

Route	Grade	Area	Page
Trickin' The Weasel	11d	OLB	252
Tricky Offwidth	10+	BSF	145
Turnin' Tricks	10c	FF	108
Turret, The	11a	CR	61
Tweekasaurus	12d	BP	34
Tweezer	11	BSF	169
Twist And Shout	9+	FF	98
Ugly Route, The	10b	BP	26
Under The Big Top	10a A0	BSF	151
Under The Eye Of The Vulture	8	KB	203
Under Water Ninja Moves	13+?	FF	124
Undeterminable Monster	11c	KB	211
Unnamed	10a	BSF	143
Unnamed	9+	DR	238
Unnamed	8	DR	238
Unnamed Corner	9	BSF	145
Unnamed Mixed Line	11d	CR	62
Va Voom	12a	BP	32
Vanderbilt Wall Area	5	SG	228
Vanishing Breed	12a	LF	45
Vapor Lock	12a	FF	111
Vapor Trail	11a	DR	237
Vertical Imbalance	9	DR	237
Vertigo	10 A2	BSF	156
Vine Line, The	11	BSF	143
Viper	13b	BP	29
Visions Of Jesus Freaks	8	LF	47
Vividly Grey	9+/10	FF	118
Vols And Chains	8	BP	38
Vols To The Wall	8	BP	38
Vulcans Do Not Bluff	11b	SM	180
Vulgarian Crack	11b/c	BSF	158
Walk The Plank	10d	KB	213
Way Out Back	11a	BP	30
Wayne's World	11 A3	BSF	156
Webs We Weave	12b	LF	48
Wedgie	10b/c	FF	103
Weenie Boy	9+	BSF	166
Welcome To The Jungle	11d	DR	236
Wet Willie	9	FF	103
Wet Willie	10a	DR	237
Whadyathink?	8	KB	205
Wheatward Bound	12b	OLB	250
When Old Friends Meet	10b	KB	208
Whippersnapper	11a	OLB	249
Whirlwind	10c	KB	193
White Corner	9	CR	75
White Line Fever	11c	KB	203
Who Shot Bambi?	10d	BP	25
Wide Corner	A1	BSF	142
Wild Horses	10a	SM	184
Wild Man	11d/12a X	CR	62
Wild Thing	12a	BP	31
Wild Virus	11b	BP	29
Winter Solstice	10d	BSF	166
Wired For Sound	9	KB	205
Wish	11b	CR	65
Witchy Woman	10c	FF	105
Wit's End	10b	BSF	166
Wonders Never Cease	8+	KB	208
Woody	8	FCF	221
Wristlets	11c	FF	86
Yakuza	12b	OLB	251
Yaller Jambo	9	BSF	169
Yeller Feller	11b	BSF	148
Yellow Streak	11b	KB	211
You Big Dummy	11d/12a	FF	104
You Enjoy Myself	11c	BSF	169
You Only Get Two Tries	10a	KB	203
Young And The Restless, The	9	FF	108
Zach Be Nimble	8	BSF	166
Zombie Stomp	11c	DR	237

ABOUT THE AUTHOR

Chris Watford began climbing at the age of thirteen, inspired after seeing the Clint Eastwood classic The Eiger Sanction. Born into a family of outdoor enthusiasts and fortunate to be part of a very active Boy Scout troop, his interest in climbing was a natural extension of his early camping, hiking, and backpacking experiences. The love of climbing quickly took hold. His formative years were spent traveling and climbing all over the southeast, exploring, developing routes and establishing new areas. He is a founding member of the Access Fund, having attended the first Access Fund Fixed Anchor Symposium in Boulder, Colorado in 1993, as a delegate from the southeast. He served as the Southeastern Regional Coordinator for the Access Fund from 1993 until 1999 and has been extensively involved with access issues and cliff preservation through his affiliation with the Southeastern Climber's Coalition.

Though the steep sandstone and granite of the south are his first loves, Chris has traveled extensively throughout the United States. Yosemite, Moab, Rocky Mountain National Park, the Shawangunks and the City of Rocks are just a few of his favorite areas. Climbing has presented many opportunities over the years, among them a dual career as a high angle climber/rigger for specialty camera contractors in the sports, video and film industries. This work has led him all over the world – Malaysia, Australia, Japan, Korea, Italy, Qatar, China, Greece, South Africa, Poland, Ukraine and London for the 2012 Olympic Games. Naturally, these trips include a healthy sampling of local rock climbing as well.

Chris graduated from the Kennesaw State University School of Business with degrees in finance and management, and post-college, owned and operated a family business - an outdoor specialty retail store, until 2008. These days, through his company ClimbSouth, he designs and builds climbing walls, publishes guidebooks, consults with schools and universities regarding outdoor and climbing programs, travels for camera and video work and manages real estate properties. He currently resides in Roswell, Georgia with his wife Mary Ann and two little girls, Ava and Liza. His non climbing interests include soccer, music, reading and all things guitar related.

NOTES